PARENTS' GUIDE TO
College
Life

PRAISE FOR PARENTS' GUIDE TO COLLEGE LIFE

"With savvy advice, great tips, and tell-it-like-it-is practicality, this book is a must-read before college begins!"

—Soledad O'Brien, Co-Anchor, *CNN American Morning*

"A handy reference book that anyone with a child in college will want to check out."

—*Kirkus Reports*

"Forget about the kids—this is an essential college survival guide for you."

—Janet Chan, Editor-in-Chief, *Parenting Magazine*

"Consider this book required reading if you're sending a child off to college."

—Michael Lafavore, Founding Editor, *Men's Health Magazine*

"An invaluable book for any parent with college on their mind."

—Mary Beth Wright, Publisher, *FamilyFun Magazine*

"Destined to become the bible for long-distance college parents."

—Stephanie Izarek, Executive Editor, *Scholastic Parent & Child Magazine*

"A benchmark guide for 21st-century college parents. Raskin delivers her recommendations with wit, intelligence and love."

—Claire Green, President, Parents' Choice Foundation

"No longer does sending a child off to college have to feel like a jump into an abyss. . . . This book not only answers every question we want (but are afraid) to ask, it tells us what we don't know we need to know."

—Jenifer Marshall Lippincott, Author,
7 Things Your Teenager Won't Tell You (And How to Talk About Them Anyway)

"Raskin helped teach millions of families about technology. Now she's helping parents navigate their kids' college experience. As a parent with two kids in college, I can say with certainty that we need all the help we can get."

—Larry Magid, Technology Columnist, CBS Radio

PARENTS' GUIDE TO
College Life

181 straight answers on everything you can expect over the next four years

— BY ROBIN RASKIN —

RANDOM HOUSE
information
G R O U P

The Princeton Review, Inc.
2315 Broadway
New York, NY 10024
E-mail: bookeditor@review.com

© 2006 by The Princeton Review, Inc.

ISBN: 0-375-76494-1
ISBN-13: 978-0-375-76494-3

Publisher: Robert Franek
Editor: Lisa Marie Rovito
Designer and Production Manager: Scott Harris
Production Editor: Christine LaRubio
Illustrations by Udo Drescher.

Manufactured in the United States of America.

9 8 7 6 5 4 3 2 1

ACKNOWLEDGMENTS

I wish I'd written this book six years ago, or at least read it. That's when our first daughter headed off to college. Since then two more kids have followed.

I can't say whether or not they're smarter now (though I think they are) but I know that I am. I've worked through the problems and prospects posed by summer vacations, winter breaks, and semesters abroad. I've survived the roller coaster rides that go along with meeting a variety of their significant others (including the canine variety), and we've somehow reached parity on every decision from meal plans to credit cards to mountain bikes and cell phones. They found majors, and, much to my surprise, they even found good jobs and apartments—except for the one who's still finishing up.

But it wasn't until I began working at The Princeton Review that the commonality of my experience hit me. Every day parents, the press, and even the colleges would call looking for the nuggets of information that are contained in this book.

Creating a book is that rare mix of slugging it out alone and depending on the encouragement, talents, and contributions of others. I talked and listened to many people while writing this book but there were a few knockout contributions.

Robert Franek, the Editorial Director and Publisher of Guidebook Publications at The Princeton Review, deserves a big thanks for letting me plunk down a list of 181 questions I thought parents needed to have answered, then giving me a shot at tracking down those answers. The deans, administrators, and other staff of the colleges who are quoted throughout this book took extraordinary pains to help parents understand both the simple and the not-so-simple facets of college life. They come from many different types of colleges and they represent some diverse opinions, but they all rank high on the "wise" scale. Lisa Marie Rovito, my editor and sounding board, had more questions than a 2-year-old on a walk after reading my initial manuscript, but my answering each one made this a better book. Harriet Brand, my colleague at The Princeton Review, should have (but never once) showed that she was getting tired of sharing my latest findings, and Linda Nessim deserves thanks for allowing my "evening" project to creep into my day job.

Then, there's my own family—all too used to seeing me become a midnight-oil-burning champion of some project or another. Thanks to Kari, Arli, and Reed who, not without a certain degree of embarrassment, finally agreed to enlist their friends and their friends' friends to talk to me about the mundane and the sublime of their college experiences. It was an honor to have them share with me.

Last but not least, thanks go to two special guys: John Katzman, CEO and founder of The Princeton Review, who follows his own passions and let's others do the same, and to my husband, Kaare. We did okay on the college thing, and now maybe others can, too.

—Robin Raskin

TABLE OF CONTENTS

CHAPTER 1

A Parent's Role During the College Years

Children begin by loving their parents; as they grow they judge them; sometimes they forgive them.

—Oscar Wilde

My mother told me I should have called this book, *Do As I Say, Not As I Did*. It's hard to believe I was that bad in school. She said it was often painful to watch as I chose a wild, overgrown path throughout my college tenure. Short of a few mild letters my parents sent that alluded to the fact that I was making immature, costly mistakes and not taking full advantage of the education that they'd worked so hard to provide, my mother and father let me find my own way.

In hindsight, could my parents have prevented the headaches that ensued when I transferred from a small school to a large school and then back again? Or the hardships I had when I decided to live on a farm twenty-five miles from campus? Should they have? No doubt, they could have put a foot down, but they gave me the space to move from high-school kid to real-world adult, even if I didn't do it gracefully; kids need that. Sometimes I think my parents' generation and their willingness to let things take their natural course made the next generation of parents feel the need to overcompensate on issues of parental control.

Welcome to the world of long-distance parenting, where the key to survival is the unwavering belief that, just like they outgrew diapers and learned how to read, they'll outgrow their college problems, too—and they'll get through each one with the life skills you packed up for them.

One of your greatest tasks over the next four (or more) years will be trying to maintain a sense of balance. In the past, parents were much more willing to abdicate responsibility come college time, proclaiming to their kids: "You're in college now; I'm checking out." There was an implicit trust in the school and in the kids, who, their laissez-faire parents believed, would outgrow any experimental or rebellious phases and get it right.

There was, perhaps, too much trust. Now that the pendulum has swung and parents are at the other end of the spectrum—wanting to hand-hold from move-in day to graduation—you'll need to check yourself from time to time and scooch back toward that desired middle ground.

The person you are parenting no longer lives under your roof or by your rules, but he or she is still your responsibility—financially and otherwise. As a matter of fact, most parents will never pay more per year/per kid than they do during college years. How ironic it is that just when they cost the most, you see and control them the least.

When you first drop your children off at school, you'll naturally be asking yourself whether the college is up to the task of managing this student in your absence. In loco parentis is Latin for "in the position or place of the parents," but it's obvious that the college is not going to have day-to-day contact with your son or daughter in the same way that you did.

History tells us that it's tough to rule from a distance. (Just look at what happened when the British tried to oversee the American Colonies.) You won't be there to enforce the rules you've made, and truth be told, there aren't many that you can dictate successfully from afar. Instead, you'll rely on three things:

- Your child's good judgment
- The school's ability to service in loco parentis
- A host of communications strategies

Don't underestimate the power of parental radar—the ability to read the signals of a conversation without the benefit of face-to-face communication. Each time the phone rings or an e-mail arrives, you'll need to read between the lines or hear the tone in her voice, and ask the right questions in the right way.

WHY PARENTS CAN'T LET GO

Colleges and universities complain that parents have become "helicopters," hovering over their children's college years and zooming in closer to take a look whenever they sense danger below. In fall 2005, *The Wall Street Journal* ran a story that mentioned the University of Vermont's use of "parent bouncers" whose job was to stop parents from going to register for classes with their children. The article even relayed stories of students who, while in a meeting with their advisors, would conference their parents in with a phone call on speakerphone. (Don't let this be you and yours.)

Thomas A. Smith, PhD, Associate Dean, College of Arts and Sciences Loyola University, New Orleans, echoes the sentiments of many educators when he comments that the current generation of parents seems, from a faculty perspective, "to be amazingly over-involved in the minutiae of students' lives." Making the case that college should be the time for fledgling adults to make their own decisions, Smith says that these days the best advice he can give parents is to let their children grow up.

"Administrators everywhere can tell stories of parents who have taken over too much of their students' lives, stifling opportunities for their growth," says Williams College's, Jim Kolesar, Director of Public Affairs. Kolesar makes his point with a student's story:

"Last summer we sent a letter to one hundred or so first-year students who would be living next to a building about to be taken down and replaced. The purpose was to let them know the schedule and say that the college would work with them to ensure that the project would disrupt their lives as little as possible. One parent called immediately to say that this was unacceptable and to demand that his daughter be moved to a different building. The following day, this father e-mailed to say 'forget about it.' In his words, his daughter had told him to 'knock it off.'"

With two children attending Williams College where he works, Kolesar can see both sides of the coin. "Maybe," he says, "when we parents are deciding whether to inject ourselves into some aspect of the students' lives, we should ask ourselves whether we'd be doing so for our students' sake or our own. If the latter, then it's better to simply 'knock it off.'"

What makes this generation of parents so obsessively involved in the long-distance college relationship? After talking to parents around the country, here's the snapshot:

Parents are educated consumers.

This is a generation brought up to be informed consumers. Whether they're buying cars, computers, or a child's college education, they are doing their product research and following up to make sure that the product lives up to its claims. They have warranties and guarantees for everything else, now they want the same for college. They've researched schools ad nauseum, and they're sticking around to see if they made the right purchase. That's just one part of the equation...

College is really expensive.

The cost of college has more than doubled in a generation. With a four-year private school often ringing in at more than $20,000 a year, and a public school ranging somewhere between free and $10,000 a year, college tuition is, understandably, a burden for most parents. Raised to make smart investment in the future, these parents want to know that they are going to see a return on that investment.

Colleges are not transparent.

This generation of parents is America's best educated ever. They're not going to assume that the college is doing a good job; they want proof. They've been there themselves, and they've seen what happens with their own eyes. They've demanded accountability in their children's lower schools, and this mindset will migrate to college.

Communications are faster and better.

When I drove back to campus during my college years, my instructions were to place a collect call "from Aunt Rose" when I arrived back safely at my dorm. That was the code. My family wouldn't accept the charges, but they knew I was okay. When I actually spoke to them, it was at best once a week—and briefly. A long-distance call was not to be taken lightly. Today—with track-'em-down cell phones, e-mail, and instant messaging—it's not uncommon for parents to check in daily. In turn, kids are speed-dialing their parents to get their blessing on the smallest of situations that, by now, they should be well-equipped to handle on their own.

The world is a scarier place.
Columbine, the World Trade Center, London bombings, college suicides, date rape, frat parties…it's not hard to make a list of reasons to lose sleep over your college student's safety.

Ignorance may have been bliss for my parents. After all, the more parents know, the more they worry. But many of today's parents of college students must like to worry—because they certainly want to know.

Still, the educators want parents to chill out. Scott Nelson, an Assistant Dean of Students at Elon University, is one of the most strident. He says, "Stay out of the way for a while, and let them find their way. They can—and will—succeed if we let them. They need to learn that they can do things (request a room change, drop/add classes, etc.) without a call from mom or dad. The 'helicopter parenting' by parents who hover around to mend all of the mistakes their children make, should stop now. It's not healthy!"

This book was written to help better define that fine line between micromanagement and an appropriate level of concern during your child's college years. Deans and college professionals who represent a wide variety of colleges across the country and log in hundreds of years of cumulative experience have offered some advice on a parent's new role and the process of letting go for this chapter, and on a world of other topics for the others. Many of them are, or have been, parents of college students themselves.

THESE ARE NOT THE BEST YEARS OF YOUR LIFE

"Once the acceptance letters are in, the process of letting go begins," says Dr. Linda Bips, a psychology professor and former director of counseling at Muhlenberg College. It's not an easy process. Here are her action items for parents:

- Start saying good-bye now, in your own ways.

- Talk about the good times, and anticipate the new ones.

- Talk about money—who will pay for what and how much.

- State your expectations regarding grades; remember that college is not high school and adjust those expectations accordingly.

- Challenge your child to change a possible problematic behavior for six months while he or she thinks about new values.

- Be a good listener, but don't be a fixer.

- Promise to send lots of mail or e-mail and set up a weekly telephone call.

- Make sure your child finds the career development office and before his senior year. He should talk to career professionals and professors about graduate school and careers during his sophomore and junior years.

- Don't worry if your child hasn't picked a major or profession by the end of her freshman year. Encourage her to take a variety of classes.

- Remember: The administration is not the enemy. Most administrators are in the business because they care about the students. Most are willing to help whenever possible. But, by the same token, just because you don't get your own way does not mean the administrator didn't listen, didn't care, or didn't try to help.

What shouldn't you do according to Dr. Bips?

- Don't call faculty or staff on your child's behalf. Students need to fend for themselves and take responsibility.

- Don't give him the old "These are the best years of your life" speech—even though they are. (Cynthia Cherrey, Vice President of Student Affairs at Tulane University adds, "If we give them that line," it not only adds pressure, but "what do they have to look forward to for the rest of their lives?")

- Remember that this is their college experience, not yours. (Another good one from Cherrey.)

- Discuss class choices with your student, but keep in mind that they have advisors to help them deal with majors and require-ments, graduating on time, and being prepared to enter the work force.

Most of all, Bips says to remind yourself that even "wonderful kids make mistakes during college." Good colleges, she believes, will allow stu-dents to make a mistake, yet provide a safety net so they can recover and thrive.

GUIDELINES FOR YOUR NEW ROLE AS LONG-DISTANCE PARENT

Seldom do parents feel just one emotion when the kids head out the door and off to school. Instead, they swing between mourning the empty nest, loving their reclaimed freedom, and all points in between. Here are fif-teen rules for your new role, straight from the colleges. Remember that you'll be experimenting just as much as your kids will be, and you're bound to make some mistakes of your own along the way. Be easy on yourself.

1. Get in touch with your own feelings.

University of Dayton's Robert Johnson, Head of the Enrollment Management Division, acknowledges that parents have complex feelings when their kids are in college. He specifically sites: apprehension about their student's chances of success; worry; envy of their opportunity; being more comfortable with things they are familiar with; and feeling more skeptical or critical of things that are not familiar. Not to get touchy-feely, but parents should be aware of these feelings and know other parents are experiencing them, too.

2. Become a friend and supporter.

Over and over again, the single biggest piece of advice that educators offer is for parents to begin to shift their role as authority figure to that of supporter, role model, admirer, and friend. J. Ann Hower, PhD, Director of New Student Programs at the University of Michigan, says that the parent's role during the college years becomes that of a mentor—someone who can provide encouragement, advice, and support without taking over the new responsibilities that belong to their son or daughter.

"While the easy decision is to call home and ask a parent to intervene, it is an important part of students' personal development and growth to address problems and conflicts on their own," say administrators at Babson College. At the same time, parents should make no bones about letting kids know that they're in for some tough times as they encounter roommate conflicts, course registrations, disciplinary concerns, and grade disputes.

Elon University's Smith Jackson, Vice President and Dean of Student Life, observes that the nature of the parent-child relationship shifts to a more equal one during college. "Parents have to give their son or daughter the opportunity to succeed, which sometimes means the opportunity to fail. Students are much more likely to ask for their parents' opinions and help if they feel their viewpoints and decisions will not be criticized." Elon's Chaplain, Rev. Richard McBride adds that, "the hardest part for parents—but eventually the most liberating for themselves and for their sons and daughters—is to realize that their place is to be the most loyal fans in the stadium, extending their trust to the new coaches on the field."

In a rather odd sort of metaphor, some administrators think of college a sort of second toddlerhood. "The securely attached first-year student is much like the securely attached toddler who can tolerate her mother's departure from a room, engage purposefully while she is gone, and then welcome her back," says Elizabeth Feeney of Mount Holyoke.

In a nutshell, says Swarthmore College, "Do not do for your student what your student can do for himself or herself!"

3. Don't compare your child's needs to others.

Hampshire College administrators caution that some students may need more support from their parents than others. One parent can expect anxious phone calls for advice on how to handle the situations he encounters, especially during the first year—and last year (when he has to adjust, yet again, to entering the working world). Another parent will only get a call from a student looking for that quick vote of confidence now and then. While some students crave communication from home, other students, while they may appreciate an occasional e-mail, may offer only one-line replies until they are confident that they have clearly established their independence.

4. Moderate your communications.

In this age of technology overload, it's getting harder and harder to distance ourselves from anyone, never mind the kids. "But that's okay," says Christine Schramm, Assistant Dean of Students and Director of Residence Education at the University of Dayton, "as long as you're aware of what 'instant' communication means. It means that your student is in the moment," she says. "When they call you, which they will do (a lot), they may be in the midst of an emotional moment, i.e., a roommate disagreement, a boyfriend/girlfriend argument, a disagreement with a university office. They may be calling you to vent or to ask for your help in solving the situation. You may not be able to figure out which one." Either way, their emotion du jour may not be at all representative of the overall college experience he or she is actually having.

Schramm says that the instinct of a good and supportive parent is to respond immediately and try to fix things. Instead, she says, "give it 12 to 24 hours and let your student an opportunity to resolve it themselves. You may find that it was not as big a 'crisis' as they reported. "One of the things we find is that college life moves quickly," continues Schramm. "Students go in and out of favor with each other quickly . . . they love their roommate, then they hate their roommate. They are in love and out of love, they are in trouble then out of trouble. The tendency for a parent to hover over or swoop in is very strong, but if you are truly interested in 'letting go,' then do it for awhile and see how much of what happens will unfold on its own."

5. Make adjustments on the home front.

Purdue University—West Lafayette says there are adjustments that need to happen at home even before the kids are away at school. "As they progress from being dependent on you to being independent and on their own, expect some changes."

"Understand that the person who you drop off on the first day of school won't be the same person you see at Thanksgiving—and allow that to happen," say Elena Sharnoff, Public Affairs Officer, and Nancy Pike, Dean of Students at Marlboro College. Once they're back, it's a good time to reexplore curfews and other pre-college rules. You both might have changed your point of view.

"Parents will be surprised at how easy it is to live with their college students if they allow them to be themselves, rather than expecting them to conform to parents' values and standards," say the staff at the University of Dayton's Counseling Center.

6. Set some grade expectations.

"External pressures from parents regarding grades or choosing a major can backfire or place undue pressure on students during a challenging time," cautions Sarah Griesse, Associate Dean of Students and Director of Residential Life at Macalester College. Grades, as she sees it, are just a portion of the college experience and students should experience all of the campus community along with their focus on academic success.

Mount Holyoke's Director of College Counseling Services, Elizabeth Feeney, PhD, says it's important to let your child know that you expect her to do her best instead of expecting her to achieve a certain quantifiable outcome. "Instead of saying, 'A 3.0 GPA? What happened? You were a straight-A student in high school!' try to reflect on the 3.0 with your child." If your child feels that she did her best, says Fenney, she should be praised for her efforts. "So many of the students I see today have been building their resumes since kindergarten and they are exhausted, disillusioned, anxious, and depressed," Feeney continues. "The healthiest students I see are the ones who allow themselves to have fun, explore new interests, make mistakes, build relationships and carve out an identity slowly and holistically. These students are willing to do these things and take care of themselves even if it means a less than perfect academic performance—unfortunately, I am seeing fewer and fewer of these students these days."

Fenny suggests the following: "If your daughter calls home to announce that crew tryouts are over and she has made the team on the novice boat, bite your tongue before saying 'Why aren't you in the Varsity Boat—I'm going to call that coach first thing tomorrow.' Or worse, 'Crew? What about your grades!?'"

"I've worked with many students who are proud of their efforts or accomplishments because they are aware of and realistic about the competition," she says. "However, these same students are devastated when a parent makes it clear that they are putting a negative, judgmental spin on the situation."

7. Accept that things aren't always fair.

University of Dayton's Assistant Dean of Students and Director of Residence Education, Christine Schramm says parents need to realize from the get-go that at college—as in life—there are going to be injustices. And as parents, they should help their students realize the same thing. "You can work hard to mitigate them and prepare for them, but they will happen. Such is life. The best lesson you can teach your student is how to handle those injustices" and move on.

8. Believe in the first eighteen years.

Without the belief that you've sent your child to school with a strong foundation of beliefs, values, and skills, college is going to be very tough on a parent. Jeffrey C. Mincey, Director of Admissions at Grove City College, says that "You have had them for eighteen years, and you have taught them and raised them with the values and principles that should motivate them to make the right decisions."

"I always tell parents: You gave your child terrific roots, and now be sure to allow them the wings they need to succeed," says Charlotte G. Burgess, Vice President and Dean of Student Life at the University of Redlands. "One of the major problems for today's parents seems to be that they perceive that they can solve problems better and more quickly than their students," she continues. "I shudder to think how these students will ever be as competent as their parents at problem-solving if we don't let them get some good practice."

Seattle University says parents should do a flashback: "Remember handing your teen the keys to the car the first time? You stated your expectations, offered your best advice, told him you were there for him, and took a deep breath as he headed down the road. With any luck, you managed to keep yourself busy enough to avoid looking out the window every few minutes." Your job now is the same. "Be available, offer love and support, and try to remember that the keys are now in their hands," say Seattle University administrators.

"Frequently, families are so bound up in the transition process, so preoccupied with the logistics, that they fail to stop, breath deep, and reflect on the meanings of their new relationships," says Purchase College— State University of New York's Ron Herron, Vice President of Student

Affairs. "The parent who knows how to provide ground support for what is essentially a solo flight will—despite occasional feelings of loss—be exhilarated by the way their child does fly!"

9. Know that knowledge is empowering.

Contrary to some parents' belief, colleges want them to know what's going on. "Attending a parent orientation is a way of obtaining practical information about the services of the counseling center, student health services, dean of students' office, university chaplains, etc. Learning about resources and conversing with other parents who are on the same journey is a helpful way of not only gaining information but creating a connection to the university community," says Jeffrey Lanfear, PsyD, Director of University Counseling Services at DePaul University. Obtaining this type of information is helpful in striving to be a good coach, rather than a rescuer.

10. Shift into listening mode.

"Listening can be a difficult role," says Dr. Nancy B. McDaniel, Assistant Vice President of Student Affairs at Auburn University. "Students sometimes want problems to be solved immediately rather than learning to work through things independently."

Start by getting a good knowledge of college policies and procedures so that you know when and how to become involved, say Jacqueline Kiernan MacKay, Assistant Vice President for Student Services, and Wanda S. Ingram, Associate Dean of Undergraduate Studies at Providence College. They point out, for example, how important it is to understand FERPA (Family Educational Rights and Privacy Act—see Appendix A for the full text) and the parent notification policies at your particular school. They say "during those first few weeks it is important to listen, listen, and then listen some more!"

To Fairfield University's Mark Reed, Dean of Students, listening is all about *not* taking action. "Sometimes parents can misinterpret a quick call or message for a need to intervene and solve some problem, when, in fact, the student just wanted someone to listen."

When you do talk, make sure to ask the right questions. Mount Holyoke's Director of Counseling, Elizabeth Fenney says, "Try not to ask: 'Where exactly were you last night when I called at 1:00 A.M.?' Rather, ask gentle leading questions such as: 'Is there anything you need? Is there anything you are struggling with? Anything you are proud of? Do you want to hear the hilarious thing that your crazy dog did last weekend?'"

Fenney says parents should think through their means of communicating carefully. Although e-mail and instant messaging are time- and cost-efficient, she points out that they can also be emotional and reactive. "I have worked with many students who have sent an angry e-mail that they later regretted, and I have seen many wounds inflicted by an angry, impulsive e-mail from a parent. I am quite sure that if either party had been forced to put pen to paper, find a stamp, and drive to the post office and mail the letter, they would have also been forced to calm down and write a more rational response. E-mail and instant messaging can be dangerous ammunition, so slow down and be sure that what you send is what you want your child to hear."

11. Refuse to see college life as one big emergency.
Vanderbilt University's Chancellor, Gordon Gee, asks parents to "Recognize that distance imparts a sense of urgency and sometimes a desire to overcompensate. Surely if she took the time to tell you about it, it must be urgent! And you are doubtless in the habit of helping out anyway, of carefully overseeing your son or daughter's affairs, or you would not be reading a book like this one," he says. But Gee would like to see parents retrain their parental reflexes. "Your impulse will be to try to remedy every issue your young person has, no matter how small. But you have to resist that impulse!...Save your big guns for real crises." This is especially true since you don't want to risk undoing the good work that is happening on campus. "Professors think of students as adults and fellow scholars," says Gee. "That is a deep compliment to a student, and it's the reason why professors are flummoxed when a parent appears on the scene to intercede!"

12. Don't live vicariously.

Hampshire College finds that "What is often hardest for parents is to let go of their own secret dreams of who their children will become, letting them find their own paths. Yet the ultimate gift of love is to learn to play facilitator to your child's own steps toward an independent future." Hearing about a great class, a weekend spent hiking in the mountains, or being surrounded by so many new friends can set off a pang of envy for the college lifestyle. But there's no going back, so you have to push on ahead.

As much as you know exactly what you would do if you were in your child's shoes, "remember and understand that you don't know everything. There are limits to your knowledge about the various situations your child will face during college," say the administrators at Swarthmore College. "Empower your children to meet their challenges themselves and solve their own problems. Trying to micromanage their lives or run interference is not helpful—not helpful to them, the college, or yourself."

13. Lose the tendency to guilt trip.

We all know that guilt works, but Mount Holyoke's Fenney also reminds us to be careful and not put too much pressure, stress, or guilt on your child about the cost of her education—or anything else. "I have been alarmed recently at the number of students who feel paralyzed by the sacrifices that their parents, extended family, and sometimes even their entire community, have made for their education. This paralyzing effect often leads not only to failure, but to depression and anxiety as well," she says.

In a similar vein, Fenney believes children should be informed and connected to what is going on at home, but not overly burdened by it. "Too many students fail because they are overly concerned with the caretaking of a parent or a sibling, or they are completely overwhelmed by a crisis at home." Quick updates are fine—the harrowing details should be kept to a minimum.

14. Laugh it off.

The College of Wooster's Dean of Students, Kurt Holmes, doesn't under-estimate the importance in keeping your sense of humor. "You will be very proud of your kids come graduation day, so don't be too hard on them at Family Weekend when they have been through three majors in a month, are sporting a new piercing, or they have long hair, no hair, or blue hair," he advises. "They're just finding out who and what they want to become in life."

15. Partner with her school.

It's not hard to see the college as an adversary when information is scarce and tuition is high, but if you don't think of your child's education as a partnership, the student will lose. Elon University's Rev. Richard McBride, University Chaplain, believes that a parent's job is to say to their children: "Here is your life; welcome to it!" The college's job is to say: "Here are opportunities for you to grow intellectually, socially, and spiri-tually. We can teach you how to make wise choices!" Often times, parents and colleges are saying the same things in different ways because they want the same things for their students: success.

"Collectively, everyone wants the student to be academically and social-ly successful, to learn personal accountability and responsibility, and to be equipped with the skills necessary for a productive life after college," says Susquehanna University's Tracy Tyree, Dean of Student Life. "Parents should think of themselves as partners with the college or uni-versity in the students' success."

What's your role in this partnership? "I tell parents to try to relax, even though it's difficult to hear and almost impossible to do," says Dr. Michael Freeman, Vice President and Dean of St. Mary's College of Maryland. "College is meant to be a place for young people to experiment and test boundaries—and they do. There are people on campus with the charge to watch for their safety and to guide them when they try to extend or move the barriers. Parents need to partner with those professionals, and try to establish and maintain honest and open communication with their son or daughter."

Unconditional Love

Elizabeth Feeney, PhD, Director of College Counseling Service at Mount Holyoke College, puts it this way: "Your role as a parent during the college years is to be just that: a parent. You need not be the coach, tutor, academic advisor, matchmaker, cook, private investigator, or therapist. Instead, your main job is to love your child unconditionally as only a parent can do—because that is the one thing that no one else will be able to do for her."

Certainly, much of the foundation of secure attachment and unconditional love is laid down in the early years of a child's life, but there is still a lot that a parent can do during the college years. In fact, channel the voices of former students talking about what parents can and should do during the college years, and near the top of the list would be the following 15 parent "shoulds" and "should nots" as reported by real former students.

During college, my parents should:

1. Set limits and stick to them ·

2. Be as interested in their own lives as they are mine

3. Model what they say. Take care of their own demons, addictions, short-comings, etc.

4. Have other connections in their life—otherwise they will smother me

5. Work together as a team, even if they are divorced. Get support if they are single

6. Ask questions

7. Listen and pay attention not only to my words, but also to my silences and my behavior

8. Convince me that they care

9. Let me know their values, but still love me if my values are different

During college, my parents should not:

10. Air their (or other family member's) dirty laundry with me

11. Expose me to their doubts and insecurities

12. Depend on me

13. Try to be as cool and hip as I am

14. Try to be my best friend; I have friends—I need a parent

15. Nag, interrogate, or judge me

These students have also illuminated the main reasons why they shut their parents out:

1. Shame or embarrassment about something that has happened

2. Fear of being cut off financially and/or emotionally

3. Fear of being judged

4. Protection of the parent based on the belief that the parent is too weak or vulnerable to be involved

5. Belief that the parent does not care

6. Poor communication skills or a lack of experience with sharing personal information

7. Fear that the parent will tell others

ENOUGH WORDS, TIME TO DO

Love your child hard, well, and unconditionally. Be her advocate when she needs you, be her cheerleader when she succeeds, and be her confidante whenever she allows you that privilege. Expect nothing in return. (Every student appreciates gestures of love, but few are capable at this point of consistently expressing that appreciation or reciprocating the gesture.) Be patient; it may be years before they can tell you how much your support means to them—but rest assured—it does mean a great deal. Parental love and support are part of any student's recipe for a fantastic college experience.

Letting Go (of their bedrooms, that is...)

As children move from kindergarten through high school, the day-to-day changes are subtle. Heading off to college, in contrast, is anything but a subtle change. It's a now you see 'em, now you don't phenomenon. Once they're out that front door, their feelings will vacillate wildly between total exhilaration and total despondency, not to mention hitting all points in between. You? You'll have your own vacillations. The euphemism for this flurry of emotions is "letting go"—and most professionals speak of it in terms of parents letting go of their children. But—putting emotion aside for a moment—what about all of their stuff? Few people address the aftermath of letting go, always so evident when you push open their bedroom door.

"Stuff" turns out to be a great topic of conversation for parents with kids in college. Parents will talk of walking into their children's empty rooms, inhaling a faint whiff from the few remaining clothes in the drawers, circling the floor aimlessly as they pick up their notebooks, trophies, and souvenirs from family vacations. Their thoughts at this point tend to fall into one of two camps: either, "I miss them so much every time I walk in here" or "This is a bonus room in the house now. What should I do with it, and where will I put all this stuff once I decide?" Most parents, over four years, experience both.

Most parents also struggle with the limbo-like existence between these two states of mind while their kids are in college. Speaking generally, college is an eight- or nine- month annual affair, which leaves your child seeking alternatives (at home or otherwise) for approximately one-third of the year.

With the room empty for such a long stretch, some parents release their creative energies (and whatever budget is left after tuition) to transform the former bedroom into something a bit more functional—a sewing room or entertainment room, meanwhile leaving a small corner with a pull-out bed for those visits home. In urban areas, where real estate is scarce, kids joke that their parents threaten to redo their bedroom before their last bag is packed for school. Other parents—the sentimental types—tidy up, shut the door, and keep the bedroom as dust-gathering shrines. A last group of parents realize they're now living with too much empty space in general. These parents choose to downsize, moving out of their larger, "kid-based" homes to a smaller dwelling—sometimes in whole other cities or states. It's their chance to choose a town they might have moved to sooner if they weren't worried about traumatizing a child by pulling her out of high school when she finally got asked to the homecoming dance by the cutest boy in her chemistry class.

There is no one correct answer to the empty bedroom dilemma, but the general guideline is to let your child in on your decision early on as well as the thought process you used to get there. This is a full conversation you should have, not a unilateral action plan. Getting their buy-in on the plan is crucial to avoiding resentment or confusion down the road.

Regardless of the outcome, it's good to let them know that they always have a place in your home should they need one. Most of the more long-term thinking parents wait at least for a year or two after the kids head off to college before deconstructing the room. (They're often trying to gauge the likelihood of "the revolving door syndrome"—a child moving back home after college or after a bad experience living elsewhere.) Parents with younger children still living at home often see this as a hand-me-down room, upgrading a younger child to a bigger, better room.

A survey conducted by www.findyourfurniture.com found that empty nesters' most popular choice for redoing an empty room was to create a library or reading room. Other popular choices included a hobby studio, a guest room, a home theater, or a home office.

Here's a cheery thought: If you're an average baby boomer (1946–1964) who lives to an average age, you'll spend more time as an empty nester parent than you did as a roost-full parent—so get used to the extra space and enjoy it!

READY, SET, CHANGE!

Here are some ideas for helping you fluff the nest to your liking and start your new life.

Practice.

If your kids haven't spent much time away from home and you still have a bit of time left, get them out for some practice runs. A travel program, a summer school college experience, a trip to a friend or relative in another city, perhaps? Getting them out of their comfort zone—and out of the house—is good preparation for you both

Create a "stuff reduction" plan.
Talk about what you'll do with their things when they're gone—their drawers, their closest, their bookshelves—before they go to school and let them help with the plan if they're willing. Also instigate and pack-and-pitch plan. Require them to weed out their old things and get rid of some excess stuff while they pack for college. You can even set a big box outside their door and tell them you want to see it filled by the time the day comes to drive to school.

My husband and I asked each of our children to go through the possessions they were leaving behind and create one "memory box" filled with important bits of memorabilia. We stored these big plastic crates in a safe place for them. And while we left their rooms in tact while they were at school, we did make numerous trips to thrift stores and used book stores with the stuff they left behind that fell into the "they'll never want to see this again" category.

Students attest that it's disconcerting to see their rooms dismantled and to feel as if they have become a guest in their own homes. Parents can respond by doing things to show them it's still their home—be it cooking their favorite dinner or rearranging the space to make them more comfortable when they return. If they're sleeping on a different bed or a pull-out couch when they come home, let them pick out some new sheets, choose a new color to paint the room, or put a TV in there so they'll have a place to go and do their own thing, even if it's not their old bedroom. Obviously, don't eliminate all traces of their existence either. Keeping some of their favorite things out on display provides a subtle reminder that home is a constant.

Remember who your friends were and what your hobby was.
Many parents report that they feel a burst of energy and creativity when the kids leave home. They sign up for classes, begin fitness programs,

redecorate, volunteer, or throw themselves into their work with a new fervor.

Your kids can be your biggest fans and champions as you start your next act. Mine will actually cheer when I say I'm starting a new project or I've signed up to take a course. They go wild in the stands when I say I'm having dinner with a friend, since I spent much of their lives working and parenting, leaving little time for friends. Your kids will be thrilled that you have your own life, and they'll undoubtedly find you a better conversationalist for it. (At least some of the emphasis will at last be taken off of them.)

Look in the mirror, but not too hard.

Friends tell me that, even though I'm older, I look a lot better than when my kids were younger. I look at my peers and notice the same thing. "That," I tell them, "is because I can now exercise, make sure my pants are clean, zipped, and my shirt is tucked in, and I don't feel compelled to cook pounds of food each week." No wonder I look better!

"The newfound time for yourself can be disconcerting when you're not used to it," remarked a friend of mine. "But there's no doubt you have a bit more time to put yourself together—which is good—because at our age we need it!" And if you don't, you'll have some free time for something else.

Remember the spouse.

There's a good chance that, on the long list of life's chores, your spouse slipped down in pecking order when your kids were still at home. Once that first one goes off to school, it may be time to reinvestigate that order. Psychologists who've pondered this question all suggest that it's a time to reacquaint yourself with your spouse. (It's fun once you have some time to get going...) If you're not married or you're divorced, it may be time to reacquaint yourself with the adult world at large.

Vacation Time

School-aged children provide a rhythm to life, and that rhythm goes berserk when the kids head off to college. Holidays and vacations will take on a new form, but they're still important...

Should we still take family vacations?

In the U.S., we have only limited vacation time to divvy up, unfortunately. But most experts believe that family reunions and vacations are just as important as the kids get older as they were when they were younger. Sure, they'll want to head off for spring break somewhere with their friends, or spend the summer working away from home. In between, try to squeeze in a few days of family time together away from home. You'll break the daily grind and get a chance to talk and experience each other in a new surrounding. Plus, if you can swing it, take your vacation when school first gets out in May. It's less crowded, and the prices haven't skyrocketed yet.

What can I expect over the holidays?

Holidays take some getting used to on both your part and your student's. It's not atypical for kids to feel depressed, a bit "out of it," and like strangers in their own home. Patience, some good food, and a little coaxing to go out and shop, see a movie, or call an old friend can help speed the acclimation.

CHAPTER 2

Life in the Dorms

Borrow your razor?

When my oldest daughter was a sophomore in college, she became ill. While she was hospitalized, her roommate honored me by allowing me to stay in their dorm room and sleep in my daughter's bed. This way, I could zip over to the hospital, and as the medical bills were adding up, at least I wasn't paying for a hotel on top of it. I will never forget her kindness—nor my week as a dorm member. I am now convinced that there's a good reason why you go to college and live in a dorm at age 18. It's much more difficult—both mentally and physically—as you get older.

What did I learn in the dorm?

One: Dorm life is not a life of the mind. It may, in fact, be a life of the anti-mind. Who can think there? Studying is nearly out of the question. Nothing—not the sound of boots clomping or sneakers running through the halls, not the peals of laughter and shrieks, not the constant background (or not so background) music—makes it easy. Deterrents to studying dot the field like an obstacle course. You develop amazing concentration skills or you fail trying.

Two: You need to be a bit oblivious and immune to dirt. It must be that your eye for dirt gets keener as you age. These kids don't mean to be dirty—their eyes simply aren't attuned to seeing dust-balls under the bed or mold on the bathroom tiles. Their noses don't smell rotten food and it's not on their list of priorities to care that it is festering inside the fridge.

Three: There's not much place for modesty in the dorm. There are no attempts to hide who is sleeping with whom or who's got cramps. Keeping a secret about your health or your family problems is tough to do. It's quite a public life despite anyone's best efforts.

Perhaps the biggest eye-opener were the little things—like the regularly replenished fishbowl full of condoms in the bathroom. Like the sound of alarms (and snooze alarms) going off at all hours of the day. Like the zany décor with "no parking" signs, neon lights, and advertising posters that found their way from some refuse pile to their new home in the dorm. This is how our children live.

For parents mired in their habits who relish their privacy, the dorm can be unsettling. Despite the fact that they're filled with smart, engaging, generous, and kind students, my five days as a dorm-mate made that "Survivor" reality show look like a cakewalk.

Another way to think of it: Other than summer camp, and perhaps a stint in the military, dorm life is probably as close to communal living as your children are going to get, and the transition is never a gradual one. One day, they're hanging out in the comfort of their childhood bedrooms; the next, they find themselves thrown in with a random group of strangers in a stark dorm setting where they're expected to live in peace and harmony. They'll all have age and maybe a few test scores in common, but that's about it. Yet these students will suddenly be sharing a room the size of their bedroom closet back home with one, two, or even three other kids they've never even met. As an added stressor, they'll be sharing the most sacrosanct of teenage places—the bathroom—with a gaggle of others who may or may not share the same levels of modesty, hygiene, and neatness. Ah, college!

The transition to dorm life hits freshmen the hardest. This new arrangement often triggers a jumble of emotions, especially at the larger schools where students can't help but feel processed by number in the housing game and are rather stripped of their personal identity overall. They'll each be issued the requisition ID card, bed, closet, desk and trash can. Then they're off and running.

This chapter looks at life in the dorm, especially for freshman who are living away from home for the first time, as well as how upperclass students should approach their housing options. We'll cover:

- What kind of dorms and living arrangements are available
- How colleges pair roommates
- How to deal with roommate problems if they arise
- What to expect from life in the dorms
- Alternative living situations like fraternities, sororities, and off-campus housing

Dorm Life 101

Most colleges require students who aren't commuting to spend at least their first year on campus living in the dorms—or what schools now like to call their "residence halls." Whatever you call them, dorm living is a truly unique experience, and the more a student knows about it, the more likely she is to embrace the best and be aware of the rest.

The upside of dorms is that the students who live in them become equals in jump-starting their new social lives. Each student has been instantly placed in a situation designed to help them meet people, with Residence Advisors (RAs) to help them through any rough patches. Freshmen living on campus meet some of their best friends in the dorms and often find someone with whom they decide to room the following year. While your child may not adore every single person he passes in the halls, a sense of camaraderie naturally develops among peers who are all "in this together."

What they'll trade for the benefit of living in the dorm community is any sense of privacy. Every stomachache, headache, and bad day the residents have become everybody's business in a college dorm. On the other hand, when a couple of Excedrin are in order, your child will find a number of mini drugstores along the hall where she can go searching for relief.

Parents seem to worry more about dorm life than students do. Plenty worry about it even more than they fret about academics. Maybe that's because they trust the professors to teach more than they trust their kids to become an adult with his own "crash pad" overnight? Or maybe they recall their own dorm lives with a "do as I say, not as I did" mantra.

Students will undoubtedly have their share of complaints and have colorful tales to tell about "the dorm weirdoes." They'll be thrown together with people whose cultures, habits, and personalities may be vastly different from their own. But despite all of the emotional and physical ups and downs, most students who experience dorm life find that they make friends for life and find out something about themselves in the process. The truth is, some of the most important things they'll learn in college will be learned in the dorm room, not in the classroom.

Not Your Grandfather's Dorm

Schools aren't calling them dorms anymore. Today the fashionable term is "residence hall," a less institutional sounding name. For our purposes we'll stick with the four-letter word.

The name isn't the only thing that's changing. Dorms themselves are getting facelifts faster than Hollywood has-beens. The formerly old, drafty, claustrophobic spaces are making way for a new generation of housing designed to meet the needs of a much more demanding clientele. We're seeing more private or semi-private spaces, fewer people sharing those large institutional bathrooms, and lots of amenities designed to make students feel "at home." Today, it's not uncommon for a dorm to look more like a condo replete with Internet connections, cable TV, security gates, workout gyms, and covered parking lots! Here's a few of the new dorm amenities popping up in college housing across the country:

SUNY—Purchase College: Has multicolored U-shaped buildings that form a courtyard dotted with storefronts. The idea is to create a small-town atmosphere.

Case Western Reserve University and University of Massachusetts at Dartmouth: Both have new residence halls where students can have a full-size bed.

University of Wisconsin—Milwaukee: New dorms have a fitness center with massage, free movie theater with first-run movies, branded coffee shop, and a convenience store.

Pennsylvania State University: New dorms feature single rooms with private baths.

University of Wisconsin: Manicures and pedicures on campus.

Baylor University: One dorm has an amphitheater, a Chili's restaurant, and ten different floor plans from which to choose.

Kennesaw State: Dorms come with a full refrigerator, range, microwave, and washer and dryer.

Florida International University: Campus housing includes pools, sundecks, reserved parking, convenience stores, computer labs, and 24-hour reception.

Michigan State University: TVs in the bathrooms and Jacuzzis in the residence halls.

Oklahoma City University: New dorms include large-screen TVs.

If dorms are palaces, then the public spaces around the campus are like kingdoms. Ohio State University's new Recreational and Physical Activity Center offers massage, three pools (instruction, leisure, and spa), outdoor equipment rentals, and a climbing center. Washington State University has a fifty-three-person Jacuzzi. Indiana University of Pennsylvania has a golf simulator with fifty-two courses from around the world. At the center of Penn State's Student Union is a salt water coral reef aquarium—a living replica of a barrier reef.

The bottom line is that today's campuses are more intimate and less institutional, but there's a touch of a country club creeping in at more and more schools. Students may find themselves wanting to trade colleges with their friends just to upgrade their current housing.

Note: Dorms are a college profit center. Some of these flashy new dorms cost more to live in than the older variety, leaving educators speculating on whether this luxury housing will cause a further socio-economic rift between more and less wealthy students.

The Modern Dorm

Below, is a list of amenities and a percentage that indicates how many of the dorms built in 2004 will feature them according to a "College Housing 2004" study available from the Peter Li Education Group, an educational publishing and media company in Dayton, Ohio.

Laundry 100%

Vending 96%

Study Room 96%

TV Room 83%

Rooms Air Conditioned 83%

Card Access to Building 79%

Kitchen 75%

Rooms Carpeted 71%

Computer Center 54%

Video Surveillance 52%

Classrooms 42%

Card Access to Rooms 38%

Fitness Center 25%

ATM 13%

Dining Hall 8%

WHAT KIND OF DORM CHOICES ARE THERE?

Your children will have a number of choices, but make no mistake about it: Freshmen have the least choice and typically get the worst dorms on campus. As they rise through the upperclass ranks, however, their situation should improve.

A freshman's biggest choice, at least in coed schools, begins with whether to live in a same-sex or coed dorm. Same-sex dorms often have restrictions against all-night visitors of the opposite sex. A coed dorm can mean anything from a floor or one wing that's designated for males and another one for females, to a room-by-room mix of males and females with rooms on the same floor. In addition to coed and same-sex dorms, many colleges offer themed dorms which cater to a students' interests or lifestyle. Students with certain pursuits (international studies) or beliefs (Judaism) may find these of interest. They are not usually available to freshman.

Dorms come in many configurations as well. Single rooms are usually in short supply for freshmen. (If the point of dorm life is meeting people, schools don't want to give newbies on campus a chance to hole up alone in their own little rooms.) Doubles, two students in one room, is the most common configuration. Some dorms—especially newer ones—are designed as suites: a cluster of single or double rooms around a shared common space. Suites are often the province of upperclassman. They are much in demand because they allow ample privacy for study and sleep, but offer the benefits of a shared space for entertaining and relaxing.

SHOULD OUR CHILD CHOOSE A SAME-SEX OR COED DORM?

As stated earlier, coed dorms can mean a spectrum of different things. If you and your child are straddling the fence on the gender question as far as housing goes, the deal-breaker is to visit the college's dorm bathroom— the place where your student is most likely to feel the full impact of coed versus same-sex living. When your child walks into a fully coed bathroom full of boys and girls who are showering, using side-by-side stalls, and walking around in various states of undress, he will get a pretty good gauge of their comfort level.

The Catholic University of America suggests that your child try to experience both coed and single-sex dorms and choose the type of dorm in which she feels most comfortable.

Most schools offer programs for incoming freshmen in which they will host prospective students overnight in the dorms. It's not always possible, but if a student can swing it, it's the best way to get a sense of what living in a dorm would be like. Students can always request a coed or single-sex dorm for the visit, and the school will try to accommodate.

At Worcester Polytechnic Institute, the Residential Services Department sums it up by saying, "a coed hall offers students an opportunity to live in an environment that is very diverse" despite the fact that "some students come from backgrounds where cultural differences may not allow them to live in a coed environment." WPI also mentions that "some students prefer a same-sex environment because it gives them an increased sense of privacy. If the school your child chooses has a coed campus, there will still be plenty of opportunities for coed interactions, no matter which dorm he decides upon."

There are arguments to be made in favor of both coed and single-sex dorms. A coed dorm lets students experience the other sex as just another bunch of "folks" with different anatomies. Same-sex dorms bring out more of the flavor of an individual gender. So, while it sounds a bit stereotypical, there really is something of a general perception that girls' dorms are catty and cliquey, yet calm. Then, there's the stereotype of guys' dorms as loud, stinky, belching havens for practical jokes. Both extremes become subdued in mixed company. Coed dorms temper the extremes often found in single-sex dorms.

For some students, same-sex dorms offer a haven from the opposite sex where many students say they can more easily relax and be themselves. Whether that means wearing curlers in their hair at night, putting on ratty old pajama bottoms, or wearing an orthodontic night-brace, in a same-sex dorm, students seem to do these things with a bit less inhibition.

In the end, remember that regardless of college policy, dorm rules, and their parents' grandest wishes, kids tend to develop their own rules once they're out of the house and living on campus. That includes bringing boyfriends or girlfriends into the dorms after hours. A single-sex dorm will make it harder, but far from impossible, to have visitors dropping by.

ANY ADVICE FOR GETTING USED TO A COED DORM?

Is this advice for you or for your child? Without a doubt, you'll have a harder time adjusting to a coed arrangement than your son or daughter will. By the time they reach college age, teens are used to mingling and hanging out in a variety of situations. At Washington University the school's housing staff finds that it takes very little time for students to adapt to mixed dorms. They say that students rank the opportunity for interaction and to meet others as one of the most important things about living on campus. Coed dorms help fill that bill.

So, take a deep breath and exhale. Look around and see how

> **TIP:** Just like dating at the office, it's probably a good idea to advise your children that if they are going to date, it's probably best to avoid dorm-mates and housemates.

comfortably your children mix in this environment. Think about how nice it is for them to have the chance to experience the ultimate diversity—enjoying the opposite sex in a place where friendships are valued above dating and intimacy. In the best possible world, living side by side in the dorms will help break down one more barrier to understanding.

Famous Roommates

Be nice to your roommate because you never know...

Tommy Lee Jones roomed with Al Gore at Yale. Ana Paquin and Julia Stiles went to school together, too.

A Don't Tell Policy

Several years ago, Wesleyan University inaugurated a "gender-blind" dormitory for incoming students who weren't sure what sex they were or who wanted a room assignment made independently of identifying their sex. In 2004, the decision to create special transgender housing was reversed, and that dorm is no longer for transgenders only.

Are Special Interest Dorms Like "International," "Honors," or "Outdoor Interest" a Good Idea?

In this age of niche marketing and self-selecting cliques, you shouldn't be surprised to learn that most colleges offer "special interest" dorms where like-minded individuals can live together under the same roof.

Almost every college has some form of self-selection. There are quiet dorms, wellness dorms, substance-free dorms, and nonsmoking dorms. These allow students with a certain preference or interest to take shelter in the same building. Is segregating oneself on campus based on what you do or don't ingest a bit odd? That isn't for me to say, but the colleges feel it allows communities to grow and minimizes intolerance.

You'll also find dorms segregated by dietary preferences such as vegetarian and kosher dorms, or by a cause, such as an environmentally friendly dorm. There are international dorms, where foreign students can feel a kindred bond as well as African-American dorms. There are dorms based on hobbies and passions ranging from outdoor activities, computers and technology, academic study dorms, and those geared toward volunteer service. If your child is considering a special interest dorm, have her talk to as many of the residents as she can to get a feel for what life in this dorm will be like. Students with only a mild interest in the dorm's theme might start to feel suffocated or that the theme is overkill after a few months. These students might be better off in a dorm without a special interest.

Are special interest dorms a good thing? To their credit, they allow students to immerse themselves in the things that define them. Timothy Spears, Dean of Middlebury College, reports that the school has several academic interest houses oriented around foreign languages, environmental studies, and multi-culturalism. Students are eligible to live in this type of housing after their first year. "These 'living and learning' environments offer important educational opportunities," for some students says Spears.

The flip side is that special interest dorms can pigeonhole or type-cast students and create situations where they spend all their time with folks just like them. It's hard to foster race relations if the various races all live in their own campus cliques. Special interest dorms tend to surround the student with people just like them, who share the same interests.

The best advice is for your child to spend freshman year in a traditional dorm. After that, if your child expresses interest in a dorm like this, discuss his motivation for living in a special interest dorm. Be aware that some students choose a special interest dorm for housing, not ideological, reasons. It doesn't take long for students to figure out that the Spanish language dorm has the best views, or the international dorm has the best food. There are plenty of kids who will suddenly embrace eco-living or quiet hours if it means a bigger room or a private bathroom. Is that so wrong? Not necessarily. But a discussion prior to the special interest commitment is never a bad idea.

Interest-ing Dorms

These theme dorms at UC—Davis are typical of the offerings you might find at many larger colleges:

African American and African

Agriculture and Society

Asian American Studies

Communicating in the Twenty-First Century

Education In and Out of the Classroom

Engineering

Environmental Connections

Leadership Exploration

Health Science Community

Science Community

Agricultural Interest Program

Asian Pacific-American Theme House

Casa Cuauhtémoc (Chicano-Latino)

Davis Honors Challenge

Hammarskjöld International Relations

Health Science Community

Integrated Studies

Multiethnic Program

Music, Arts, and Performance

Outdoor Experience Programs

Quiet Program

Rainbow House (lesbian, gay, bisexual, transgender)

Science Community

Wellness/Substance Free Community

Women's Community

HOW ARE FRESHMAN ROOMMATES PAIRED UP?

Freshman year is typically the only year that colleges make the room-mate choice for students. While incoming freshmen can request to room with a friend from high school or a cousin who will be attending as well, it rarely happens: Schools want students to experience new people and not get caught in their comfort zones.

With a year of school under their belts, sophomores through seniors can request roommates, and the school makes every attempt to make sure that it happens. There's a pretty good success rate, too. If a sophomore doesn't want to live with anybody in particular, she can abdicate and ask the college to make a match for them. Remember that by sophomore year, there's a different system for assigning rooms. Unlike freshman year when the school is matching unknowns, the system shifts to accommodating the pairs or groups of students who want to room or dorm together.

In addition to who a student wants to live with, there's the question of what kind of dorm she wants to live in. Again, freshmen are typically bottom-feeders here, often segregated into the least desirable dorms on campus. For sophomores and higher,

> **TIP:** No Smoking?
>
> What if your child selects a smoking dorm and you don't approve? You do have some choice. You have the luxury of telling him that you won't pay for him to live in a building where he can smoke. He can pay the dorm fee himself, or choose a non-smoking dorm. This may not stop him from smoking, but at least he won't have permission to do it inside.
>
> On the other hand, be aware that non-smoking dorms typically impose a fee for smoking violations. John (last name withheld), a student and RA at College of the Atlantic in Bar Harbor, Maine, says that when parents put their kids in a where dorm they don't belong—typically a substance-free or non-smoking dorm—there are bound to be violations of the rules and the students end up paying the price for that mistake.

there are a few systems to help select rooms in a somewhat ecumenical fashion. The two most popular are a lottery (by far the most widely used system) and some sort of point system (sometimes tied to grades).

Colleges swear that choosing students to room together freshman year is part art and part science. However, after meeting their roommates, most students believe that it's not much more scientific than picking names out of a hat.

How can they rig it so that a neat freak doesn't get paired up with the campus slob? The teetotaler with the beer guzzler? The drinks-coffee-at-

11:00 P.M. girl with one who teaches a 6:00 A.M. aerobics class? It's no accident, they say! Colleges, much like online dating sites, gather basic profile information and do their best to make a match. Middlebury College's Spears says, "Incoming students are asked to fill out a roommate questionnaire the spring before they matriculate." Like most other colleges, Middlebury asks questions like: "Are you an early bird or night owl? Do you have an interest in sports, music, theater, or dance? Do you play video games? Have you ever shared a room?"

> **TIP:** Teaching Roommate Etiquette
>
> Since there's not an Emily Post of the dorm room, you may have to do some coaching, especially if your child is not used to sharing his space. A good roommate will...
>
> - Leave the room quietly when the other person is fighting with her parents or girlfriend/boyfriend on the phone.
> - Use a book light if they're a late-night reader.
> - Never hit the snooze button on the alarm when the other person is still sleeping—or at least not more than once.
> - Always have their key.
> - Be careful about bringing their dates home too often.
> - Clean out their share of the fridge before it gets moldy.

Parts of the questionnaire revolve around the physical building. At the University of Redlands, the basic factors for pairing first-year students are whether they prefer air conditioning, old or new architecture, a hall close to eating facilities, athletic facilities, or classroom facilities.

Colleges look at lifestyle over personality or academics when making roommate selections. "We survey students about things like their need for neatness, their sleep habits, study habits, and smoking," says Deborah Olsen Nolan, Associate Dean and Dean of Students at Ursinus College.

"Shared hobbies and interests help make great friends, but they aren't critical in a roommate relationship. It doesn't matter if you like the same music or play the same sport, if one roommate is a slob and the other is a neat-freak," says the Residence Life staff at Union College. Union asks incoming freshman about cleanliness standards, noise tolerance, normal bedtime, and study habits, but don't promise that all of these preferences will be met. For all of their questioning and matchmaking, schools admit there is no perfect science to pairing up two complete strangers to live together for a school year. Keith B. Humphrey, Sr. Assistant Director of Admissions at The University of Arizona expresses some of his frustration: "For some reason, students in high school will tell us they have no problem getting up at 7:00 A.M., but something magical happens to them when they come to a college campus and they lose this ability!" All the same, he says the school finds it important "for students to learn more about others, so living with students who may be different from themselves provides a prime opportunity for this personal development."

HOW CAN PARENTS HELP WITH THE ROOMMATE SELECTION PROCESS?

Keep out! Or, as Charlotte G. Burgess, Vice President/Dean of Student Life University of Redlands puts it: "The best way to help your child choose a dorm is to make certain that he or she completes all the paperwork. If you fill out the housing form for them, it's almost guaranteed that roommate conflicts will exist."

Burgess suggests parents manage their expectations, too. Freshman dorms, even the ones at the most elite colleges, are typically small and furthest from the campuses' prime real estate.

The questionnaire needs to describe who your child is, not who they want to be. Burgess says that students sometimes don't answer the questions honestly because they think that their parents will be upset with their choices. She's known parents who found out, for the first time, that their kids were smoking cigarettes just because they looked at the questionnaire.

There are always those students who decide they want to turn over a new leaf and become an early riser. So they check it off on their roommate questionnaire as if that will make it so. (Enter: Their enraged roommate who actually *does* get up early to study and has to listen to this other student pounding down the snooze button for two hours every morning.) There are other students who are sure that the college is going to make some post-acceptance judgment about them because they say they are beer drinkers. So, they take on a false persona to fill out the questionnaire.

A parent's job is to give kids the leeway to be honest. There is one caveat, however: If the school asks for information about your child's mental health, prescription drugs, learning disabilities, or other things that you wish to remain personal, you've got a dilemma. You need to balance your right to privacy with the trust that disclosure places on the school. There is no right answer here, and, in fact, there could be legal ramifications if any problems were to occur down the road surrounding a situation you hadn't disclosed. If, for example, you didn't disclose that your child had violent tendencies and was on medication and there was an incident at school and your child was involved—you would potentially be liable. Whether you decide to disclose or keep private, you and your child should decide together.

TIP: Snooze You Lose?

Freshman Move-In Day etiquette would ideally dictate that even if you get there first, your child be kind enough to wait until her roommate arrives before claiming anything like a bed or a dresser. Try to plan to arrive at similar times so you can get off on the right foot. On the other hand, it might be easier to move in to the dorm room with only one family hauling things in and out rather than two or more sets of parents and sibs standing by in the peanut gallery. Plenty of students understand that it's finder's keeper's and that the first person who arrives just might take the desk with fewer dings in it and the bed by the window with a view. If your child can discuss how she wants to coordinate this with her roommate ahead of time, all the better. (Some students agree that if there is a clearly better bed or desk locale, for instance, they will switch halfway through the year.) If not, encourage her not to let a less desirable piece of furniture sour the roommate relationship from day one. If she steps up and lets her roommate take the clearly nicer half of the room, she might score some brownie points toward better camaraderie with her new roommate down the road. If nothing else, remind her that it's dorm furniture, for heaven's sake! This isn't like drawing straws for either a Chevette or a Lexus to be driven around the next four years. It's a temporary situation and the level of desirability is only relative—and it amounts to very little in the grand scheme of her college life.

SHOULD MY CHILD CONTACT HER ROOMMATE-TO-BE IN THE SUMMER BEFORE FRESHMAN YEAR?

Most schools encourage this sort of contact. That's why they send the names out midway through the summer, leaving plenty of time before move-in day. Of course, your child will say she wants her roommate to call her first. In which case, Tracy Tyree of Susquehanna University says you can suggest that she e-mail the other student; it's often an easier icebreaker than a phone call. "But don't forget to use the phone, too, since e-mails can be misunderstood and lack intonation and gesture."

> **FACT:** Students who are accustomed to sharing bedrooms and bathrooms at home tend to make an easier adjustment to school.

Administrators at Babson College assert that contacting her roommate will not only ease some of that first-day anxiety but may better help her decide what to pack. (Who should bring the TV? Who has the better DVD player or stereo? Should someone bring a fridge to share?) Some roommates even get into discussing décor and color coordination of sheets and comforters. Whatever they discuss, an initial phone call can help break the ice before the big day arrives.

SHOULD I CALL THE PARENTS OF MY CHILD'S FUTURE ROOMMATE AND INTRODUCE MYSELF?

They're roommates, not getting married, right? Nearly every college takes the same platform on this topic: "Don't do it." College after college has told us they flat out believe that it's a bad idea to get involved in this way.

If you feel you must do something, however, Christine Schramm, Assistant Dean of Students and Director of Residence Education at University of Dayton gives a nod to placing a brief call to the other parents "as long as the call is about you getting acquainted with the parents, not with the roommate through the parents." Schramm explains that "Introductions are fine as long as they are coupled with something more, such as a time to meet on move-in day to have more formal introductions. Discussing too much too soon may set up your student with some false expectations. Keep the conversation about you and your hopes and expectations as parents and not about the students. Leave that to the roommates to figure out and negotiate."

In other words, don't turn it into a gossip session about your kids and don't, in your zeal to be friendly, suggest the kids spend Winter Break at your house or that you all vacation together next summer. (Yes, well-meaning but slightly overbearing parents have actually done these things!) Your kids will have to create the bonds that tie you and the other set of parents together and not vice versa.

If you do decide to get in touch, Dr. Robert Pearigen, Dean of Students at Sewanee—University of the South, urges parents to get the approval of their child first, instead of contacting the parents behind his back.

Icebreakers

Robin Jones, Associate Dean of Residential Education at West Virginia University says roommates-to-be should think long and hard about how easy-going they want to be once they get to school. Is the old "what's mine is yours" adage going to apply to their belongings or will they label even the pens on their desk with their first and last name?

Below are conversation topics for new roommates to discuss before they get to school:

Their own backgrounds: This includes hometown, hobbies, high school activities, and friends. It's a good icebreaker and can give roommates clues about each other's lifestyle.

Sleeping hours: Knowing whether they have an "I'm unbearable without ten hours of sleep!" type or a "I usually go to bed at 2:00 A.M., and I'm never taking an 8:00 A.M. class" type can go a long way toward envisioning what life with their new roommate is going to be like.

Who's bringing what: The stereo, the refrigerator, the vacuum.... No sense in having two of everything when a simple call can take care of the redundancies, right?

Lifestyle topics: Elena Sharnoff and Nancy Pike of Marlboro College also suggest asking about their study habits, music listening habits, level of neatness, early bird/night owl tendencies, smoking, free time pursuits, and whether there might be a steady boyfriend or girlfriend who will be visiting regularly.

"Hi, My Name Is Control Freak..."

Many parents ask whether "it would be nice" to introduce themselves to their child's roommate's parents. Parent to parent, my advice is to resist the temptation (and it is tempting if you're a parent who likes to be in control). To be honest, there just isn't a need for parents to initiate contact through the other parents. The impetus and motivation needs to come from the students. It's fine to meet at the roommate's parents at an orientation or Parents' Weekend, but never try to micromanage the roommate relationship. It's a beast of it's own and the fewer who enter into the lair, the better off for everyone.

IF SHE KNOWS OTHER STUDENTS WHO WILL BE ATTENDING THE SAME SCHOOL, SHOULD I ENCOURAGE THEM TO ROOM TOGETHER?

An emphatic "No!" from St. Olaf College's Dean of Students, Greg Kneser, among many others. "Living with someone in a twelve-by-fifteen-foot box is very different from knowing that person from home, or even from being his or her friend," he says.

Although choosing to live with someone from high school may initially provide a "comfort zone" for your child, often times this is not an ideal situation. According to Dean of Residence Life, Father Ken Sicard, of Providence College, "Living with friends from home can sometimes set unrealistic expectations, which can only serve to complicate the living situation for new students. Students may be unfamiliar or surprised by some of their friends' habits, and in some cases the situation may preclude students from making new friends. Although it may appear risky, having a roommate randomly assigned by residence life may be the best way to go."

Elon University's Smith Jackson observes that roommates from the same high school are less likely to get out and make new friends and may be seen as homebodies. Kneser says a compromise might be reached with a child who is adamant on the issue by suggesting he live near someone from home. He explains, "The housing office will usually consider such requests, assuming they're made well in advance, to put buddies in the same residence hall or even on the same floor. But part of the college experience is to expand your horizons and meet new friends. That won't happen if your student rooms with someone she or he already knows."

If you know the other parent, it can be helpful to call them and discuss the problems of living with a close friend from home. With the two sets of parents in cahoots on the issue, there's a better likelihood of listening. A compromise situation you might want to consider is asking for the friends to have housing in the same building, offers College of the Atlantic.

TIP: Studying in the dorms?

Like the old adage about not sleeping where you eat, most kids probably shouldn't make a habit of studying where they hang out and sleep. The temptation to close the textbook and take a little nap is too great and the dorm distractions are many. (Although some dorms, especially honors ones, have study rooms that the students actually use for studying!) Your child will probably figure this out on his own, but you can always suggest that she find a place away from the room for serious studying. Libraries, after all were designed for this purpose (though many campus libraries play a dual roles as the center of the social scene). An alternative would be to find a special quiet nook or cranny that they associate with studying.

IS IT BETTER FOR MY CHILD LIVE ALONE OR WITH A ROOMMATE? WHAT ABOUT MORE THAN ONE ROOMMATE?

For the most part, having a roommate is ultimately better than going it alone. If your child arrives at school knowing no one, he will know at least one person as soon as he moves in. Even if they aren't best buds, cordial roommates can be a good source of information on everything from where a certain class building or coffee shop is to how to best haggle with the financial aid office. After meeting this one person, there is naturally an exponential effect. The more kids you put in a room together, the more people they will meet. (Plus, they will probably end up meeting each roommate's friends, and so on.) That can be a good or bad thing depending on your child's personality and their tolerance for socializing.

When it comes to the numbers of roommates in a space, there is also some truth to the law of even numbers. Two kids sharing a room will be fine. Three often end up making one feel like the odd person out. Four is a nicer number with more combinations for mixing. The majority of dorm rooms on the average campus are doubles, which speaks to the chances of success of the two-per-room formula. Administrators at Valparaiso University mention that "the new lifestyle of living on a college campus is challenging enough with one roommate—without bringing in the challenges associated with more than one."

So, how much say will you and your child have over the number of roommates he or she is assigned? It varies by school. Often in the case of freshmen, you can request a certain type of room with a certain number of roommates, but it doesn't mean that your wish will be granted. As your child gets a couple school years under his belt, however, his requests will carry more weight. Schools have a certain economy of scale that they need to make work. As you read this, there are schools that are cramming four kids into rooms that are more appropriately sized for two, and there are those that have so much excess housing that even freshmen get their own rooms. The size of the entering class of freshman and the number of upperclass students living off campus affect the numbers.

It's also worth noting again that there will probably be a price differential that corresponds to the number of roommates and/or type of dorm. Single rooms are the most expensive, and extra fees may be added for dorms with special amenities like an outdoor deck or gourmet kitchen. Quads and triples tend to be cheaper than double rooms, though that should not be the main reason for requesting one.

WHAT IF MY CHILD HAS A PROBLEM WITH HER ROOMMATE?

Roommate issues are one of the most common problems on campus, especially during freshman year. And most every school has the same answer for students with roommate complaints: Work it out.

No can do? Talk to an RA and have them help you work it out. See a pattern developing? Schools have been around the block. They've heard every roommate story in the book and they have their party line perfected: Feuding roommates should improve their communication and come to a civil agreement.

> **FACT:** Cleanliness at a Price
>
> At University of Michigan, a few lucky students are each given $100 cash for the school year to keep their dorm rooms presentable so prospective students and their parents can take a peek during campus visits.

And if they call you to complain? Carol Casey, Associate Dean of Students at Rhodes College advises parents to at least listen to your child's gripes. But, "Remember that you are hearing only one side of the issue. Help your student to be rational, encourage prompt action, and let him or her resolve the issue. Parental involvement in roommate conflicts can heighten the problem."

In an effort to prevent conflict in the first place, many schools, like UC Davis, ask RAs to meet with students at the beginning of the school year to go through a roommate "Agreement Form." This document covers topics such as: Is it okay to use my computer without asking? When I'm away, can someone else use my bed? May I put a poster on your side of the room?

As far as resolving issues between roommates goes, schools like the University of North Carolina at Asheville follow a several-step process. The first step is a preventative one: Draft a contract that outlines expectations and responsibilities, such as cleaning chores. If a problem does arise, roommates should first discuss their issues with each other, using the contract as a point of reference. If the discussion stalls, it is time to bring in outside help.

The next line of defense for tense roommate situations is usually the RA, who acts as mediator. (This is step two.) If the RA cannot help, the third step refers the issue to other campus professionals. Requesting a roommate change should be the last resort to solving the problem. That said, schools do not make it easy on students who clearly have a personality conflict and not an unfair living situation.

Of course, the magnitude of the problem needs to play a part in its resolution. Learning to accommodate another person's idiosyncrasies is one thing. Living with a violent, psychopathic roommate is another. If your child suspects a serious problem with the roommate, and you concur, you need to urge your child to lobby for a room change.

What's a serious problem? A roommate who is harming themselves or others: self mutilation, selling and using hard drugs, and experimenting with violent cults are just a few examples. Getting involved goes against the "parents stay out" rule, and a serious problem should be the only exception. Before you get involved, let your student make every attempt to manage the situation herself. If she didn't get results and you feel that the situation is jeopardizing the well being of your child and/or others, then call the Dean of Residence Life or Housing and make your issues known. The squeaky wheel will usually get results in these situations.

Another avenue is to talk to the parent liaison at the college, if the college has one. According to a survey done by College Parents of America, about 70 percent of four-year schools have at least one staff member working nearly full time with parents. You can find these personnel on the college's website.

IF MY CHILD IS GAY, HOW MIGHT THAT AFFECT ROOMMATE ARRANGEMENTS?

This may or may not be something your child has decided to share with you. Or, it may be something that they will discover about themselves while away at school. Either way, if your child is gay and is rooming with someone who isn't, there may be some tension. Many students who found themselves in this situation say that they manage to get through their first semester or year and then make other living arrangements where they feel more comfortable.

In general, schools do not ask students to specify a sexual orientation on the freshman room request questionnaires. After freshman year, students may request a special dorm where they might find a better fit. Many schools do have a themed dorm or a floor in a dorm devoted to gay, lesbian, and transgender students.

Most schools do offer their RAs some training on how to manage gay/straight roommate combinations and how to be sure that discrimination of any kind (religious, gender, race) is not tolerated in their dorms.

The Princeton Review surveys approximately 110,000 students each year, asking about their schools and reporting that information in our book, *The Best 361 Colleges* and on our website. One of the sixty-two ranking lists in that book is a list of schools that students have told us are gay-friendly. While this may not help the roommate situation at any given college, it may help students know what they might expect from a roommate on one of these campuses.

In 2005, New College of Florida (Sarasota, FL), Macalester College (St. Paul, MN), and Wellesley College (Wellesley, MA) came out as the top three gay-friendly schools on our list of twenty schools. On our list entitled "Alternative lifestyle not an alternative" for the same year, Hampden-Sydney College (Hampden-Sydney, VA), University of Notre Dame (South Bend, IN), and Baylor University (Waco, TX) were reported by students as the three least gay-friendly schools. (You can see the full lists at www.PrincetonReview.com/college/research/rankings.asp.)

Do Upper Class Students Live Side By Side With Freshman?

Most schools treat incoming freshmen as a special subset of the population. "The issues faced by new students are fairly universal, so a living group comprised of all first-year students can be a wonderful support mechanism," says Kurt Holmes, Dean of Students at The College of Wooster. "Likewise," he continues, "life is changing for seniors, and senior centers (not to be confused with retirement homes) are a great idea to promote positive transitions at that point in life." At most schools, freshmen will find themselves in a dorm comprised exclusively of fellow first-year students. Check with the individual school to be sure.

What Is a Housing Contract?

A housing contract is a document that gets signed by your child at the beginning of each year. It specifies all policies for the dorm. There are sections that elaborate on everything from quiet hours to what can hang on the walls, to what type of appliances can be used, to which computer services are available. It's an important document that you should read at least once. Violating the contract, especially if there's damage to the dorm, could be costly.

Are There Quiet Hours in the Dorms?

There are more schemes to enforce quiet and respect in the dorms than there are Eskimo words for snow. Every school has their own version, and the rules regarding quiet hours can usually be found in the housing contract. Though weeknights and weekends follow a different set of rules, quiet periods typically start after 10:00 P.M. on weeknights and after midnight on weekends. Some schools are stricter; some more lenient. Many schools have programs like American University's 24/7 "courtesy hours," which means you can always ask someone to "turn it down" and they will comply. American also mirrors other schools in that individual dorm floors may elect to have earlier quiet hours but never later. During finals week and Study Days at American, quiet hours are 24 hours a day.

Remember that "'quiet' is a relative term," say administrators at Georgia Institute of Technology. With 100 to 500 students living together in one building, there will always be someone listening to music or watching TV or talking on the phone. During designated quiet hours, however, the noise should be notably subdued.

Who's the enforcer of the silence? Typically it's the RA, but students should be able to ask one another to be quiet and have their requests honored as well.

WHO IS RESPONSIBLE FOR CLEANING THE DORMS?

As long as there have been dorms, there have been questions about who's responsible for keeping them clean. At most universities and colleges, students are responsible for cleaning their own individual living space. "Common spaces that are utilized by multiple residents (such as a hall bathroom that is shared by all students of a particular floor) are generally cleaned by university custodial staff," says Tavia Sessoms, Director of Housing Assignment at the College of Charleston. But, reminds the Student Affairs staff at the University of Puget Sound, "these services should not be mistaken for 'maid services.' And it is hoped that any extraordinary mess created by residents will be attended to by those responsible."

Saint Louis University takes the state of the dorms seriously says Argyle Wade, Director of Housing and Residence Life. This school, like many others, "will check the students' rooms several times a year for health and safety reasons. Students may be asked to address problems or pay for a professional cleaning service if necessary."

At NYU, a group of enterprising students formed a maid service catering to other students on campus. Harvard students protested when they discovered that a student-run business called Dormaids was employing other students to clean rooms for a fee. The protesters felt that it created a gap between wealthy and less wealthy students.

A few schools, such as Warren Wilson College, are innovative in that the students maintain all the campus facilities and spaces. Each student works fifteen hours a week at a school job—which could mean doing anything from collecting garbage to gardening to maintaining the school's website. Students get paid for their hours, which in turn, keeps tuition much more reasonable. For other colleges like this go to www.workcolleges.org.

The biggest problems in shared spaces on campus tend to be the kitchen and bathroom since they take more than their fair share of use and abuse. Sometimes, according to John (last name withheld), a student and RA at College of the Atlantic in Bar Harbor, Maine, the problems can even be cultural. Different students from different backgrounds have differing standards of cleanliness. He tells the story of one Eastern European student who would routinely leave raw meat on the counter for long periods of time; this offended the other student's sense of cleanliness, but was perfectly reasonable in the student's native country.

A parent's job is to encourage students to be mindful of others who need to share their space. If a dirty toilet seat, a hair-filled drain, or a sink full of dirty dishes are not what they'd want to find, then they should not leave it for others. If your child hasn't been responsible for shared spaces like the bathroom or kitchen at home, it's time to get her in the game.

The Student Dorm-Cleaning Kit

"The person who cleans your student's room at home is the same person your student will expect to clean his or her room at school," says Wendy Seligmann, Associate Dean of Student Development at Earlham College. So, if you don't want to spend Family Weekend cleaning your student's room, Seligmann advises that you supply your student with the basic tools for cleaning his personal space and your expectation that he will do it (at least before you visit). Our suggestion is the First Year Independent Cleaning Solutions kit, better knows as a Quick FICS kit:

glass-cleaning wipes

anti-bacterial wipes

furniture dusting wipes

bleach wipes

toilet bowl tablets

liquid dish soap

dishwasher soap tablets

several sponges in different colors

permanent marker to label sponges to be used for different things

solid air-freshener that can be exposed gradually

laundry soap

dryer sheets

A deluxe Quick FICS kit can include a hand-held vacuum (often cost can be shared by roommates/suitemates). All can be easily packed in a laundry basket, which students will also need!

WHO WILL BE MY CHILD'S MAIN SUPPORT PERSON IN THE DORM?

Meet the RA, an upperclass student who lives amongst the freshman in exchange for a stipend or scholarship. RAs are paid to play the roles of big brother/sister, police warden, psychologist, and surrogate parent, all at the same time. They receive some serious training and have the back-up support of the campus community. They typically report directly to a Dean or Associate Dean of Residence Life. In addition to keeping an open door to students under their charge, they are responsible for holding weekly meetings with them to resolve any issues. They often schedule activities or trips with the dorm members.

Of course, RAs vary greatly in their own maturity. While they elect to take on this challenging role, they are still students after all. And as college students, well, they do college things. If an RA stays out late or sleeps at her boyfriend's apartment every other night, she's not going to be around much when the students on her floor might need her most. The majority of RAs out there, however, demonstrate insight, helpfulness, and maturity. They are in these positions because they genuinely want to help their fellow peers to have the best experience they can while in school.

Dorm Design

Many researchers, academics, and architects have written extensively about the changes taking place on the campus as new dorms are built to coexist with the old. Witold Rybczynski, a professor of urbanism at the University of Pennsylvania, recently wrote about dorm architecture in *The Chronicle of Higher Education* saying that students—especially those having grown up with more money, more space, and lots of entertainment—are shaping the design of modern dorms.

One campus design firm talks of the new "total-package dormitory" where colleges and universities are beginning to acquire and build real estate equity in much the same way that apartment dwellers did when the condominium industry gained momentum in the mid 1970s and 1980s (RTKL, an architecture and design firm www.rtkl.com).

For students, the new dorms mean larger living spaces, furniture that's built into the space, central air-conditioning, private bathrooms, and parking garages to name a few. Some newer buildings at schools like the University of Pittsburgh and UC Santa Clara are "green designs" with solar heating, biodegradable materials, and water conserving bathrooms and showers.

While there are spates of new dorms being built, the old ones retain their unique character. Your child may find themselves in one of the following distinctively different styles:

Gothic: Just like you'd a imagine college was hundreds of years ago. Stone construction, often ornately carved, with bell towers and stained glass. Sometimes even reminiscent of living in a church. University of Chicago is a classic example.

Prewar Originals: Think University of Pennsylvania or Harvard's Quad. The spaces can be a bit gloomy but ooze with character. Sometimes damp and overheated, the plumbing creaks, and the technology is all retrofit, but you feel smarter just being in them.

1960s Bauhaus: These dorms look like an Eastern European postwar city. Single rooms behind metal doors are the signature. Metal and Formica are the main building materials, and don't even try to hang any pictures on these cinderblock walls. The Illinois Institute of Technology is the classic example.

SHOULD MY CHILD CONSIDER LIVING OFF CAMPUS?

College is all about the transition from adolescence into adulthood. One way to expedite that process is for students to leave the security of life in the dorm and strike out into the "real" world of off-campus housing.

Most colleges require that students live on campus for the first year or two. By junior year, most schools feel that their students have earned the right to live off campus. (Some actually require that students live on campus all four years.) Off-campus housing is housing that's rented from a private landlord. The college is not responsible for or responsible for or involved with maintenance, utilities, or other routine landlord/tenant agreements.

TIP: The Campus Housing office usually maintains a list of some off-campus housing options, but they tend to get snatched up quickly. If your student is planning a move off campus he should think early.

Like stores and restaurants that struck it rich by operating alongside railroad tracks in the days of westward expansion, many landlords do quite well renting houses or apartments in college towns. Some of the landlords do a great job providing services; others earn a slumlord status. You need to help your child research the landlord and make sure that the students living in the house or apartment will be well accommodated. Finding out about utilities, snow removal, trash, damages, sublets, parking, and so on may not be a part of your student's experience repertoire. If you're in doubt about a situation that sounds a bit sketchy, ask to speak to the landlord yourself. (Oftentimes at least one parent needs to cosign the lease, anyway.)

Rent for off-campus housing can vary significantly, and the cost of collecting enough stuff to operate a functional household is not trivial. Students often need to supply everything from pots and pans to furniture. There is a ritual of passing a home's furniture along from one set of renters to the next, but if you've ever looked at some of the mattresses and sofas that are being willed to the next generation of students who live there, you'd probably be on the phone with the Board of Health.

As liberating as off-campus housing can feel to a student, there are definite downsides to consider. The biggest is that your student will be removed from daily campus life. It's easier to miss classes or skip a trip to the library or computer lab when the campus is out of sight. What's more, students will miss out on some support functions that are provided by the school, such as the set up and maintenance of their PCs and access to high-speed Internet connections.

Nearly every college we checked with had a strong preference for students to remain on campus. True, there could be a financial motivation for saying so, but research helps back them up, says Earl Johnson, Senior Associate Dean of Admissions at The University of Tulsa. "Research regarding on-campus living has revealed that students are more successful in college, more apt to complete their degree in four years (good news for mom and dad's bank account), more likely to earn professional degrees, more likely to achieve a higher grade point average, and that they participate in more extracurricular activities than a student living off campus," he says. Johnson goes on to add that at Tulsa, the retention rate of students living on campus has consistently been 10 percentage points higher than that of students living off campus. "Besides," he reasons, "students will have plenty of time to experience 'the off campus life' once they leave college and enter the real work world."

Some colleges like Clark University offer hybrid solutions for students itching to break free of the confines of the dorm: free-standing, apartment-style living with the college serving as landlord. It's is a nice compromise that many kids seem to enjoy just as much (if not more) than they would "real" off-campus housing.

So why live off campus at all? Many students have found that it does save money when compared to room-and-board costs for the dorms, especially in a house shared with three or four friends. They also declare that there's no better preparation for the real world and essentially that "playing grown-up" is fun once they feel ready for it. It seems that, finances being equal, living off campus is the domain of the more restless and the less group-oriented members of the student body. Students who live off campus report that they like to distance themselves a bit from the day to day of the group gestalt. Your job as a parent will be to weigh the costs involved and but even more so to weigh your student's ability to conduct himself as a conscientious adult once he's away from the school's watchful eye.

For the Student Who Wants to Live Off Campus...

Make sure you and your child consider all of the costs including rent, the upfront security deposits, how much furniture and household goods you'll need to buy, and whether utilities like heat and electricity are included.

Find out if you'll be responsible for maintenance like snow shoveling and mowing the lawn.

Will you be able to walk to campus? If not, is there ample free parking? Is it near conveniences like a supermarket? What sort of laundry facilities are there?

Think about housemates. Are they all fiscally responsible? Can you count on them for the year-long lease? Does the lease belong to one person or is it shared amongst house members? Does a parent need to cosign?

Remember that landlords and property owners are not responsible for your personal property and, unlike in the dorms, there are no security personnel. Check into buying renter's insurance or seeing if you're eligible for coverage under your homeowner's policy.

SHOULD I BE WORRIED IF MY CHILD IS CONSIDERING A FRATERNITY OR SORORITY?

Before you have nightmarish visions of *Animal House*, you should know that not every fraternity is a haven for chugging beer, loose women, and juvenile pranks, nor is every sorority is a claw-scratching, gossip mill either. That said, there's usually—not always—at least a grain of truth in these stereotypes. Fraternities, in particular, have played a large part in a range of campus problems. For some fraternities, what starts out as guys having fun has ended in everything from vandalism and drunk driving to hazing incidents and date rape. While there are some known for community service, outstanding academics, and a true brotherhood among members, others seem bent on breeding a reckless kind of culture (not to mention zero desire to keep their house in the realm of livable cleanliness!). Sororities also run the full spectrum. From those whose members excel in sports or music, throw big charity fundraisers, and are devoted to bettering themselves through challenging courses, real-world experience, and career development to those houses that have earned a stereotypical reputation for narcissism, self-centered snobbery, and not much else. Are these stereotypes deserved for every Greek house across the board? Absolutely not! But, Greeks are an easy group for administrators to target because they are a defined group of people and because most have a high-profile social scene attached to them. College administrations, for many reasons, have been under increasing pressure to stop heavy drinking and raucous partying at fraternities, and to a lesser degree at sororities. At schools like University of Colorado—Boulder, fraternities are being asked to delay their rush so that students can take the opportunity to get involved with their studies and mature a bit first.

> **TIP:** GradeReport: The University of Rhode Island reports a higher proportion of students in academic distress that happen to be first-year male students in the Greek system. At the same time, they note that members of Greek houses often have higher than average grade point averages overall.

Overall, fraternities have begun to lose new applicants. In response, the frats have been pumping up the public relations on their own behalf— stressing community service, good grades, and friendships in order to paint over the damage that's been done. Today, there are still over 400,000 students who are fraternity members; some schools have as much as 30 percent of their student population participating in the Greek system of sororities and fraternities. For the right student, a fraternity or sorority can become a safe and close-knit environment.

Get involved with your child's choice in this matter. Not all campuses have fraternities and sororities, but if your child attends one that does and he wants to join, you will both need to research the frat carefully. Frats that stress their roots in literature, academia, and public services may prove less troublesome than some of the other alternatives.

> **FACT:** The majority of campuses with Greek systems are those of larger schools. The smaller campuses that often don't have a Greek system report having a plethora of other extracurricular activities to help students meet each other in diverse settings. Of the 10 schools we randomly asked to answer questions about Greek life, four of them—SUNY—Purchase, St. Olaf, Xavier, and Fairfield—had no Greek system on campus. This is relatively indicative of the nationwide ratio overall.

WHAT IS RUSH?

Rush is the recruitment process that one goes through in order to join a fraternity or sorority. (This usually happens second semester of freshman year, but could be sooner or later depending on the school.) The process works differently for sororities and fraternities, but basically your student will visit the various fraternity and sorority houses during the rush period. They will get to meet the house members, find out about more information about their houses, and possibly allow themselves to be wooed to join. Typically lasting a week, rushes can involve going to some great parties, sporting events, trips to the beach, and more.

> **TIP:** Greeks Rule
>
> The Princeton Review's book *The Best 361 Colleges* ranks the top 20 schools with the most active Greek scenes as reported by students. The top 3 schools for 2005 were: DePauw University (Greencastle, IN); Washington and Lee University (Lexington, VA); and Birmingham-Southern College (Birmingham, AL). This list and the other sixty-one ranking lists can be found in the book and on www.PrincetonReview.com.

At the end of the rush, students may or may not receive one or more bids—an invitation to join a certain fraternity or sorority. By accepting the bid, he can then "pledge" to join. If the pledge is honored, the student enters a pledge period (of varying lengths at varying schools) in which he shows an eagerness to be initiated. On one end of the spectrum, he might sit through informational meetings to immerse himself in the culture of the house or, on the other end, he may engage in activities like "Hell Week" in which members are asked to prove their allegiance by doing some pretty wild and creative things. At the end of the pledge period, students are initiated into the fraternity or sorority.

WHAT IS HAZING?

Rushing and pledging have become much tamer in recent years. A decade ago, hazing—the act of harassing a new pledge by pushing him to extreme and often dangerous physical and mental behavior against his will—were the norm to be endured by those rushing. There was a time when pledges might be hit with a wooden paddle, have to perform physically exhausting tasks, streak naked, vandalize property, or serve as slaves to their elder fraternity or sorority brothers or sisters. This extreme form of pledging involved elements of hazing. Today, the entire rush/pledge process is considerably more staid on most campuses—and closely watched by college administrators to make sure nothing is amiss. Groups like www.stophazing.org have documented incidents at colleges all over the country and have a load of resources available for parents and students who want to ensure that hazing is a bygone phenomenon.

TIP: Most universities that have an active Greek system belong to councils that are governed by student leaders and overseen by a staff member of the university. If your child chooses to rush, he or she should look for an affiliation with the PanHellenic Association for sororities, or the Interfraternity and/or National PanHel for fraternities. These organizations have councils that are governed by student leaders and are overseen by a staff member of the university.

If He Joins, Will He Live in the Fraternity House? If so, for Which Years?

While most sororities and fraternities have houses on campus where members can opt to live, some merely have meeting rooms. Most of them require that students pay dues into the organization, regardless of whether or not they live in the house.

For most Greek houses, members first have the option of moving into the house for sophomore year. The upside to living in a fraternity or sorority house is that students are surrounded by a group of people they essentially chose, instead of the random hodgepodge of students they would be surrounded by in the dorm. The down side is that because they are hanging out and living with the same group, they may not be making—or even wanting to make—new friends outside the house. If you find that Greek Life is not for your child, he can leave the house and drop out of the organization, but you will typically lose the housing deposit and some amount of dues you have already paid.

Is Joining a Fraternity or Sorority Expensive?

The fee for room and board is probably similar to the dorm or slightly higher. Most of the more established fraternity and sororities have smaller bedrooms for their members, but large and inviting public spaces. They have a staff that includes a cook and a resident "mom" who sort of watches over the house in one way or another.

The dues surrounding the membership in the organization, however, can get pricey. They vary, but on average, dues can be around $700 year. The fees include social dues for activities, chapter insurance, national dues, and other various items. Fees are generally higher during new membership to cover the initial pledge dues and initiation fees. It's also common that there are additional fees throughout the year to cover house parties and special events.

How Can We Weigh the Pros and Cons of Greek Life?

It's always a good idea to question your student's motivation for joining something that requires such a significant, multi-year commitment in terms of time and money. "Students should join a fraternity or sorority only if it their intent is to establish a group of 'brothers' or 'sisters' for social interaction, leadership possibilities, and community service involvement. A student knows it is right if he or she feels comfortable, finds a sense of belonging when amongst the members, and is committed to the larger goals of the Greek system," say administrators at Bradley University.

As a word of caution, Jayne Richmond, Dean of University College at the University of Rhode Island explains: "Students who tend to be swayed by peer pressure, who tend to work hard to 'fit in' as opposed to being motivated by their own goals, may find they lose sight of the academic priority of the university. My suggestion is that students wait until they adjust to the first semester, and then determine if this is the right decision for themselves."

> **TIP:** Parents should look up the history and reputation of the fraternity or sorority your child hopes to join. You'll find a good list of fraternities with links to their respective sites at the National Institute of Fraternities (www.nic.org) and a good link to sororities at the National Pan Hellenic Council (www.NPC.org).

As far as the pros and cons go, Greek life gives students:

- The opportunity to find a very small group with whom to identify while remaining a part of a larger, more diverse school. Fraternities and sororities can be a way to cultivate a close set of friends and lifelong relationships.

- An opportunity to grow in leadership positions due to the steady stream of service events, philanthropy events, and intramural activities that need to be planned and executed. At larger schools, where students are more apt to feel lost in the shuffle, a Greek system can help to foster a sense of self.

- A chance to be cost-effective while possibly living in a lovely setting. Some fraternities and sororities are even housed in beautiful old homes that are listed on the National Register of Historic Places.

- "Having been in a fraternity can even help in your post-college job search," quips Jeff Gates, Senior Assistant Director of Admissions SUNY at Binghamton.

On the other hand, Greek life can:

- Chew up valuable time with meetings, social activities, and community service requirements. There may also be social pressure to fit in or conform—not to mention an obligation to spend gobs of time at social functions related to the organization. Greek life is recommended only for students who have a firm grasp on time-management and are confident in making their own decisions.

- Make you lose your sense of self. The more negative side of the cliché fraternity and sorority image is that of a bunch of followers obeying a master. In reality, frats and sororities meet regularly to make decisions as a group. But if your child has a weak sense of self and is easily influenced by the crowd, a fraternity or sorority is probably not the best idea.

- Members are hit with initiation fees, monthly dues, house fees, and need to follow a set of living-in requirements. Plus there are outfits to buy for formals, souvenirs from special events, and so on. These fees will affect the overall cost of your child's education. Be clear with your child upfront about what portion of these costs you are willing to pay and what portion they should think about coming up with on their own.

When making a decision, says Jana Lynn Patterson, Associate Dean of Students at Elon University, students considering Greek life "should keep an open mind about the groups they are considering and to research them well. Simple stats such as a sorority or fraternity's aggregate grade point average is public information and should be available online. All national fraternities and sororities have websites that can provide other information about costs, volunteer and philanthropic activities, and activities of their college chapters."

WHAT IF I DON'T WANT MY CHILD TO JOIN A FRATERNITY OR SORORITY?

"Parents won't know what the right decision is, but their son or daughter will," says Scott Nelson, Assistant Dean of Students at Elon University.

Make a concerted effort not to put your foot down before you know all of the facts. Some fraternities truly do build a strong sense of brotherhood and some sororities offer outstanding chances for leadership. For starters, do the research. Look into the policies that schools have regarding the rush period, says St. Olaf College's Dean of Students, Greg Kneser. Do they allow students to rush in their first semester or during their first year or do they wait until students have a year to adjust to college life? Also take a look at the school's alcohol and hazing policies related to rush. Has the college had dangerous situations with rush in the past? Are there academic regulations related to the school's Greek system?

At Loyola University in New Orleans, Thomas A. Smith, PhD, Associate Dean of the College of Arts and Sciences explains a parent's responsibility in clear cut terms. "Generally, if academic performance declines after joining a Greek organization, parents will do well to set a clear standard: improve your grades or we will not fund your Greek experience." But don't necessarily assume your child will not be able to handle Greek life and academics. Houses with a strong academic culture may actually boost a student's study time and even his GPA.

Nelson also suggests that students do their share of research by watching the Greek system from the day they arrive on campus. Are Greeks involved in other campus groups, and not just socializing amongst themselves? Do they assist with student orientation and new student move-in day? Do they host programs and activities aside from social events and parties? Are members serious about their academics? What is their standing with the campus and their national organization? Simple information about the group's aggregate grade point average is public information, and is available on many student life websites.

Whatever you decide—together—it's best not to rush into Greek Life, so to speak. And if your student really wants to join the Greek system—and you can afford it—think about a compromise that would enable him to do so.

Freshman Move-In Day: A Glimpse from the Parents' Point of View

There's nothing that can make you feel more inadequate than college move-in day. And for good reason. It's an endurance test like no other.

First, it's physically exhausting. If you're like most parents, you'll have spent the past 24 hours lifting boxes heavier than any you've lifted in decades. Then, with a bicycle poking into your lumbar and a stereo knocking against your neck, you'll drive an overstuffed car for a great many miles on unfamiliar roads. Adding insult to injury, you're probably eating up vacation days to do this.

There's a good chance you'll cram the whole family into one room at a cheap chain motel, dine at the nearest greasy spoon, and set the alarm for 6 A.M. No one will sleep that night.

Arriving on campus, the pressure is on to look fresh and composed and, worst of all, smart and well-educated. You'll stand in snaking lines filling out form after form, writing checks, and getting keys.

Your feet will ache. Your head will swim. Your jaws will hurt from smiling. Your child may or may not be talking to you by this point. (Isn't this exciting?)

At the orientation, the Dean will introduce himself or herself and a swarm of other administrators whom you'll probably never hear from again. Each will sermonize about the next four years, quoting everyone from Homer to Homer Simpson. Next, it's off to the bookstore where you'll drop a cool $600 on "Intro to Everything"—and other important tomes.

Then there's the business of unpacking all those things you just packed up and brought with you—a chore best left to those half your age. With any luck, your child's room is on the first floor. With more luck, you can all fit all of her stuff into the room, and the roommate that shows up fits your description of reasonable.

> **TIP:** If you bring a small tool-kit you'll gain instant brownie points from the other kids and their parents.

In the dorm, it's natural to eyeball the other parents and suddenly feel either underdressed, overdressed, inappropriately dressed, or not sufficiently parental. You'll wonder how all these parents can afford to be here at these tuitions prices and be wearing clothes at all. You'll eyeball the other students' possessions and be reminded of the 100 things you forgot to remind your child to pack or that your family never owned in the first place. Your kids will eyeball the other kids' possessions and hone in on the kid with the $5,000 computer setup and the $1,000 mountain bike.

As usual, anything you say or do is completely embarrassing to your child. "Try not to speak, Mom." (She just wants you to unpack the car and go.) You'll be making snap judgments as to

> **TIP:** These days, nine out of ten four-year campuses offer a special orientation for parents.

whether the school may be too artsy, too liberal, too geeky, too rural, or whatever other "too" has been plaguing you. And you'll be reading every sign on every bulletin board like tea leaves, hoping to be able to divine the future of the child that's about to start living here as a true adult.

And then, one by one, the stereos and iPods start pumping a cacophony of sounds, the Frisbees start flying through the air, and the computers beep back into existence. The sun is setting and, for the first time in years, you and your kids are not a nuclear unit in the quest for the perfect college. They're about to continue that quest as you watch from a distance and keep sending money. Your job? Keep up that sense of humor as you turn back to the car and make the reverse trip home. Give yourself a day before you tackle the mess they left behind. And remember, if you see an overstuffed car on the road or an adult wiping a tear from their eyes anytime during the last weeks of August you can bet another parent has just moved their child into a dorm.

A Taxonomy of On-Campus Parents: Can You Spot Yourself in the Line Up?

The Darters

With eyes that dart frantically, these parents take it all in and never stop checking comparative status.

The Exhausted

Telltale marks are dark circles under eyes. Often seen with chin tucked into chest, eyes at half-mast or closed, and a head that nods then jerks up at attention. Results in one of the species to be seen elbowing another during long orientation speeches. Occasional snorts and snores.

The Germ-inators

Spotted by the weapons they carry—Lysol, broom, and various disinfectants. Fanatics about cleanliness they often will stay hidden in the nest while the others are out at festivities. An antibacterial room is mission numbero uno.

The List-Makers

List-makers have two variants: the electronic and the paper-and-pen varieties. Both can be seen copying phone numbers, websites, and e-mail addresses off campus bulletin boards, making list after list of supplies needed and tasks to complete, and taking copious notes on the President's welcome remarks.

The Pied Pipers

Usually glimpsed with a group of freshmen in tow, this species plies students with dinner and snacks hoping to win their friendship and be treated as one of them. Ah, youth!

The Fixers

They come bearing tools and are a coveted species. They are handy beyond belief and delight in repairing a desk drawer that sticks and in hanging curtains, pictures, and just about anything else. Can be dangerous if hammers and levels are snatched from them.

The Weepers

Given away by their running eyes and noses, these overly moist parents can be heard sobbing and sniffling, even throughout the happiest moments of the weekend.

ON A SIDE NOTE, WHERE SHOULD MY CHILD VOTE? WHAT'S HER LEGAL RESIDENCE?

Students can vote in their college town or their hometown—but not both. Some find it simpler to vote by absentee ballot, obtained from the county election office at home. Others prefer to take a more active role in their new college community.

To vote, most states require proof of legal residence—often a driver's license and some proof of a local address are required. Before a student decides between their hometown and their college town, she should consider these factors:

- Do you claim her as a dependent on your tax return? If you do, then her address in your hometown will probably work best for voting purposes to maintain the status quo.

- Does she have a scholarship that would be affected if she changed her residence? Some scholarships require that the student be a resident of a particular town, city, or state.

- Would anything change regarding her or your existing health, automobile, or other insurance coverage? If she is covered by your insurance policies, you will probably need to change her address on the policy in order to continue coverage.

- Is she close to graduation and does she intend to live and work in her college community after graduation? If she is close, then you may want to use the college address as the legal residence.

WHAT ABOUT JURY DUTY?

If she is registered to vote, your child may also get a jury duty notice at school. If she serves on a jury at college, she will be exempt from serving in her hometown and vice versa. All things being equal, it would be ideal if she could serve at home in the summer when there are no classes or exams.

CHAPTER 3

Sex, Drugs, and Drinking: The Darker Side of College Life

If it's against state law, it's generally considered a breach of etiquette.

—Miss Manners

I write this chapter with a certain amount of dread. First, I'm not a trained psychologist or counselor. Rather than prescribe advice, I can only give you the data—and this information is not always comforting. Second, if you look at the trends and listen to students' stories, you'll get a different picture than the one that school administrators will paint. When choosing a college, try to balance the information you're getting from all sides with your own gut instinct. And once your child is there, the best you can do (and it goes a long way!) is stay in close contact with your child. Try to have some interaction (by phone or through e-mail) with your child each week—at a minimum. Find out what he is up to, and make yourself available to listen when your child wants to talk. From there, all you can do is trust that your child will use good judgment and make sound decisions.

Advise your child to be wary; but don't spend all of your time worrying. It's true, college kids have always been, to some degree, risk takers. They've always believed in their own invincibility, and that has always given their parents a cause for concern. James Matthews, a college counselor consultant and author of *Beer, Booze and Books* reminds us that while the media often make college out to be a big booze fest, this snippet of college life doesn't tell the whole story. It's just that real learning and educational accomplishments don't add up to juicy news stories.

"Most students either don't drink or do it at a low-risk level," offers Matthews. That's not to say it's not a problem. But "campuses are learning how to help change kids' dangerous behaviors," says Matthews. "We'd love for them not to indulge at all, but it's more realistic to try to delay their use of substances, reduce the amount ingested, and hence reduce the seriousness of the problem."

Parties, drinking, drugs, casual sex...there are any number of ways our children can get into serious trouble. Even students who have been dutifully running to classes and study sessions all week may find themselves looking for ways to let off some steam and explore new sides of themselves. Away from their parents' curfews and rules, they have a newfound freedom that, for many, may be intoxicating.

There's been a darker side to college life ever since there have been colleges. But now with media and the Internet to publicize it, along with laws that require colleges to publish reports of campus incidents, we are much more aware of the problem. Hardly a day goes by when there isn't a story of date rape, drunken driving, drug overdoses, overmedicated or depressed students, campus suicides, and casual and often unhealthy sex. You might wonder if this is what we've been saving up to pay for all of these years.

Concurrent with increased awareness about alcohol and drug abuse problems has been a shift in the relationship between parents and colleges. For many years, parents sent their children to colleges with the expectation that the college would act as interim parents and fulfill the role of guardian.

Today's parents are much less trusting, much more educated as consumers, and much less willing to give schools carte blanche to run their campuses and protect their students. Schools are also much more willing to involve parents. Colleges are facing pressure to curtail drinking on campus and institute preventive programs, as well as to implement stricter punishments for those who violate campus policies. You're seeing the beginning of a phase in college relations that I suspect will have more communication and interaction between parents and schools.

Kids will experiment in college. That is, to be realistic, part of the experience. Our job as parents is to make sure that we're giving our children the good judgment they'll need to stay healthy and safe long before they get to the first party. Once they leave the house, it's up to us to check in (often, but not too often) and use that long-range parental radar to spot the telltale signs of trouble. We need to be very clear in telling them what behavior we expect, and what the consequences will be if those expectations are not met. We need to be there when they need us, even if the news they bring isn't always what we want to hear. And we need a little bit of luck, prayer, or whatever works for you.

To help you understand how you can help your child stay safe, this chapter covers:

- College drinking—and what colleges are doing about it
- Drug use among students
- Sexual activity on campus

HOW DANGEROUS A PROBLEM IS DRINKING ON CAMPUS?

The most dangerous part about campus drinking is not necessarily the drinking, but what happens while students are drunk. Talk about sobering statistics! The National Institute of Alcohol Abuse and Alcoholism (NIAAA) found that 1,700 college students between the ages of 18 and 24 die every year as a result of hazardous drinking. Another 599,000 suffer unintentional injuries under the influence of alcoholism. College campuses report 600,000 cases of assaults under the influence and 97,000 cases of sexual assault or acquaintance rape. (These numbers incidentally have all risen fairly dramatically in the past few years according to a new report by the NIAAA.) And that's just the stuff that students actually report. Many instances—especially those of sexual assault and rape—are never reported.

> **FACT:** Drinking and Grades: Cause or Correlation?
>
> A study by the Core Institute at Southern Illinois University surveyed 65,000 college students and found that students who reported that they has received Ds and Fs on their report cards consumed an average of nine and a half drinks per week.

The list of alarming facts about college drinking compiled by the NIAAA doesn't stop with death and assaults either. Other widespread effects of excessive alcohol on campus include:

- Unsafe Sex: 400,000 students between the ages of 18 and 24 had unprotected sex and more than 100,000 students between the ages of 18 and 24 report having been too intoxicated to know if they consented to having sex.

- Academic Problems: About 25 percent of college students report academic consequences of their drinking including missing class, falling behind, doing poorly on exams or papers, and receiving poor grades.

- Drunk Driving: 2.1 million students between the ages of 18 and 24 drove under the influence of alcohol last year (the percentage relative to all college students, by the way, mimics the general population and drunken driving statistics).

- Vandalism: About 11 percent of college student drinkers report that they have damaged property while under the influence of alcohol.

- Alcohol Abuse and Dependence: 31 percent of college students met criteria for a diagnosis of alcohol abuse and 6 percent for a diagnosis of alcohol dependence in the past 12 months, according to questionnaire-based self-reports about their drinking (Knight et al., 2002. www.collegedrinkingprevention.org).

WHY DO STUDENTS DRINK?

Drinking on many college campuses has become as much a part of the culture as English 101. Students may be experimenting for the first time, trying to impress new friends, or simply letting loose after a tough week of classes. A 1998 study found that two-thirds of students believe alcohol is an ice breaker in social situations. So a drink here or there may be their way of enjoying a taste of newfound freedom. In the peer-pressured world of college, the feeling of being relaxed and the loss of inhibitions that liquor brings with it is often highly desirable. Half of the students surveyed in this study thought alcohol contributed to having fun and to facilitating sexual opportunities.

Let's not overthink the reasons why college kids drink. A keg or a bottle adds a touch of celebration and an element of excitement to what might be an otherwise boring party. Compared to other weekend entertainment, it's relatively inexpensive and requires little advance planning. The truth is, many college students drink for the same reasons adults do: to relieve stress, to loosen up in any number of social situations, and because it is there.

WHAT MAKES DRINKING SUCH A TOUGH ISSUE TO FOR SCHOOLS TO RESOLVE?

We've all seen (and quite possibly been) an intoxicated person at some point in our lives. Most often, it is not a pretty sight. But when the drunk is a young person, one who's not very experienced, things can easily get out of hand.

Modern society's messages about drinking on campus are very mixed. Even though it's illegal for anyone under 21, kicking back with a few beers seems to be more socially acceptable than other forms of escapism. Many parents and

> **TIP:** Drinking Games
>
> There's no end to student creativity when it comes to thinking up new ways to turn drinking into social sport. From bathtubs filled with "poor man's punch," to drink-downs (chugging a beer a minute), to standing cups on their heads and tag-team drink-offs, drinking has become a competitive sport on campuses nationwide. The object of each of the countless drinking games is usually very simple but set a dangerous premise: Whoever can consume the most and still remain standing wins.

college campuses take the quiet view that drinking is just a part of the college rite of passage. They remember their own college drinking episodes fondly, and have probably enjoyed a few reminiscences within earshot of the kids.

The college years are also at the apex of the transition between childhood and adulthood. Culturally, we tell kids that they're old enough to make their own decisions, and we fully expect them to do it. We remind them it's high time for them to live on their own, exercise their right to vote, gain some professional skills, even marry or head off to fight a war—but they're too young to have a beer. Adding to the temptation is the fact that they live on a campus where the population is divided between upperclassmen that are old enough to drink and underclassmen that aren't. And adding to the accessibility are the many upperclassmen that are willing to make a run to the liquor store on behalf of their younger buddies.

Next, you've got Madison Avenue tacitly promoting drinking as sexy, fun, and the cool thing to do, with some pretty powerful messages that appeal directly to college students. Every college student knows that Red Bull, the energy drink, is best when it's a mixer for vodka (you can get drunk but still stay awake), and that those sweet drinks like Smirnoff's Vodka Lemonade are created and marketed to appeal to college students.

You can thank computer graphics, scanner technology, high-quality printers, and PhotoShop for the masterful fake IDs that so many students have in their wallets. Needless to say, it's not easy for colleges to monitor who has fake IDs, along with what is happening behind closed doors in the dorms, at off-campus parties, and at the bars downtown. Can a school know what is going on in every single dorm room every single night? Can they stop of-age students from throwing parties in their own private residences? Can they stop younger students from attending? The answer, according to schools that have begun to institute tougher policies, is yes. If schools make it their business to enforce drinking policies, they believe they will see great results.

WHAT DO SCHOOL RULES SAY ABOUT DRINKING ON CAMPUS?

Every college has its own rules about drinking on campus; these rules are enforced under varying degrees of watchfulness. While none condone underage drinking, there's a spectrum of tolerance for illegal-aged drinking.

In academic parlance, there are typically areas of the campus that are "dry," "wet," or "moist." "Most campuses," says Jo Calhoun, Associate Provost at the University of Denver, "are not 'dry.' As a result, persons who are 21 years of age or older may drink on campus and in their on-campus residence hall rooms or apartments." Provided, of course, they aren't providing the hard stuff to minors.

> **TIP:** Girls and Boys and Alcohol
>
> Women get drunker faster than men— and for good physiological reason. Women have more body fat and less muscle tissue so they have a higher concentration of alcohol in their blood than men do even if they drink the same amount.

Schools take their cues from state laws. Dr. Michael Freeman, Vice President and Dean of St. Mary's College, says "drinking in the state of Maryland is prohibited by persons under the age of 21, and no one is allowed to consume alcohol in public." At St. Mary's, students who are over the age of 21 are allowed to consume alcohol in the privacy of their rooms.

Others schools like Auburn University are officially dry campuses; they do not permit the possession, consumption, or serving of alcoholic beverages on campus (though they often make exceptions for fraternity houses, some of which are housed on campus).

Other colleges ask students to follow honor codes. At Wabash College, the code comes in the form of "the Gentleman's Rule," which simply suggests that a student (of legal drinking age) conduct himself as a gentleman and a responsible citizen at all times. Some colleges impose a "group rule" that works to discourage underage drinking. At Swarthmore College, any group of ten or more is required to get a party permit, which is granted only when the students promise to abide state and college laws that are aimed at preventing underage or excessive drinking.

WHERE DO UNDERAGE STUDENTS GET THEIR LIQUOR?

If you're under 21 there are some creative ways to get liquor on campus. The first is for a younger student to ask an upperclassman of legal age to do it for her. (The nice ones won't charge a service fee.) The second is to go somewhere that doesn't really care how old a buyer is once they're standing at the counter with a couple of six-packs and cash in hand. (Flashing that phony ID is always helpful, too.)

It makes sense then that a big part of the drinking problem on campus comes from businesses that continue to sell liquor to under-age students. From in-room keg parties, to drink-ups after a game, to buying a case of beer at the Seven Eleven, to shots of Southern Comfort served at the local bar, in many college towns you'll find a pervasive laxity about serving underage drinkers—and for good reason. They'd make considerably less money if they enforced the law. College "towns" and college "gowns" often have a symbiotic relationship: The gowns (the colleges) provide the towns with an important source of income for eight months out of the year. The good news comes in the number of programs being piloted that have colleges working more closely with the towns to make sure under-aged drinkers are not served.

To boot, college campuses are essentially police-free zones. Kids feel pretty confident (and rightly so) that the police aren't going to be hanging out on campus waiting for something to happen. While colleges have their own staff of security officers, government-employed law enforcement officials tend to leave colleges to do their own enforcing, only coming onto campus if they're requested.

FACT: In 2002, the National Institute of Alcohol Abuse and Alcoholism reported that 1,400 college students die each year from alcohol-related injuries.

WHAT IS BINGE DRINKING?

One of the most troubling facts about campus drinking is not that students indulge, but that they overindulge. Binge drinking is defined as drinking five or more drinks in a row for men and at least four consecutive drinks in a row for women. Typically, this type of excessive drinking is reserved for weekend nights, after sporting events, Spring Break, and other big occasions, but surveys indicate that students can always find a good excuse to get drunk mid-week, too.

And if you think binge drinking is the isolated activity of a few students, think again. A 2001 University of Michigan survey of undergraduates found that they'd had at least one episode of binge drinking within two weeks of the survey. At Harvard University a survey found that 44 percent of undergraduates drank excessively at least once a month.

WHAT ARE CAMPUSES DOING TO CURTAIL DRINKING?

Most campuses have major efforts in place that are designed to educate students on the dangers of alcohol use and abuse. As part of these efforts, schools conduct programs, hold informal gatherings in the dorms, post informational bulletin boards, and offer counseling as necessary. "All of us (college administrators) believe that students need to understand both the personal and legal consequences of drinking" says Jo Calhoun, Associate Provost of the Student Life Division at the University of Denver.

After receiving the number-one party school ranking from The Princeton Review for three consecutive years (1993, 1994, and 1995), the University of Rhode Island instituted a comprehensive, campus-wide, alcohol awareness program that has been cited as a model for other schools. (The party school ranking is one of more than 70 ranking lists published annually by The Princeton Review that are compiled based on survey responses from 110,000 students at our best 361 colleges across the nation.) The school fell off the party school list promptly in 1996 and hasn't been on it since. In March 2004, the university's president received an award in Washington for the programs he instituted that reversed the school's party school reputation.

More recently, after coming in at number-one on the same party school list in 2003, the University of Colorado—Boulder toughened its alcohol awareness program, mandating that all incoming freshmen take an online course on awareness. The school also strengthened its penalties for underage drinking, taking it from a three-strikes-you're-out policy down to two strikes. University of Colorado—Boulder is no longer a top party school for the first time in five years.

There have been some more novel efforts as well. Recently, Colby College in Maine instituted a unique program to encourage moderation in drinking. Upper class students of legal age can enjoy a glass (a maximum of two glasses) of wine with their dinner in the cafeteria.

WHAT HAPPENS TO UNDERAGE DRINKERS ON CAMPUS? DO THEIR PARENTS FIND OUT?

On most campuses, underage drinking is viewed as a violation of campus policy and some form of on-campus action is taken. Typically, a first offense would be written up and would appear on the student's record. In most cases, the student would also be reprimanded and placed on some sort of probation, meaning that, should they be caught again, the punishment would be more serious.

The question of whether parents are notified when their child is caught drinking is up to each individual school. Some, out of respect for the students' privacy or because it is a first-time offense, will not inform the parents. For many years, FERPA (the Family Educational Rights and Privacy Act), often referred to as "the Buckley Amendment," allowed a student's records to remain private and confidential—including drug and alcohol infringements.

However, an increasing number of schools are notifying parents of drinking violations and can do so

> **TIP:** The full text of FERPA and Section 925 can be found in Appendix A.

legally. The 105th Congress passed Section 925: The Alcohol or Drug Possession Disclosure law, which permits a college to notify parents when there has been an infraction of local, state, or federal law. Section 925 was created to override the Buckley Amendment. With its introduction, if a student violated a law that jeopardized her own well being or the well being of those around her, the school now had some recourse.

It appears that parental notification is growing in acceptance at schools, and the results of this look promising. As of January 2000—according to the Higher Education Center for Alcohol and Other Drug Prevention—60 percent of 189 schools polled said that they had parental notification policies in place and reported that most parents (72 percent) were supportive when notified. An increasing number of schools notify a parent upon the student's first violation. Others have a two or three-strikes policy, notifying parents only when there are repeated offenses.

Research indicates that schools that notify parents immediately have a reduced rate of recidivism. They've also found a reduced rate of repeat alcohol-related incidents like vandalism and assault.

> **FACT:** The "college scene" is responsible for 10 percent of all brewers' revenues. (Jay Matthews. *Beer, Booze and Books: A Sober Look at Higher Education.* Viaticum Press, 1995.)

What Can Parents Do about Underage Drinking?

First off, do not take a "kids will be kids" attitude about your child drinking while off at school. The Seattle University administration suggests that parents can help by talking to their kids about the serious consequences associated with alcohol abuse and offering strategies to deal with peer pressure. Parents can also help their students to avoid distracting or destructive drinking behavior by setting clear expectations for academic performance and encouraging their child to engage in volunteer and campus activities. Suggesting that your child find a part-time job is another strategy. While he may then have additional disposable income to put toward socializing, he will also have less time for partying and will have to keep himself in presentable condition because a boss and team are counting on him to show up for work and do a good job. Finally, substance-free dorms (yes, that includes beer) are becoming popular choices at many campuses and you may want to discuss this possibility with your child. Students can still enjoy the occasional drink, they just can't do it in their dorm.

Some Advice for Schools

The National Institute on Alcohol Abuse and Alcoholism (NIAAA) created a special task force to investigate ways to reduce on-campus drinking. Here are some of their recommendations:

- Reinstate Friday classes and exams to reduce Thursday night partying. (Many schools still have limited or no classes on Friday so that students could study.)

- Implement alcohol-free expanded late night student activities.

- Eliminate keg parties on campus.

- Establish alcohol-free dorms.

- Employ older students or even adults to serve as RAs in the dorm.

- Control alcohol at tailgating parties and other sporting events.

- Refuse sponsorship gifts from the alcohol industry to avoid the perception that under-aged drinking is condoned.
- Ban all alcohol on campus, including faculty and alumni events.

HOW CAN YOU DETERMINE A COLLEGE'S ATTITUDE ABOUT THE CAMPUS DRINKING CULTURE?

If you ask your children whether there's a lot of on-campus drinking and you have a reasonably good relationship, you will get an honest answer. (This conversation shouldn't start with you asking them about their personal role in that culture, but rather about the campus drinking situation in general. As you already know, once they get into defensive mode, it's all downhill from there.)

- Parents can pick up subtle cues about the campus and the community when they visit, too.
- Look in the dumpsters. (Seriously!) Are they filled to the brim with beer cans and bottles?
- Is the campus surrounded by bars?
- Do the bars advertise college come-ons like Ladies Night, Finals Free for All, or goldfish bowl-sized beers for a buck that might appeal to college students?
- Is the school on The Princeton Review's Party School list? (This annual list is compiled by The Princeton Reviews based on students' responses on a survey that, among other things, asks them about the campus lifestyle choices. For more information, see www.PrincetonReview.com/college.)

THE CONSEQUENCES OF COLLEGE DRINKING

A 2001 analysis of existing national data estimates the annual prevalence of the consequences of college drinking for U.S. college students ages 18 to 24. Some 1,400 college students die each year from alcohol-related unintentional injuries. Other consequences are:

Assault by another student	600,000
Injury	500,000
Unprotected sex	400,000
Alcohol-related health problem	150,000
Arrest for alcohol-related violation	110,000
Sexual assault	70,000

This data has been provided by the Task Force on College Drinking, the National Advisory Council of The National Institute on Alcohol Abuse and Alcoholism. In addition to these numbers, 25 percent of college students report academic consequences, 11 percent report they have damaged property under the influence of alcohol, and 5 percent were involved with the police or campus security as a result of their drinking.

HOW PREVALENT IS DRUG USE ON CAMPUS?

It's harder to get accurate statistics about drug usage on campus; it's a much more underground scene. According to the 2001 National Household Survey on Drug Abuse, 20 percent of full-time undergraduate college students use illicit drugs. Research done by the New York State Office of Alcoholism and Substance Abuse Services (NYOASAS) found that most college students said their friends would disapprove of their "trying cocaine once or twice." Yet the same students found less disapproval with their drinking activities. Because there's less of a stigma, it's more socially approved and there are less severe penalties for getting caught: Alcohol is still the drug of choice on our nation's campuses. While drugs are found on campuses too, they tend to be used by a smaller percentage of students. "If campuses are going to exert time, effort, and dollars, they're going to put it against the biggest problem, and that's drinking," says James Matthews. "But the same messaging that colleges use to curtail campus drinking often applies to drug use."

Certain drugs become associated with college campuses as the drugs of choice. These change fast—even from one school year to the next—as kids get a hold of one, try it, then leave it for the next new substance on the block. One of the recent college-kid drugs is MDMA or ecstasy. It had a huge surge in popularity among students in the 1990s with club kids and all-night dance raves, but it still remains in the spotlight. A 2003 National Survey on Drug Use and Health found an estimated 12.9 percent of college students have taken it. It is often called the "perfect party drug" because it lets you keep dancing and remain awake and active for long stretches of time. It is both a stimulant and a psychedelic, and has replaced LSD in terms of popularity on college campuses.

Another drug that waxes and wanes in its popularity on campuses is methamphetamine, often called crystal meth, a stimulant that can be snorted, smoked, dissolved in beverages, or injected intravenously. Serious health consequences include memory loss, psychotic behavior, and potential cardiac and neurological damage. Those on the drug will often demonstrate aggressive, violent tendencies. Other drugs that have been popular on campuses in the last few years include OxyContin, a pain reliever that, according to the Drug Enforcement Administration, has become major problem particularly in the eastern United States.

Playing Their Cards

The sudden popularity of poker tournaments and Texas Hold 'Em on television and in the news resulted in a rise in the popularity of poker tournaments on campus. According to the Center for Substance Abuse Prevention, the rate of gambling among students significantly exceeds the rate for adult gamblers. According to the Massachusetts Council on Compulsive Gambling, "Teenagers have a problem gambling rate of 10 percent to 17 percent, a rate two to three times higher than the general population."

HOW ARE PRESCRIPTION DRUGS ABUSED?

One of the fastest growing categories of abused substances amongst teens and college students are prescription drugs. John will ask Sam to loan him an Adderol so he can cram for an exam. Sally will ask Samantha to lend her one of the Ambien she takes to get to sleep. Students are taking anti-depressants and anti-anxiety drugs like Prozac or Paxil in greater numbers than ever before. They're taking meds like Ritalin for Attention Deficit Disorder, and then their friends are using them to stay up all night. The Internet has made ordering a batch of drugs as easy as punching in your credit card number. Campuses have not tackled this problem in the methodical way that they have with liquor and street drugs, but my crystal ball points to this generation that has access to prescription meds in increasing numbers as a growing problem on college campuses.

The problem is further compounded by the fact that the schools have never really been charged with actively monitoring which of their students is taking which medications. Schools will ask that you list any medications your child takes on the health form you submit with her acceptance to school, but many families ignore this—sometimes for fear of the stigma of having these prescriptions appear on the student's record. Even if it is reported, the information is typically filed away for the records, but not shared with people like the RA, who might benefit from knowing.

Do College Kids Smoke Marijuana?

Of course they do! But the number of those who smoke marijuana is still far lower than the numbers who drink. According to a CORE Institute study at Southern Illinois University conducted in 2000, just about one-third of college students had used marijuana in the past year.

One of the most important things for you to know and to tell your children about marijuana on today's campus is that it's not your grandfather's marijuana. Today's variety has seen some serious botanical advances and it's incredibly potent. This means that kids don't get a little high; they can get stoned out of their minds with very little effort.

Generally speaking, the dangers of marijuana don't involve some of the rowdier crimes like assault and vandalism that liquor does. But students can have all sorts of reactions from paranoid to psychotic, with all sorts of dangerous effects. The good thing about marijuana (if there is one) is that when a student lights up, that smell is unmistakable. One whiff from under a door and an RA will smell it. It's a bit harder to hide than a bottle of rum is.

I Don't Give My Child Money for Alcohol or Drugs. Where Are They Getting It?

Drinking and drugs require money, but it's unlikely that you'll see a credit or debit card charge for an ounce of pot or a case of beer. What you might see, however, are excessive repeated credit card charges with lame excuses. One of the easiest ways for kids to get money is to charge a meal for a group of friends onto their credit card. They'll tell you that they had no cash so they used their card and their friends paid them back with cash. Then they'll tell you that they're using the cash as spending money. Which they are, but there's no way to track what they're spending it on, right? If they're using the emergency credit card for cash advances, you might also want to raise an eyebrow.

Debit cards are also a problem as they have access to cash whenever they want, either at the ATM or using the "cash-back" feature onto a retail purchase, which doesn't show up on the statement. (John could buy $14 worth of groceries with his debit card but ask for $20 cash back. The transaction on your statement simply shows up with the information that he spent $34 at the grocery store.) You don't want to start from a position of suspicion and doubt, but inexplicable money spending needs to be addressed quickly.

Obviously, if a student has a job at school, that's another place where she is getting money, but typically they're too busy to spend it. Sometimes students will get really creative and sell something they own on eBay or to another student, participate in paid experiments through the Psychology department, donate plasma at the local blood donation center, or pick up odd jobs around town such as babysitting or handing out flyers. If he is in a band or a music ensemble, he might get paid for a gig now and then, too. Truth be told, when students need money, they will find a way to get it. (Though you don't need to jump to conclusions about how that money is being used. Just because Jen gets a job at the front desk of a yoga studio for a few mornings a week doesn't mean she is running out and buying pot every weekend.)

Finally, in the most extreme cases, students can make money for drugs and liquor by selling drugs and liquor. In most cases your child is not going to do anything like this, but if you have any suspicions about illegal activity or excessive drinking you might start paying careful attention to those spending habits.

HOW COMMONPLACE ARE ARRESTS FOR DRINKING, DRUGS, AND SEXUAL OFFENSES ON COLLEGE CAMPUSES?

Drug arrests on U.S. college campuses have jumped 34 percent in recent years, according to statistics analyzed by *The Chronicle of Higher Education*. The most popular offense cited was possession of marijuana. *The Chronicle* also says that the study does not necessarily mean that more kids are using marijuana. It may simply mean that campuses are cracking down on the use of drugs on campus. Alcohol arrests also increased according to *The Chronicle*, again perhaps due to stronger enforcement. (*The Chronicle of Higher Education* reports on drug, alcohol and weapons arrests on campus using data from the Department of Education data each year. As of this writing, the most current data was for 2003.)

For a college-by-college breakdown of crime and drug data, visit the OPE Campus Security Statistics website at http://ope.ed.gov/security. Again, avoid making judgments about how safe a school is when using this data because some schools may be more stringent in their reporting of the incidents. (Look at the 2001 data and you'll see that Pennsylvania State University had the most drug arrests (173) and Michigan State University reported the most arrests for liquor-law violations (898).)

In 2001, the number of forcible sex offenses, including rape, sodomy, and fondling, increased across colleges 9 percent from the previous year to 2,125. (Campus-safety officials believe that the actual number of sex offenses is much higher because these are the most underreported crimes.) Experts have estimated that as many as one in five women experience at least an attempted sexual assault while they are in college. Women should prepare themselves for college life by knowing the facts. There are many measures women in college take to be safe including sticking together, calling each other to make sure the other got home okay, staying alert, going out with people they know well, not drinking too much, using campus escorts late at night, and taking a self-defense class.

I'm Worried that My Child is Majoring in Partying, Not Studying. Is There Anything I Can Do?

You don't want to hold the specter of good grades over your kids' heads through every conversation, but you probably want to "have the talk" before they go to school—along with an occasional refresher later on.

Dr. Mark Wood at the University of Rhode Island is involved in research indicating that parental influence has a greater affect on preventing college substance abuse than previously thought. "Before college classes start, parents need to talk frankly with their student about alcohol and drug use and make their expectations and concerns known," says Wood. "Tuition is usually a significant investment, and it is reasonable for parents to expect a good grade report in return for that investment." If necessary, Wood says parents can also seek guidance from a campus expert (substance abuse prevention educators, health services, counseling, or the dean of students).

"The kids who flunk out of school rarely do so because the work is too hard. A lot of college drinking masks other struggles, often related to depression or anxiety," Greg Kneser, Dean of Students at St. Olaf College observes. "Don't hesitate to ask your student how she or he is feeling. Trust your instincts. Pay attention to what you observe, whether it's weight loss or gain, trouble concentrating, or a noticeable drop in grades."

The beginning of freshman year is the most crucial time. Most situations of partying too much and studying too little are developmental stages through which students pass within the first few months of college, says Jana Lynn Patterson, Associate Dean of Students, and Smith Jackson, Vice President and Dean of Student Life, both at Elon University. If they don't pass through these stages, trouble could be brewing. Fran Cohen, University of Rhode Island's Dean of Students tells parents: "It is not unusual for students to have a rough first semester as they adjust to being on their own and using their time wisely. But students need to know their parents are paying attention and care about their well-being and grades." One bad semester can not only bring down a student's GPA for the remaining four years, but can also develop terrible habits that are tough to break.

"Don't hesitate to call one of those college officials who encouraged you to contact them at parent orientation. Few parents actually do—it feels like meddling to them—but you can ask questions and get advice without crossing appropriate boundaries," says Kneser. He also mentions that those first six weeks of school are also the time when students are most at risk for sexual violence. He says, "As they push their comfort zones and limits, students can find themselves in at-risk positions more often during those early weeks of their college experience."

Should I Worry About Steroids?

Parents of school athletes have particular cause to worry about steroids. At some of the more competitive colleges and universities, there is a "do whatever it takes" attitude about performance. " 'Roid rage"—the appearance of violent behavior and uncontrollable rages—has become a well-documented symptom in college athletes.

Who Can I Talk to if I Suspect My Child Needs Help?

Campuses have a directory of trained professionals who can help your student. These can include substance abuse prevention educators, health services staff members, counseling staff, and the Dean of Students.

Parents are encouraged to give them a call if there's a problem and be persistent in their search for the help they are looking for.

Unfortunately, as noted throughout this book, schools have policies in place surrounding any parent who calls the school looking for information on their child that may cause some problem. Colleges are obligated by law to keep certain information private, and private means not sharing it with parents.

If you call the Residence Life office or the Counseling Office and say, "I think my child's grades are suffering and I suspect drug use," they're likely to say, "We don't discuss grades with parents unless the student has given their explicit approval." If you say, "I think my child has a drug problem" it's likely that they'll say, "Have him call the Counseling Office and make an appointment." What's the likelihood of this ever happening? Would you even suggest it to your child?

"FERPA plays a huge role in how much you can know about your child's life on campus. Students can keep their academic and health records private. That means you can't even access their grades without their permission," says Rod Crafts, Dean of Student Life at Franklin W. Olin College of Engineering. Crafts urges parents and students to discuss access to grades, other academic information, and health information before arriving at orientation.

Due to FERPA, parents may find themselves in a Catch-22. They suspect that their child needs help, but the school can't be overly communicative and won't intervene because of existing legislation. It's a frustrating situation for both parties, and the only advice for parents is to be diligent and keep gentle pressure applied on the school and your child.

The Wall Street Journal's Work and Family columnist, Sue Shellenbarger, wrote a column in August of 2005 in defense of hovering parents who intervene on their child's behalf. While many parents do this too soon and too often, she interviewed parents who explained a multitude of good reasons (including health) about why they had to get involved and urge the administration to respond. It's the squeaky wheel syndrome that ultimately should yield a response. (Just don't abuse it.) And at the risk of sounding litigious, it's important that you document your conversations with university officials, just in case you should need that evidence later on.

When It's Time to Be a Party Pooper

"Sometimes students need a small failure on a paper or project as a 'wake-up' call, so do not be surprised if this happens," say Patterson and Jackson, both at Elon University. "If grades slip and you suspect too much partying, you need to sit down and have a sound and rational talk to assess why their academic performance is suffering."

Cheryl Brown, Director of Admissions at SUNY at Binghampton says it's a question of balance. "Students will party when they go to college. It's the way that many 18- to 22-year-olds define their social life and college experience. The problem comes when students can't balance their social life against their academic demands or have difficulty standing up to peer pressure. Students who have had some experience in high school at teen parties and social gatherings may have already outgrown some of the novelty of staying out late and overdoing it. For others, it can be devastating."

Look for Clues

Look for the warning signs. If you call and child seems to be sleeping the day away, take this as a clue. If he pulled an all-nighter finishing a big paper, that's one thing. If, on the other hand, he sounds hungover, make sure it doesn't become business as usual. Ask for a copy of his class schedule and check-in from afar once in a while. E-mail and instant messenger are also good resources. Many times students will leave telltale away messages on their IMs (like "partying at John's house") and you can see what they have been up to. You might try using Google to type your child's name in, too. If, on the off-chance, she turns up at a Spring Break brawl or topless coed site...well, it's worth knowing.

Is Sex on Campus as Prevalent as We Suspect It Is?

The best answer (though not the one you want to hear) is probably. Sex on campus has always been prevalent. Combine raging teenage hormones with physical proximity and you're bound to have a certain amount of sexual intensity. Statistics are hard to come by, but stories of casual sex and sex as a tension release are pretty common on most campuses. Every student makes his own decisions, and every campus has its own culture surrounding this. Students will tell you, however, that on the majority of college campuses, sexual encounters are the norm, not the exception.

Do Colleges Educate Students About Birth Control?

Remember: There are many different kinds of colleges that fall along a continuum of values and beliefs. Also remember that teaching your children about safe sex and casual sex versus true relationships is part of your job as Mom or Dad. That said, some colleges and universities do dispense information about birth control, while others dispense information about abstinence. On a visit to some schools you'll see that they openly distribute condoms, while others make sure that talk about sex is kept to a quiet and minimal part of the culture. Some colleges will dispense contraception including the controversial morning after pill; others will not. Check with the college or university's health department either on the Internet or in the handbook—feel free to even call them—to find out what exactly their policies are.

How Common Is Rape on Campus?

College students are more vulnerable to rape than any other age group, and violence against women on campus continues to be a serious problem. A 1998 study as reported by the Center for Problem Oriented Policy on rape in America found that women ages 16 and 24 were four times more likely to experience rape than the rest of the population. The Department of Justice has estimated that 16.6 of every 1,000 college women are raped each year. If that doesn't sound like an alarming number, remember that while colleges and universities are under federal law to make incidents of sexual assault on campus public information, it's estimated that only 1 in 100 of these crimes ever get reported. In 2001, there were 249,000 victims of rape in the United States, according to statistics from the Rape, Abuse and Incest National Network. Thirty-six percent of victims of rape and sexual assault are between the ages of 18 and 30.

What Is the "Date Rape Drug"?

GHB, gamma-hydroxybutyric acid, is commonly referred to as the "date rape drug." It is odorless and colorless, so it's easily masked in a drink. It's typically a form of horse or other large animal tranquilizer, so it's extremely potent. Some of these drugs are produced in unsanitary home laboratories (there are even recipes for it on the Internet) exacerbating the problem because of impurities and doses that vary from batch to batch.

The drug acts quickly, in about 15 minutes, and it causes intense muscle relaxation and amnesia so that the person has no recollection of events that transpired while under the drug's influence. Research indicates that a victim of rape while under the drug's influence often suffers from post-traumatic stress which can include emotional numbing, nightmares, flashbacks of the event, and avoidance of activities. Many colleges now have tests that can detect GHB in a urine sample, provided that the victim gets to the health center within a few hours of the incident. According to *The Journal of College Counseling*, in an article titled, "Drug-Facilitated Sexual Assault on Campus," GHB leaves the body within 10 to 12 hours and may not be traceable by the time a test is requested.

Perhaps the worst part of a drug-influenced date rape is that women often feel personally guilty and blame themselves for what happened. Since they can't remember, they wonder if they did anything to encourage the rape. The other alarming statistic is that frequently the perpetrator is an acquaintance. Since the date rape drug often gets slipped into a drink, many college administrators caution female students not to leave drinks unattended at a party and not to drink unless they are comfortable in a situation and know the people who are giving the party.

Other drugs like Ketamine and Rophynol are, according to the National Drug Control Policy report in 2003, used as date rape drugs as well. Rophynol depresses the central nervous system and causes an inability to remember what happened, while Ketamine is an anesthetic that can cause depression, delirium, and amnesia. Most of the Ketamine that's sold legally today is used by veterinarians.

What Are Schools Doing to Address Problems of Rape and Sexual Assault?

Much of the work is preventative in nature. Campus health officials are educating students (both male and female) about rape, what to do if a rape occurs, and what services are available afterward.

They are marketing their health services to students through posters, videos, their website, and other outreach efforts. On the Ohio University campus, for example, the Health Services department developed an effective program to advertise SANE (Sexual Assault Nurse Examination) by testing various messages on students to see which ones best resonated with them before launching their campaign about the confidentiality of the service. Many schools hold programs to discuss sexual assault during orientation week. These programs are held in dorms as well as in the fraternities.

In addition to their prevention efforts and publicizing their programs across campus, health services departments also provide medical care. Colleges have learned that students have little experience in negotiating serious medical matters alone. They are also financially dependent on their parents, but may not turn to them if they are worried their parents will disapprove of a situation. Schools have turned to offering medical assistance and counseling services under confidential arrangements.

What Can Parents Do?

Parents of girls tend to be pretty good at telling them to be careful and encouraging them to say "no" when they find themselves in unwanted sexual situations. But because boys are not put in these sorts of positions as often, there's considerable evidence to suggest that boys are rarely schooled on how to act in similar situations. A majority of boys on campus truly believe that a girl who is flirtatious, or "loose," or inebriated must have the same thing in mind as they do. Parents of boys need to make it clear that they are not to continue sexual advances if they are not want-ed—or, even if they are unsure as to whether they are wanted.

Most sexual assaults on campus occur on weekends, so it's probably a good idea to check in with your child on the weekends. Casually ask what their plans are and, if a party or a date is involved, you might ask where they plan to go and remind them to use their good sense. They'll probably come back with an, "I know!!!" but you will have said it and a parent's words often has strong sticking power.

Dating is a bit of an anachronism on most college campuses today. Hanging out with a group and then hooking up as couples is more the norm—for better or worse. If your child is going out on a date or to "just hang out," they should always tell someone in their dorm or house where they are going and with whom.

If it's a traditional date, suggest they make that first date for a public place—a restaurant or movie or jazz café rather than a dorm room. Remind them that it's never a bad idea to have a friend give them a check-in call sometime during the evening. Most of all, teach them to trust their gut feelings about the person. If they're uneasy or uninterest-ed, she should have the confidence to say "thanks and goodnight" and then move on.

Back when they were in high school, you knew that your best defense against dangerous sexual encounters or drunken parties was to keep them busy. Sports, theater, music, outdoor activities—whatever they did that kept them active and engaged was probably one of the best things you could do for them. While you can't force them to join extracurricular activities in college, you can encourage and suggest that they do. As old-fashioned as it sounds, the more time they spend in supervised fun, the less time they'll spend flirting with trouble.

CHAPTER 4

Keeping Safe on the College Campus

The first time we went to visit our son in college we found him at 8:00 A.M. outside his dorm's front door, standing in a deluge of rain wearing nothing but his underwear. We were a little perplexed (and a lot embarrassed) as other parents began to drive into the parking lot for the start of Orientation. Lips blue and shivering, arms hugging him tight, when we got close enough to hear his words he was saying that he'd walked down the hall to the bathroom, left his key inside the room, and was waiting for security to let him back in. One night on campus and our boy had already won a memorable place in the hearts of the security officers as the naked one who didn't have much "key smarts."

Taking your keys everywhere is just one part of their new college life that doesn't always immediately register with the overwhelmed freshmen who just arrived at college. We laugh when we say that college students live in their own world, but it's true. They expect doors to unlock when you need them to, bicycles to wait for them in the rack, and backpacks to be sitting just where they last left them.

Few situations are as unique as campus living; it's a world of its own. For the most part, it's a very safe and protected world, but that can lead to a false sense of security. Crime on campus does exist, regardless of the size, type, and personality of the school. Fortunately, most of it can be avoided by practicing a few simple precautions.

First, here's the recipe that brings campus crime to a boil:

- Take 1 part students who are notorious for owning the latest gear including computers, iPods, mountain bikes, cameras, brand-name clothing, accessories, and handbags/backpacks.

- Mix with 1 part students who are notorious for not remembering where their car is parked, whether they locked their door, where they left their wallet, or even—on a bad day—where they went last night.

- Combine with a "sense of trust."

Place ingredients in a dorm environment and mix. You've got your classic recipe for crime and safety issues. There's not a college campus in the world that's 100 percent safe—but knowing where trouble is likely to occur and conveying the proper precautions is a step in the right direction. The hard part is getting them to stop rolling their eyes and pay attention. Trust me: One bad experience is all it takes for them to take heed.

In this chapter, we'll look at the basics of campus safety:

- Larceny/theft
- Protecting your belongings
- Campus safety
- Insurance issues
- Building and fire safety

WHAT IS THE MOST FREQUENT CRIME ON CAMPUS?

The stealing of personal property, otherwise known as larceny or theft, is the most common crime on campus. Burglary, which involves breaking and entering with the intent to steal, ranks second.

Nancy Griffin at St. Anselm College says most campus crimes are "crimes of convenience." A student leaves his room to go down the hall to visit a friend just for a moment. He may leave his door wide open—or, maybe he just left it unlocked. When he returns, the $20 bill he left on his dresser is missing. Thefts from dorm rooms or backpacks are almost always these types of crimes of opportunity. Easily transportable valuables—cash, jewelry, small electronics, laptops—are the most common items that tend to "disappear" on a college campus.

As Griffin puts it: "Dorms, or residence halls as I like to call them, are only as safe as the students make them."

Of course there are other crimes on campus, most of them discussed in the "Sex, Drugs, and Drinking" chapter. They tend to be crimes enacted under the influence—drunk driving, vandalism, assault, or disturbing the peace,. While they do happen, only a very small number of crimes involve outsiders who don't belong on the school's campus.

How Safe Is This Campus?

Today, it's easy to get a listing of crime statistics for the various college campuses because of the Clery Act. Howard and Connie Clery's daughter, Jeanne Ann Clery, was murdered in her dorm room at Lehigh University in 1986. Her brutal murder was committed by another student she didn't know, who was an abuser of drugs and alcohol. After their daughter's death, the Clerys fought to get a federal law enacted that requires colleges and universities to disclose information about their campus crime and security policies. President Bush signed it into law in 1990. Under the federal Jeanne Clery Act, colleges and universities must disclose campus crime and safety information. Parents can use this information as a barometer of what a particular school's campus safety situation will be like. For a searchable database of campus crime, see www.securityoncampus.org.

ARE THERE MORE CRIMES COMMITTED ON LARGE URBAN CAMPUSES THAN ON SMALL RURAL ONES?

According to S. Daniel Carter, Senior Vice President of Security On Campus, Inc. (a nonprofit organization created by the Clery family after their daughter's dorm room murder and is committed to making college campuses safer), on-campus crime is often similar—in both type and in the ratio of crimes-to-students committed—across different types of campuses, with some exceptions where the college fosters a unique campus culture, such as upstanding and very devout Brigham Young University in Salt Lake City, UT.

WHO COMMITS THESE CRIMES?

Security On Campus, Inc. found that roughly 80 percent of campus crimes are committed by students to other students.

HOW CAN I TAKE PRECAUTIONS TO MINIMIZE THEFT?

You need to talk to your children in a way that sits somewhere between complete nonchalance and scaring them to death about the things that could go wrong regarding personal safety. Kids in dorms get very comfortable, very quickly. When they are comfortable, they often grow lax in their precautions. They begin to think of the dorm as a safe haven from the real world. They think: It's okay to drink too much or forget your iPod on the desk in class because it will be safe among fellow students, right?

Wrong. Remind them that while they may trust their friends in the dorm, plenty of other people they don't know can easily find ways of sneaking in and out without attracting much attention.

Here are some common-sense rules your college student should follow:

- Don't be ostentatious. Don't flaunt the gear.
- Keep doors locked when out of the room, even for a few moments. Countless students have been shocked to find something missing after just popping down the hall to put in a load of laundry. They find it hard to believe that someone who lives in their own hall would take their things! But who knows better what they have that's of value but the people who wander in and out each day? Encourage them to check their dorm's doors and windows to make sure they can be shut securely. They should close and lock all windows and doors when they're out and should keep valuable out of window view.
- Don't leave cash, jewelry, or other valuables out in the open.
- Report non-working campus lighting—crime is more rampant in darkened areas.

- Don't let anyone you don't know into the dorm.

- Buy good quality bike locks. (See the Tip box below entitled "Forget the U-Lock.")

- Anti-theft devices like chains and locks to bolt computers and stereos to the desk are a possible solution. However, kids have even found ways of yanking these things off the desk (often carrying a souvenir piece of desk with them). Plus, if it's a laptop computer, your child is quickly going to get lazy and not lock the lock.

TIP: Forget the U-Lock

Those U-shaped Kryptonite bicycle locks that everyone used to use on campus were, for a long time, the favorite. They were foolproof. In 2005, however, information began circulating on the Internet about how to use a Bic pen to hack a U-lock. In seconds, the lock, impervious to things like saws and files, was now foiled by a pen point. The Web spread the news of the U-lock's Achilles' heel like wildfire, and bikes began disappearing in record numbers. These days, the biking forums on the Internet recommend purchasing the new disc-cylinder lock rather than the older, axial-based locks.

To maximize the chance that your child will get something back if it is stolen, she should:

- Keep an inventory of big-ticket items like iPods and stereos.

- Keep receipts and a list of serial numbers of products either at school or, better yet, at home.

- Use a digital camera to take inventory. (This is simple if you bring a digital camera to move-in day and take photos of their valuables with the serial numbers. Make sure the camera is on its close-up setting (usually represented as a flower icon) to get a well-focused picture. Since move-in day is usually crazed, you could also do this right before you've packed everything in the car.

- Register that bicycle. Most campuses have a bicycle registration program. Serious riders could consider reserving one bicycle for real weekend riding and using an old junker for getting to and from classes and into town.

- Use an engraving tool to engrave initials into valuables, which can sometimes help deter thieves as well as to identify the stolen property. (Many schools have programs to do this for you. Students bring their goods to the safety office and they'll burn their initials right onto those valuable items.)

Safety Is a Team Effort

Pitzer College reminds students that safety isn't a one-man effort. It's important to talk with roommates and/or suitemates about safety (making sure the room is locked, letting the others know when guests will be coming over, etc.). Sharon Kompalla of Rochester Institute of Technology's Center for Residence Life says that students can be too trusting of roommates and floormates. It's best to keep minimal amounts of cash on hand and avoid providing temptation. Kompalla suggests that having a small, lockable file cabinet in the dorm room might prevent some theft.

WHAT CAN PARENTS DO TO HELP PREVENT THEFT? SHOULD I CARRY THEFT INSURANCE FOR MY STUDENT?

The first thing a parent needs to do is a reality check: In the course of four years, things will get stolen or lost. Think twice before buying her a brand new car, stereo, fancy television, or, heaven forbid, a Louis Vuitton handbag to take to school. The second thing on a parent's list? Plan to have some insurance.

Deborah Olsen Nolan, Associate Dean and Dean of Students at Ursinus College, says most colleges leave the decision of whether to carry theft insurance to the individual families. "Colleges generally do not cover personal theft or damage, unless it is to cover some item of equipment that is issued to every student, such as a laptop computer."

Scott Simonds, an independent financial counselor in Maine, urges parents to call their insurance companies and look into what will be covered and what won't. "Most homeowner's insurance policies will cover your kid's belongings in the dorm. Stereos, TVs, and computers add up to real money," he says, "so call your

> **TIP:** Whether you have renter's or homeowner's coverage, the optimal policy will cover the replacement cost of buying a new item rather than the cost of the actual item that was stolen. So, if a $1,000 mountain bike has been stolen, it's possible that replacing the bike with one of the same caliber would cost $2,000.

insurance agent to confirm that your level of coverage includes these kinds of items once your child takes them to school."

Provided that your child's primary residence is still your home, most homeowner policies have some provision to insure you for possessions that aren't in your home at the time of the loss. However, it's not a lot of coverage; the typical homeowner is covered for only 10 percent of the policy's value if the loss occurs outside of the home. In addition, any claims made for things lost at college are reflected on your homeowner's policy. Your rates will rise if you file a claim for something that disappears from a dorm.

A more expensive alternative that has some advantage is to purchase renter's insurance. The advantage is that any claims are independent of your homeowner's policy. A typical renter's policy can have a premium of about $150. Well before your child leaves for school, talk to your broker about your situation and assess whether your homeowner policy is adequate. (Consider the actual value of what your child is taking to school. Is everything brand new, or is much of it older things that were collected from around the house?) Also, check with the school. Some have relationships with insurance companies that can offer parents a good rate.

What Can Parents Do in Addition to Carrying Insurance?

There are other ways that parents can help being proactive about pin-pointing the potential dangers. Parents can:

- Anticipate safety problems. On move-in day, you'll want to "case the joint" to determine how easy it is for someone to break and enter into the dormitory. Address any safety concerns with real-istic precautions (like making sure your first floor window locks properly) then take up larger concerns with the RA or Residence Life staff.

- Check windows and doors for working locks.

- Make sure keys work properly.

- Be even more vigilant if the room is in an isolated location or is on the first floor in a heavily trafficked area.

- Check for adequate bicycle storage if your child is bringing a bike.

- If anything seems amiss, report it to the campus Residence Life offices.

Who's Responsible for Campus Safety?

There's a cast of characters on campus that look out for campus safety. Nearly every school hires their own security guards. Often these guards have been previously trained either as former police or security guards. They patrol on foot, bicycle, and various riding mobiles and are often sta-tioned at a front gate. There should be a Campus Public Safety Office staffed with a number of safety officers and communications officers as well. On small- and mid-sized campuses, security guards can usually spot suspicious persons more easily than on large campuses.

Many campuses also have student security personnel. These students are often asked to keep a watchful eye during events and to make sure there's an escort service in the event that someone imbibes a bit too much or has to walk to their dorms after hours.

RAs also play a part in campus security since they are responsible for keeping tabs on anyone who's missing, and they know who belongs and who doesn't belong in the dorm. At Tulane University, Cynthia Cherrey, Vice President of Student Affairs, explains that "Resident advisors make rounds each night and campus public safety officers, all of whom are fully commissioned police officers, walk through the halls on a regular basis."

Charlotte G. Burgess, Vice President/Dean of Student Life at the University of Redlands, urges parents to ask questions and pick up on the subtleties at each school. "If you find there is obsessive attention to safety, is it because there have been major incidents?" she says. "At which point you need to ask how many incidents there have been and of what kind."

What Types of Programs Are Helping to Keep Kids Safe?

Most campuses have created student safety education programs. Some programs are preventative, some address the safety of the physical plant, and some educate the students. Here are some of the more common variations on the theme; most of these are present at most schools:

- A whistle alert program in which security guards dole out whistles as protection
- 24-hours a day security patrols on campus
- Bright lighting on campus walkways with regular inspections for blown out bulbs
- Campus escorts for late-night walks and shuttle bus systems from campus to town
- Emergency call boxes around campus that provide immediate contact with police dispatchers and 911

- Campus-wide crime prevention and awareness programs held in residence halls by professionals
- Self-defense programs that might include a martial arts component
- Liaison service with the town law enforcement agencies
- Property identification programs like registering bikes and engraving valuables
- Fire safety programs
- Evacuation and disaster plans and practice drill
- Good surveillance system at dorm doors

Beyond the Safety Statistics

Mark Twain said there were "lies, damn lies, and statistics." In this case that means take crime statistics on campus with a bit of skepticism. An apparent increase of arrests on a campus can be attributed to a change in the enforcement of a law or in the reporting of crimes, rather than an increase in the actual number of incidents. In other words, the school may want to crack down on drinking by stricter enforcement of ID policies. Suddenly there are more crimes being committed that revolve around fake IDs than when the administration didn't care as much.

Statistics are also suspect because there is always the unknown quantity of incidents that are not reported to police. Also, some of the figures may include tickets or citations, which campus police officers technically consider "arrests." Finally, colleges differ widely on how they tally incidents under the crime-reporting umbrella. Some crimes, such as underage drinking, are dealt with internally and are omitted from the crime report, as are crimes that take place very close to campus, where many students live in privately run apartments.

For all of these reasons and more, one of the most reliable and informative methods of research is the word-of-mouth approach. Talk to students currently attending a college about safety issues. Ask specific questions about what actually happens on campus, and find out whether students generally feel safe on campus and in the area surrounding the campus. The students will give you the real story, and a true feel for the level of campus security. The best way to enjoy the full college experience is to feel safe and confident about your surroundings while you're there.

Reprinted with permission from www.PrincetonReview.com.

ARE THE NEW ELECTRONIC KEYS SAFER?

You bet they are. Security experts on campus say that the first line of defense against crime is the ID key card. They are better than standard keys because they can be programmed for individual access and then deprogrammed as necessary. A single key can be used at the front door of the residence hall and as the key to a dorm room. The same electronic key can get you into a library or lab with special permission.

Traditional keys are becoming anachronisms because of the strong advantages of the electronic cards. Schools have more options because the administration can selectively enable and disable the keys. If a student transfers to a different school, the school will deactivate the key; if your child loses the key, they will deactivate it. Plus, each key can have access control to other places on the campus. So, the school can give your child a single key providing access to all of the places he needs to go while keeping them out of unauthorized facilities.

Along with the ID key card, some schools are using video surveillance and/or lobbies staffed by students or campus personnel. While some students complain that they have a problem with video surveillance, it's a fact that strategically placed video cameras are major deterrents to theft.

Is This School Prepared for a Fire?

In January of 2000, a fire broke out in the dorm of Seton Hall College. Three students were killed and fifty-eight injured in what was an alarmingly fast fire, later found out to be arson. According to Underwriter's Laboratories, 1,800 fires occur in dormitories and Greek housing each year, which means that firefighters can respond to fires on college campuses five times a day somewhere in the United States. If you add in the fires that happen in off-campus housing, you are looking at an additional large number.

Here's a list of questions to consider when evaluating how well prepared your college would be in the event of a dorm fire:

- Are the residence hall and its rooms protected by an automatic fire sprinkler system?

- Does the residence hall have a smoke alarm?

- Do students receive fire prevention training and/or evacuation training?

- Is the fire alarm signal transferred directly to the fire department?

- Does the school ban any of the following items or activities in residence hall rooms: Candles? Halogen lamps? Smoking? Cooking?

- Is the furniture (beds, mattresses, desks, and chairs) in the residence hall rooms fire resistant?

- Are students given fire extinguisher training?

- Are fire safety rules-compliance inspections conducted in the school's residence halls?

The Princeton Review conducts an annual survey of campus fire safety. Visit www.PrincetonReview.com to look up the fire safety rating earned by individual schools.

It's a Crime

According to a survey conducted by the Independent Insurance Agents of America Inc. (IIAA):

- More than 100,000 property crimes on college campuses are reported to police each year.

- Thieves make off with an average of $1,250 in stolen student property per theft.

Fire Safety Is in Your Hands

According to the Underwriter Laboratories website, there are things you can do to minimize the risk of fire.

- Use a power strip with an over-current protector.

- Be wary of electrical outlets that get too hot to the touch. Unplug all appliances and notify the landlord or RA immediately.

- Do not connect multiple extension cords together. The more plugs and receptacles that are connecting a single current or a single appliance to a single wall outlet, the more chance there is for arcing and sparking.

- Extension cords are for temporary situations. Contrary to popular belief, extension cords should not be used as a long-term solution when you need another outlet. The longer an extension cord, the more chance it can be damaged over time.

- Do not route cords under doors or carpets. Extension cords can short circuit, overheat, and ignite if they are buried under carpet, if they have furniture resting on and pinching them, or if they become bunched up behind hot appliances or equipment.

- Do not staple extension cords. This damages insulation meant to protect the user from the current; potentially exposing a wire increases the possibility of sparking. It's like poking a hole in a straw while drinking a soda: No matter what you do, you're going to get leakage and, in a

crowded dorm room, you never want a spark to get near any com-
bustibles.

- Never cut off a grounding pin. Never bend, file, or cut a grounding pin
  from a three-pronged cord to plug an appliance into a wall outlet. This
  disarms the protection meant to keep you safe and presents a tremen-
  dous shock hazard.

- Don't use cheater plugs. As a general practice, refrain from using
  cheater plugs, but cheater plugs with a special screw tab that plug into
  a wall outlet are acceptable.

- Use light bulbs with the correct wattage for lamps. All UL-Listed lamps
  have wattage specifications near the bulb socket indicating what size
  bulb is the maximum recommended. If no indication is on the product, do
  not use a bulb with more than 60 watts.

- Be careful with halogen lamps. If the housing board permits them, make
  sure the halogen lamp meets updated requirements. All halogen lamps
  must be designed with a mesh guard that forbids contact with the bulb
  and with an automatic tip-over switch.

CHAPTER 5

The Healthy Student

School is not a great place to get sick, nor is it a great place to get healthy once you've been sick. Our kids all went to smaller colleges where the nurses seemed to rely on three remedies: doling out Tylenol, doing a throat culture, and advocating bed rest. Because the kids all lived on campus (and without cars), getting to an off-campus doctor was difficult. Doctors' offices seem never to be anywhere near the route of the campus shuttle bus. As a matter of fact, when one of our children got sick and needed a month of routine care, despite the fact that our daughter's friends tried to help, we racked up a couple of hundred dollars in cab fares back and forth from the hospital.

With any luck, the student you send to college will have, over the years, built up the requisite antibodies to keep him immune to the daily wheezes, sneezes, and bacteria that are so much a part of college life. They're going to need every antibody they can muster.

It's almost a given that your children will spend half of their college life tired, run down, and eating a less-than-ideal diet. They'll be living in barrack-like quarters (except that barracks are cleaner) and in the close company of at least one other student who may not have the decorum you instilled in your own. They'll abuse their bodies with stress, sleep deprivation, and the occasional high blood alcohol level. They'll miss their bed at home, their high school friends, even you—all of which can add to the already emotional carousel of college life.

It's also a given that you'll be on the receiving end of every call when they're feeling a bit under the weather, weary to the bone, or just plain cranky. If they were home, you'd know just what to do. A cup of tea, your best recipe for chicken soup, perhaps? But now, all you've got to rely on is that fine-tuned parental radar to assess the situation from afar as you struggle to dispense the right advice.

Strep throat, sprained ankles, a few lost or found pounds, tooth aches— these are the lighter sides of college health issues, the ones that you and your child will muddle through somehow. But there's a darker side, too.

Serious illness, depression, suicidal tendencies—you'll want to prepare for the worst by arming yourself with the facts, so you can then be pleasantly surprised when your preparations for the worst turn out to have been for naught.

Thinking ahead starts with an understanding of what services her college will provide and which ones they won't. In this chapter we'll look at:

- Diet and weight management

- Exercise and the student

- Mental health

- Health insurance during the college years

- Planning for medical, dental, and pharmacy coverage

- What to do if and when your child gets sick

SHOULD I WORRY ABOUT THE COLLEGE DIET?

Maybe your child should be worrying about yours! This generation of college kids stands a considerably better chance of emerging healthy and fit than many of us did when we went to college. The main ingredient in the college cafeteria of yore was grease of an undetermined origin. Snacks were limited to what could tumble out of a vending machine.

Today, the most educated part of college students' bodies may turn out to be their palates. Have you been to a college cafeteria lately? It's not unusual to see a salad bar, vegetarian fare, and a choice of everything from hand-carved deli meats to ethnic specialties from all corners of the globe. Complaining about food is an ingrained part of college culture. Half the time those complaints stem from the tedium of eating in the same place every night without a limitless budget to go eat out instead. For the most part, colleges have made dramatic improvements over the last ten years. A few have even transformed themselves into epicurean havens. When your kids call to complain, just have them compare your dinner choices to theirs.

You could worry about the college diet, but you probably have better things to worry about instead. The truth is, your child is going to eat whatever she wants to in college—just like she was probably doing at home. (Or, at least on the nights when they were left to their own devices at dinner time.) Feeling sick after sampling every dessert in the line up will eventually prompt them to make better choices, especially as the novelty of all-you-can-eat french fries wears off.

WHAT IF MY CHILD HAS SPECIAL DIETARY CONCERNS LIKE VEGETARIANISM, KOSHER, OR HALAL FOODS?

Even the airlines dutifully accommodate a bevy of special dietary requests (well, on those few flights where they serve something beyond a bag of pretzels). But, as the passenger, you can deal with their interesting interpretations of your special needs because you don't have to eat airline food for nine months in a row. If your child has special dietary needs, his school can probably accommodate him. Of course, some schools will do this with a bit more flair and imagination than others. Most colleges today offer some options for special diets, and the bigger schools can often accommodate everything from kosher and halal to vegan and lactose-intolerant diets. Many even give a nod to fads with things like Atkins and Zone selections.

If the diet is crucial to your child's well-being or state of mind, make sure the school you choose won't hit you with any surprises. "You'll want to check with the school and let them know your needs before you come," says Charlotte Burgess, the Vice President and Dean of Student Life at University of Redlands. "Try to find out what percentage of kids share the same diet, too. If a school doesn't have a sizable number of vegetarians, for example, you may find they will cook you the same meal over and over again throughout the semester."

Jody Terhaar and Jason Laker, Deans of Students College of Saint Benedict/Saint John's University also suggest requesting a dorm with a communal kitchen so your child can prepare her own food from time to time. Another alternative is to look for a school that lets your child spend meal plan points at on-campus grocery stores. This set-up is typically found at larger schools.

IS IT TRUE THAT WEIGHT GAIN IS NORMAL DURING COLLEGE?

Combine a sedentary life of classes and studying with an unlimited buffet where ice cream sundaes, waffle fries, and grilled cheese sandwiches are there for the taking and you've got a recipe for potential extra pounds. Even if the cafeteria is stocked with healthy foods, the choice to actually eat them remains with the student. But educators agree that it's not just the dining hall menu that contributes to the weight gain that many college students say they've experienced. "Changes in personal habits including eating, sleeping, and exercise, all...affect a student's weight," says Lou Ann Gilchrist, Dean of Student Affairs at Truman State University. Not to mention the stress of a total lifestyle overhaul with a whole new set of people, places, and pressures.

The Princeton Review recently conducted a study for *Mens' Fitness* magazine where we surveyed 10,000 students about their campus lifestyle. One of the questions asked was, "How much weight have you gained or lost?" It turns out that there weren't very many simple answers. Most answers could be charted like roller coasters: "I gained 5 pounds in the first semester, lost 7 in the second semester and then gained 5 more," was a typical response.

Brigham Young University was ranked as the healthiest school in the country, but all of the schools in the top ten tended to have healthy meal programs, access to high quality fitness education and facilities, and high campus safety rates. Most of them had at least some physical education course requirement. Some schools provide nutritional counseling for their students, and others offer a complete nutritional workup, often for a nominal fee.

A weekly call to tell your child what to eat, when, and how much of it is out of the question. Johnne Armentrout of Wake Forest University's Counseling Center, and Natascha Romeo, a health educator also at Wake Forest, both agree that it is students themselves who need to take responsibility for preventing an unhealthy weight gain during their college years. Tips for doing this include creating a schedule that allows time to eat healthy meals and snacks, learning how to choose healthy food options from dining services and restaurants, and controlling portion sizes and overeating. The all-you-can-eat meal plans, late-night pig outs, and social drinking are just some of the obstacles students will need to be aware of and exercise restraint toward. If you've helped them make healthy choices at home, you've probably done well in helping them to make healthy choices on their own. Many schools hold workshops on how to eat right, and more and more schools employ nutritional specialists on part-time or full-time schedules—though no one can force students to take advantage of these valuable services.

Avoiding the Freshman 15

Who wouldn't get out of shape? They probably don't need to walk very far each day and physical fitness is rarely a requirement for graduation. While some campuses are known for their active, outdoorsy students, the average college kid spends most of his time on his derrière, studying or sitting in class or the library. Students forage out of vending machines and order pizza or subs to fight the sleepiness that comes with late-night study sessions. They often gravitate towards the deepest of the fried food. Add a few beers to the recipe and you've got the Freshman 15—the code phrase for the student weight gain that's often part and parcel of the freshman experience. Though some may appreciate the newfound bulk, most, especially the girls, are despondent.

Jim Matthews, MEd, author of *Beer, Booze and Books: A Sober Look at Higher Education,* is a campus consultant, Coordinator of Health Education at Merrimack College, and all around good guy (www.beerboozebooks.com).

His advice to students:

- Know when to stop eating, and try not to eat within three hours of hitting the hay. Eating so close to bedtime can disrupt your ability to fall asleep and stay asleep.

- Eat less more often for sustained energy. Eat four small meals a day that include fruit, veggies, meat, and fish.

- Eat plenty of live foods including fresh raw fruit, salad, and either raw or slightly steamed vegetables. Packaged food that is "refined" or "processed" is often lacking in nutrition.

- Whole-grain bread and brown rice are better choices than the white stuff. And students should not live on bread alone, anyway. Balance all the bagels and pizza with the other important food groups.

- Avoid fried foods. They're just not good for you.

- Too much sugar can cause energy highs and lows, making you feel tired. Instead of that candy bar, grab a piece of fruit.

- Drink water all day long, and carry a water bottle around campus.

- Stay motivated to stay healthy. Join an intramural sport. Get a workout buddy and hit the gym together regularly. If you can't get to the gym, give your body at least 30 minutes of movement per day—walk, stretch, dance, swim, hike, bike—you get the picture. Many schools offer recreation classes as electives. Signing up for a class in martial arts or ice skating, for example, will ensure that exercise is part of that busy schedule.

HOW PREVALENT ARE EATING DISORDERS ON CAMPUS?

The National Eating Disorder Association says that 5 to 10 million adolescent girls and women struggle with eating disorders and borderline eating disorder conditions. While not as prevalent in males, there are 1 million boys and men struggling with the same conditions. To put this in perspective, these numbers are triple the number of people living with AIDS, says the association.

While they vary in magnitude and some are borderline disorders, at their worst, eating disorders are more than peculiar eccentricities or a passing phase; they can be completely dehabilitating, even causing death. High school and college students, especially girls, are likely sufferers.

Here's why: College is a place where—ideally—the self-doubting high schooler turns into a confident college kid, and self-image plays a big part in that. It's also a social place where students are out to meet and greet, whether they're in class or going out to clubs. They want to look good, which for them, because of our popular culture and current beauty trends, often means looking as thin as possible.

Further contributing to the scrutiny of how they look is dorm living, where body type comparisons are part of an unavoidable routine. Weight gains and losses are duly noted by a watchful community of peers. Add it all up and appearance is one the most frequent topics of conversation on campus. Whether it's a "Did you see that body?" or "Does this outfit look okay?" or the ever popular "Do I look fat?"—the language of body image is very much a part of the campus fabric.

According to www.CampusBlues.com, a website that helps troubled students find resources at their schools, Americans spend $40 billion dollars a year on dieting and dieting products. Educated young men and women are opening their pocketbooks, even on college campuses.

Eating disorders take dieting to an extreme and dangerous form. The two most recognized eating disorders are bulimia and anorexia nervosa. Students suffering from anorexia obsess about being thin to the point of starving themselves. They'll perceive themselves as fat regardless of how little they weigh. Bulimic students aren't afraid of eating the way anorexic students are. Instead, they will binge eat and then force themselves to throw up or take laxatives and diuretics to eliminate the food from their bodies.

Eating disorders can—and should—be treated with therapy, and it's important that the person gets help. Because students live in such a tight community, friends and roommates will often be the first to detect an eating disorder in a peer.

Your child may come to you with questions about how to handle a friend in the dorm with a suspected eating problem. Encourage her to go to her RA or health services department and seek professional help for their friend. Or maybe she's caught up in it herself. There have been instances where an entire suite of roommates decide to "go on a starvation diet" together. Your children need to have strong self-images to buck these situations and stay healthy. It's frightening to think, but friends tend to be complicated enablers in eating disorder cases. A student with an eating disorder is usually afraid their peers are watching and making judgments and, in fact, that is often the case. A student who asks her roommates to constantly watch what she eats and measure her eating intake—regardless of how well meaning the roommates' intent is—can result in really dysfunctional patterns. This is why it's so important that a professional gets involved.

If your child comes home for break looking a little lighter, it's not going to help to cross-examine her the moment she walks through the door. Chances are she just came off a rough semester followed by a grueling week of exams. Casually ask her how she's feeling, watch her behavior, and look for other changes that have occurred since she was at home last—especially when it comes to her mood or energy level. You definitely don't want to jump to conclusions, but you don't want to miss any warning signs either.

Help for Eating Disorders

The National Eating Disorder Association reminds friends and family that they cannot change a person's behavior, but they offer these tips:

- Learn as much as you can about eating disorders. Read books, articles, and brochures.

- Know the differences between facts and myths about weight, nutrition, and exercise. Knowing the facts will help you reason against any inaccurate ideas that your friend may be using as excuses to maintain their disordered eating patterns.

- Be honest. Talk openly and honestly about your concerns with the person who is struggling with eating or body-image problems. Avoiding it or ignoring it won't help!

- Be caring but be firm. Caring about your friend does not mean being manipulated by them. Your friend must be responsible for his actions and the consequences of those actions. Avoid making rules, promises, or expectations that you cannot or will not uphold. For example, "I promise not to tell anyone." Or, "If you do this one more time, I'll never talk to you again."

- Compliment your friend's wonderful personality, successes, or accomplishments. Remind your friend that "true beauty" is not simply skin-deep.

- Be a good role model in regard to sensible eating, exercise, and self-acceptance.

- Tell someone. It may seem difficult to know when, if at all, to tell someone else about your concerns. Addressing body image or eating problems in their beginning stages offers your friend the best chance for working through these issues and becoming healthy again. Don't wait until the situation is so severe that your friend's life is in danger. Your friend needs as much support and understanding as possible.

The Weight Game: What's Your Role?

Weight is often a parent's first, and sometimes their only, measure that all is going well, but here are few more practical tips you might use as part of your "stay well" action plan.

Don't send packages of junk food. There is no shortage of junk food on campus. Some home-baked cookies are nice on occasion, but a weekly batch is a bit much.

Many schools offer care packages you can purchase for your child. They may even send you postcards reminding you to send these during high-stress exam weeks and to celebrate birthdays and holidays. Typically these are rather pricey and are heavy on the junk food. You are paying for the convenience of not sending your own food, so use them sparingly. Websites like collegecarepackages.com provide the same service and are also expensive. Why not create your own care package of healthy snacks, new pens and highlighters, and a gift certificate for a CD or DVD?

Good care packages could also include things like soups or chicken broth, granola or energy bars, nuts, and dried fruit. (Go ahead and toss in a nice dark chocolate bar, too. Its antioxidants are said to block the free radicals that breakdown normal cell reproduction.)

Don't make weight a constant topic of conversation. Instead, focus on the importance of staying healthy and strong at school and how exercise and good eating help that. If your child has gained or lost excessive amounts of weight, you might want to tactfully mention it once and then move on. No dice? Sometimes a sibling might have more success broaching the topic with them.

Don't be afraid to call the Dean of Residence Life if you suspect an eating problem. She may have some suggestions simply because she's seen so many students in so many different situations. Here's a real-life example of a simple explanation for a perplexing problem: A college freshman was burning through his meal-plan dollars, but he was actually losing weight. When his parents spoke to the dean, the dean suggested that perhaps this student was buying the pricey coffee and tea drinks putting him over the spending limit but not giving him enough to eat. Sure enough, when his parents asked if he'd been drinking those "exotic lattes and smoothies" they got a sheepish "yes" for an answer. You can guess who got a nudge to cut the caffeine and grab some dinner instead.

Which Meal Plan Should I Choose?

"The best meal plan is the one that helps your child remove food from the list of stressors," says Kurt Holmes, Dean of Students at The College of

Wooster. For some that means a full plan (twenty-one meals); for others it's the one-meal-a-day plan. "If a student is always worrying about whether they have enough money on their meal card, or whether the hours fit their needs, then the meal becomes much more inconvenient and much more of a chore," agrees Charlotte G. Burgess, Vice President/Dean of Student Life at the University of Redlands.

What's most important is to know your child's eating style and plan accordingly. Burgess says, "You don't want to be subsidizing the schools' football team by paying for a fully loaded meal plan when your child doesn't use it." At the University of Redlands, amongst other schools, students have the opportunity to change their meal plans during the first two weeks of school to allow for an adjustment that better suits their lifestyle.

So go to the source and ask the student how she prefers to eat and what kind of eating habits she feels she's had over the last couple years. Sure, college life will change things—but this is a starting point. Some kids love to eat a big breakfast while others skip it or would find it easiest to eat a piece of fruit or bowl of cereal in their room than make an extra trip to the dining hall. If your child eats three square meals a day, you should count on her taking most of them in the dining hall; it's often a new student's most convenient option for mealtime.

After determining what kind of eater your child is, it's important to look for meal plan flexibility. The campus should be able to accommodate the spectrum from 5:00 P.M. early dinner eaters to midnight-run eaters. It's good to ask how many locations there are where students can eat, when the facilities are open, and whether there are dining room alternatives like grocery stores and delis that are on campus or nearby. (Almost certainly, there will be. Where there are college students, there are plenty of ways to feed them.)

At first glance, meal plan options are almost as confusing as course offerings. You'll wish you had a PhD in on-campus dining to decipher some of the options. Some schools use a point system to tally up items, some offer unlimited food per meal, and some ring up charges, restaurant-style, for each individual item. Some schools have a meal plan card with points that can be used toward food purchased at stores on campus; others have even arranged for your meal plan to work off campus in select restaurants and carry-outs. Some provide you with a balance of food money left, in real time online. Some ask you to pay by the semester; others let you pay-as-you-eat from a fixed amount debit card.

Many schools now use their student ID to keep track of meals; you can add money to their card if it runs low. It works out fine as long as students understand that losing an ID card is like losing their lunch...literally. The card should be replaced immediately if lost or stolen. If someone picks up your student's lost card, they will be able to use it for meals. Schools will typically deactivate a card that's reported missing and issue another one with the balance intact.

Whatever the set-up, choosing the right meal plan all boils down to estimating the number of meals per week your child generally eats and how many of those meals he will eat in the dining hall. The school's website usually offers some rules of thumb for heavy eaters versus commuters, and so on. Most schools will help you switch or try to accommodate you if you find the meal plan to be inadequate or overkill.

What's New on the College Culinary Scene? Ask U. Mass!

As a parent, you may be existing on a diet of macaroni and cheese now that you're on your new, tuition-paying austerity budget, but your child, meanwhile, is probably surveying a long line of tasty choices at his comfy new school. If that makes you a tinge jealous, a visit to the NACUF (The National Association for College and University Food Services) website, www.nacufs.org, won't make it any easier.

There you'll learn that at U. Mass—Amherst's award-winning dining halls, the chef recently added chicken with coconut milk, pasta stir-fry with different sauces, and tofu fricassee to an already impressive menu that includes dim sum brunch and all-you-can-eat fresh sushi!

You can find some great recipes (suitable for large groups) on the NACUF site as well. (You never know when they might decide to bring all fourteen of the international student Thanksgiving orphans to your house, right?)

If you know any U. Mass. students, it just might be worth having a meal on their card. Here's a few more reasons why...

- Certified kosher meals are available Monday to Friday, for lunch and dinner. The school's kosher (non-dairy) kitchen is under the strict supervision of a mashgiach from Springfield, Vaad Hakashruth.

- Franklin Dining Commons is famous for vegan dishes.

- Worcester Dining Commons, one of the most popular dining facilities on campus, offers sushi, pho noodles, and create-your-own stir-fry.

- The school employs "mystery shoppers"—students paid a small amount by U. Mass—Amherst Dining Services to secretly review the food and service of the dining commons on a weekly basis, a great way to keep quality up to snuff.

- U. Mass was recently the winner of the Loyal Horton Residence Hall Dining Award from the National Association of College and University Food Services for overall dining experience, including quality of food, presentation, and innovative menu concept.

- When students said they wanted the dining commons to be open later, they began staying open until 9:00 and even 10:00 P.M. on some nights.

- In response to student requests, more vegetarian dishes are offered than ever before; soy milk is available; canola oil has replaced vegetable oil to reduce trans fats; omelettes are made with less oil; and artisanal breads are offered, with olive oil available as well as butter.

- And for the kicker, students have even clamored to the dining hall for Lobster Night—complete with fresh lobsters in tanks.

How Can I Be Sure My Student Is Getting Enough Exercise?

There are some pretty unhealthy college kids out there—the ones who loathe the walk to the library so they study in their rooms, or who wait for elevator to take them up their second-floor dorm room. But is it really possible to change their behavior, or more importantly, their mindset?

Short of hiring a private eye, you'll have to resort to asking them if they're staying active and to causally nudging them toward a few heartbeat-raising activities every now and then. At the risk of sounding like a manic health nut, encourage them to take the stairs instead of the elevator, walk into town, or organize an impromptu game of girls-versus-guys soccer. Sending them a kite, a suped up Frisbee, or some other outdoor play toy could make them a hit on the quad.

Exercise is undeniably important for good health. But remember that your child is busy trying to choose classes, get good grades, and honestly, make friends and socialize. Be supportive. But at the same time, go easy on the get-in-shape mission, especially during that first semester.

Is the Campus Gym Just for Jocks?

The gyms and facilities at a number of today's colleges are incredible, going far beyond the clunky treadmills and exercise bikes of yore. In addition to competitive inter-collegiate sports, most schools offer casual intramural teams that anyone can join if they're willing to put in a little sweat and learn a new sport. In fact, more and more colleges are going beyond the basic team sports to offer esoteric fitness options from ultimate Frisbee, to African dance, to scuba diving and winter camping. Sometimes there's an extra fee required, but many schools offer massage, Pilates, and other spa-like activities, too. There are so many wacky physical education classes available from colleges that there's an inside joke about "underwater basket-weaving" classes as an example of how far things can go to make courses appealing to non-athletes.

Schools in areas where outdoor adventure is popular often have a recreation center that loans equipment to students, from kayaks and cross-country skis to tents, sleeping bags, and backpacks. Some snow belt schools even offer discount ski passes to students and a bus to shuttle them to the mountain on weekends. Almost any school will offer at least a few outdoor adventure clubs as well.

You'll find a few schools that have physical education requirements, but many do not. If that's the case with your child's school, why not suggest taking a recreation course for a nice break in their course load and a good way to blow off some steam? Many schools offer physical education classes to register for pass/fail or without receiving academic credit.

It's true that some less-than-athletic college students may actually have a true fear of the college locker room, where brawny athletes seem to occupy a larger-than-life space. They should look for "open swim" hours and time slots when the teams are not infiltrating the gym.

Off-campus exercise is another way to go. Maybe she'd like a new bike for her birthday so she can zip around town, or a gift certificate for a local yoga studio or martial arts center. Some of these places may have an arrangement in which they let students take classes for free in exchange for a few hours of work at the reception desk each week. It pays to inquire.

WHAT SORT OF MENTAL HEALTH COUNSELING SERVICES CAN I EXPECT TO FIND?

Faith Leonard, Assistant Vice President and Dean of Students at American University, reminds us that life in college is filled with developmental challenges that sometimes require new coping strategies. College counseling centers are there to help students traverse that sometimes rocky terrain and build new skills for the future.

While almost every college has some sort of counseling facility, Elizabeth Feeney, PhD, Director of Mount Holyoke College Counseling Service, reports that the number of sessions, the modalities (kinds of treatments) offered, and the credentials of the counseling professionals can vary greatly from institution to institution. A visit to the college website or a phone call to the school will answer some of your questions, but here are some of the things you'll want answers for:

- What type of help is available? Do you offer individual therapy, group therapy, outreach, consultation, and referral services? Anything else offered?

- What are the credentials of your counseling service professionals? (Licensed social worker, licensed psychologist, board certified psychiatrist, certified nurse specialist, psychology interns, social work interns, etc.).

- What is the ratio of staff to students? (The national average is 1 to 15,111—smaller schools usually have better ratios.)

- How long is the wait to get an appointment? Is there an urgent appointment/triage system for students who need to be seen quickly?

- Who is eligible for services? Is there a limit to how many sessions a student can receive? (Approximately 40 percent of centers currently have limits.) What resources are available off campus if a student reaches the maximum of care that is offered on campus?

- What services are available after hours? Does the counseling service have an on-call system?

- What are the school's policies on parental notification, medical leave, and hospitalization?

- Is there anyone on staff who can prescribe medication? (Approximately 54 percent of centers currently do have a prescribing staff member.) What are this person's credentials?

- Is there a charge for services? If so, how much and for what?

If your school is not fully equipped it will sometimes do an initial assessment, offer short-term counseling, and then give a referral to the community for ongoing or specialized care, Leonard explains.

WILL EVERYONE KNOW MY CHILD IS GOING FOR COUNSELING?

All treatments at the college counseling center are kept confidential. Their peers may see them walk in to the center, but that's about it. Under the Family Educational Rights and Privacy Act (FERPA) privacy laws, a counselor cannot share information with anyone, even the parent, unless there is written consent of the student to share that information. The only time schools modify this policy is in a situation where they've determined that the student has the potential to do bodily harm to themselves or other students. Each school has its own way of determining when parental notification is required, and the subject is hotly debated amongst the higher education community.

Parents have expressed frustration over these policies, and arguably they've had to endure great tragedy because of FERPA. There's a twisted irony to knowing that you, the parent, could be the first one to recognize your child's problem, suggest that he get help, and yet not be privy to the details of the treatment. It's parental nature to want to know about the state of your child's health and the nature of the treatments. At the same time, it's important to understand and respect the need to give your emerging adult some privacy around the sensitive issues he is facing. Take comfort in the fact that schools are allowed to break confidentiality agreements and notify you if the situation is deemed as becoming a threat to your student's well being or to the well being of students around him. Schools take this notification very seriously. (See Chapter 3, "Sex, Drugs, and Drinking" for an overview of FERPA.)

It's also disconcerting that the school cannot approach your child on hearsay of a problem, either. There are numerous stories of parents whose children were obviously in psychological distress, but, because the college could not do anything until the child came forth for help, the situation was left unattended. There have been stories of parents who suspected their children were doing drugs at school but could not get the schools to confront them. Other parents have claimed that their daughter's many friends and acquaintances knew she had been the victim of a date rape and was seriously depressed, but couldn't get the administration to help until they'd been approached for help by the girl herself. It's times like these that a students' right to privacy may cause them serious harm. If you can maintain open and accepting lines of communication while your child is at college, you will hopefully be privy to their triumphs and disasters.

Finally, even though on paper and by law, what happens in the counseling center stays in the counseling center, students know that's not always the way things work. In the dorm, plenty of students know who's taking which medications and have a pretty good idea of each other's class schedules. Despite a college counseling center's commitment to confidentiality, students love to share information—especially when it's about another student's covert operations. Many counseling centers employee work-study students who know very well who among their peers has been walking through those doors as of late. So despite a school's best efforts, you can't absolutely, 100 percent, count on things staying private.

WHAT SIGNS SHOULD I LOOK FOR IF MY CHILD IS HAVING PROBLEMS WITH DEPRESSION, EATING, ETC.?

A parent gets that gut-wrenching, helpless feeling when the child they're hearing on the other end of a phone isn't quite the same child they sent off to school. "Are they hanging out with the wrong kids? Drinking too much?" The thoughts run like wild fire. And listening to the teary meltdown of your child on the other end of the telephone calls for measured calm even if your own fears—and tears—are rising.

Even kids who never had emotional meltdowns before have been known to let them fly in college. First, check your school calendar. Meltdowns and midterms or final exams have a natural correlation. Knowing this doesn't make the meltdown any less real, but at least you can point out that feeling anxious during exam week is normal, even expected. It sometimes helps to brainstorm on a block-and-tackle strategy for surviving exam week "Why don't you write your first draft and then do something relaxing for a while? You can study for your test after that." This might be the sort of step-by-step they need when the schedule seems overwhelming. Remember that a large part of your role for this four-year stint is as comforter/cheerleader/and "buck up" evangelist. Hear them out and then give them the strength to go back and do it again.

At the same time..."If a parent notices a significant change in their child's emotional behavior (lots of tears, negative attitude, a sense of hopelessness, anger, disinterest in studies, not sleeping well, excessive alcohol/drug use) or the child sounds as though he is rather isolated (eating meals in his room, not participating in floor/dorm activities), that parent should be concerned," says Associate Dean of Student Affairs/Dean of First-Year Student at Bowdin College, Margaret L. Hazlett. She and others suggests that parents contact the professionals on campus directly.

Remember, contacting the school officials does not mean that they're going to dash over to the dorm and rescue your child. What they may be able to do is to give you some generic advice that you can apply to your situation, which is important because you may need to prove the school's negligence at some point. You will also have a documented record of alerting them to a potential situation. There are a number of cases pending where parents feel the schools were neglectful in not reporting a problem.

One recent high-profile case where parents accuse the school of being negligent involved Elizabeth Shin, a student at Massachusetts Institute of Technology, who committed suicide in 2000—just four days after she had attempted a suicide and failed. Shin had been receiving counseling and treatment at school, but her parents had not been notified. At this writing, the suit has still not gone to trial, but the judge in a preliminary ruling found that the case should be allowed to go forth. Furthermore, the court ruled that the university will not be tried, and the suit is limited to the individual psychiatrists and administrators, not the institution.

When the system works best, parents and schools should be working together to help students when they are in need. Schools are constantly juggling and reevaluating what their responsibilities to the parent and to the rest of the campus community should be when a student has mental health problems. It's likely that there will be continued friction in this area and that the court decision in the Shin case and others like it will help redefine school policy.

Will School Counseling Remain on My Child's Record?

Most of the time the answer is "no"; school counseling is not a part of the permanent transcript. However, while schools respect confidentiality and do not inform parents or professors of counseling services, there is the matter of insurance records. Grove City College's Dr. Warren Throckmorton, Director of College Counseling, offers that "much depends on the policies of the school concerning payment. If the college's counseling services are paid for via health insurance, then any services would be a part of the insurance record. If the services are free to the student because the college takes the costs from the student's regular activity fees, then the services are potentially more private." Another instance in which records stay public is when there's a public health issue like a communicable disease.

Those are the exceptions. Generally, all counseling services are confidential, and the records of these services are subject to release only under certain, legally defined circumstances or by written consent of the student. Parents do not have access to this information unless the student gives written consent. In the case of a serious crisis involving risk to self or to others, then confidential information may be shared with those who can protect the student or others at risk. This, of course, would make the situation more public and involve records that would be kept by other agencies or institutions (hospitals, physicians, etc.). Thus, there is no simple answer to this question, as so much depends on the nature of the crisis and how life threatening it is.

One relevant caveat is that the American with Disabilities Act generally forbids prospective employers from asking questions about mental and emotional illnesses or crises. If a student is resisting counseling because of future concerns about employment, this fact should be explained. A student may have counseling but is under no obligation to report it as an aspect of seeking employment in the private sector. Sewanee—University of the South's Dean of Students, Dr. Robert Pearigen, adds that counseling records are not the same as disciplinary records. Disciplinary records are not bound by the same professional expectations as a counseling service.

TIP: Suicide Prevention Resources

The Jed Foundation is the nation's first nonprofit group dedicated solely to reducing suicide on college campuses. The group, founded by the parents of a college sophomore who committed suicide, seeks to expand the mental-health "safety net" by offering online services for students. Visit them at www.JedFoundation.org.

Campusblues.com, a for-profit company, also uses the Internet to direct students to appropriate services on or near their campuses.

Active Minds on Campus is a student-run mental-health awareness group based in Washington, DC. The organization, founded to destigmatize mental illness, is establishing chapters on campuses nationwide. It was founded by Alison Malmon, when she was a 23-year-old graduate of University of Pennsylvania, after her brother committed suicide. Their website is www.ActiveMindsOnCampus.org.

Does College Take a Toll on Mental Health?

In our media-driven world where no subject is taboo, it's always tough to know whether conditions like depression and mental illness are on the rise or whether more students are now willing to talk about what's always been there. Either way, the numbers are startling. In 2004, the American College Health Association conducted its National College Health Assessment, which was completed by 47,000 students at 74 colleges and universities. The study found that almost 40 percent of men and 50 percent of women reached a level of depression one or more times during the year that made daily activities difficult. Ten percent of students answered that they had seriously considered suicide. Sixty-three percent admitted to having felt hopeless at times, and ninety four percent said that they were overwhelmed at times.

In a speech that's been widely covered in the media, Richard Kadison, Harvard's Chief of Mental Health Services, gives parents of incoming students this reality check: "I tell them, 'Look at the person next to you. One of your kids is going to get depressed to the point that they can't function in college. There's no shame in that. The only shame is if you don't recognize the problem and do something about it.'"

Of course, one of the major treatments for anxiety and depression on campus are drugs: Prozac and Celexa to name just two of dozens. There has been little conclusive data published about students taking prescribed psychotropic drugs for anxiety or depression, but the anecdotal data points to a staggering number. Psychologists and psychiatrists have written widely about the fact that today, because of the use of psychotropic drugs, more students who previously wouldn't have been able to function in college are now able to attend. And while the college health centers are reluctant to release figures, off the record they generally talk about numbers like 1 in every 4 students is on some sort of medication for depression, anxiety, or learning disorders. Students confirm this and suggest it might be even higher.

HAS THERE BEEN A RECENT RISE IN STUDENT SUICIDES?

Student suicides are certainly not a recent phenomena, but the widespread media attention they receive is a relatively recent phenomena. Suicides are more widespread on college campuses than you would think. A recent *Newsweek* special said that, according to estimates by mental health groups, more than 1,100 college students commit suicide each year.

The situation was brought into the national limelight a few years ago when, according to a *Newsweek* report, six students committed suicide by jumping to their deaths at NYU in a single year from September 2003 to September 2004. There was talk in the media of copycat suicides—kids who imitated the original. Since then, NYU has become something of the poster child for campus suicide prevention. In 2005, they made news again when they closed the balconies in two of their tower buildings and put up Plexiglas in the library's atrium in an attempt to make jumps and falls less likely. They also instituted a variety of new wellness programs, including one that lets counselors visit the students in their own dorms.

Mental Health Fact: The Numbers Add Up

Statistics about mental health on campus are troubling. We know that more kids are going to college than ever before and that the pressure to do well, fit in socially, and remain competitive is greater than ever. Schools and parents are going to need to pay attention to how to integrate the student's total health—including mental health—into their academic lives. This topic is being investigated by educators and various pilot programs are being initiated.

A recent *USA Today* article reported the results of a decade-long study from Kansas State University's counseling center. It found that the number of depressed students had doubled and the number of students who'd thought about suicide had tripled over the past decade. In 2003, the American College Health Association found that 61 percent of college students reported feeling hopeless, 45 percent said they felt so depressed they could barely function, and 9 percent felt suicidal.

Data collected from other studies are equally troubling. A recent UCLA study found that more than 30 percent of college freshmen reported feeling overwhelmed, especially during the beginning of college. Johns Hopkins University reported that more than 40 percent of a recent freshman class sought help from the student-counseling center. At Cornell University, a full 12 percent of the university's 20,000 students sought mental health services in 2003. A University of Pittsburgh study found that 85 percent of college counseling centers surveyed reported an increase in the number of students coming in with severe psychological problems including depression. At University of Michigan, over 20 percent of the students seen at Counseling and Psychological Services (CAPS) have depressive illnesses.

WHAT ARE THE REASONS FOR THE HIGH PERCENTAGES OF STUDENTS REPORTING PROBLEMS?

The studies cite trends including increased competition, a breakdown of the family unit's support systems, the social pressures of living on a college campus, and the fact that more students who have problems are going to college in the first place.

There is some evidence to suggest that one explanation for the increase in students being treated for depression is simply knowledge. There's more known about symptoms and treatments for depression and anxiety than ever before, and dealing with depression is less stigmatized than it was just a few years ago. *The New England Journal of Medicine* adds credence to this with a report that says that American sufferers of mental ailments are being treated for their illness more today than they were 10 years ago, according to a federal and drug company-funded study.

Whether more kids are seeking the service or more kids are suffering from depression, the result is that college counseling services are feeling the pressure of a more troubled population. In response, they're increasing the kinds of services they offer and they're marketing the services aggressively so that kids use the center before their problems become overwhelming. A recent article in the *Boston Globe* (April 2005) looked at schools in the Boston area and found:

- Harvard hired more therapists within the past five years, and this school year added a new high-level position to oversee and better coordinate disparate mental health services.

- Harvard sends "wellness-resource tutors" into the dorms. They help students deal with issues from procrastination and stress to depression.

- At MIT, teams of physicians and counselors hang out with students in the dorms. And some of the dorms have been redesigned to foster more interaction and less isolation.

- MIT has also added stress-reduction and relaxation classes such as yoga, meditation and tai chi.

The Globe also reported that, programs are similar elsewhere in the country. Columbia, Cornell, and New York University also station counselors in dorms. Emory University and the University of North Carolina ask students to fill out anonymous mental health questionnaires. A credited course at the University of Maryland helps freshmen deal with stress and time management. At Tufts University, Jonathan Slavin, Director of the Counseling Center, said the campus has reduced the stigma associated with mental illness to the point that 750 of 6,000 undergraduates have received counseling. "If you can make a counseling service commonplace and ordinary, and students can just drop by," he said, "that is the best prevention. That means you made the place something other than this kind of scary, mysterious place you got to be crazy to go to."

Campus mental health professionals agree that treatment usually involves short interventions, which are, by and large, positive. They also stress that kids can take some comfort in numbers. They are not suffering alone; feelings of loneliness and anxiety are shared by many in their peer group.

Interestingly, it seems that colleges are now going to begin placing some value on a students' emotional health as a factor in the admissions process. In a 2004 *Newsweek* article, Dean Marilee Jones of MIT commented that she was looking to enroll "emotionally resilient" students. "If we think someone will crumble the first time they do poorly on a test, we're not going to admit them," she says. "So many kids are coming in, feeling the need to be perfect, and so many kids are medicated now. If you need a lot of pharmaceutical support to get through the day, you're not a good match for a place like MIT."

After looking at the data, there's a strong temptation to lock your kids in a closet and let them out when they're 25. But it's important to look at it another way. Parents have a role to play in creating mentally healthy students. If a student has never been taught how to cope with stress, how to break a large task into smaller pieces, and how to stand up for their own beliefs and not kowtow to peer pressure, they are going to have a more difficult time "keeping it together" in college. One of the double-edged swords of an involved parent is that they may not be fostering the independence a child needs to face their own issues.

Whether it's their social life or their academic life that has them feeling overwhelmed, a parent needs to be there as the one who sees the light at the end of the curriculum (no, that light is not an oncoming train!). They need to foster optimistic, positive, can do attitudes and spread the mantra of "there's no problem so terrible that it can't be resolved." Even if it's out of character for you to be the optimist, you need to try out for the part. It's the most important role you'll ever play.

WHAT CAN I EXPECT IN TERMS OF MEDICAL CARE AT COLLEGE?

The scope of the medical care that college health centers provide is all over the map. Typically, the centers are set up to deal with everything from mental health issues to sexually transmitted diseases, and to offer basic care to a student population suffering from everything from migraines to mono. "Most student health services define themselves as primary care facilities that offer services for acute primary care issues such as bronchitis, sprained ankles, or the flu," says Jennifer Berkman, Director of Student Health Services at Salisbury University. Generally speaking, the centers offer a few different types of services:

- Primary medical care for when your child gets ill
- Counseling services for psychological help or help with substance abuse
- Preventative education to teach students good health practices

In addition, some of the larger schools have sports therapy components to their health centers.

Many campuses outsource some of their medical services, contracting with local physicians in family practice, gynecology, dermatology, orthopedics, and psychiatry, as well as with dentists, optometrists, physical therapists, and pharmacies. Schools will make recommendations to local specialists for more difficult problems.

TIP: Filling Your Student in on the Details

Of course your medical insurance isn't going to be as valuable if your child doesn't know what to do when they need medical attention. Linda Mackenzie, Director of University Health Services at SUNY Binghamton, says you should make sure your student knows who the providers are that your plan identifies and how to use them. (For example you may need a referral or a call to the insurance company before treatment.)

"It is also advisable that students carry information about a medication allergy or any chronic medical condition in their wallets or on their person, in case illness or emergency occurs away from the campus health center or when the health center is closed," she says.

Remember that a large number of kids make it through their entire college career never even knowing where Health Services is located. Hopefully, your child knows where the building is, and if they haven't done it yet, this would be a good time to find out exactly which services their school offers. Colleges that dispense antibiotics, for example, can save a student days of running around off campus to secure a doctor, a throat culture, and medicine, even for a relatively minor ailment.

> **TIP:** Mandatory Health Services Fees
>
> Many schools assess full-time students with a student health fee to cover the cost of basic university health services. This is different from and should not be confused with health insurance. At Georgia Institute of Technology, for example, all students taking more than four semester hours are assessed a student health fee. All visits to a physician, nurse, or nurse practitioner are covered by the health fee, along with all X-rays, many laboratory tests, and medications. The student health fee covers ECG, spirometry testing, blood pressure monitoring, IV fluids and observation, and suturing. If your school has a health fee you should find out exactly what it covers and factor that into your decision. Jana Lynn Patterson, Associate dean of students at Elon University says that "to keep out-of-pocket costs low, encourage students to visit health services first. Many basic health care services are provided quite competently at the student health center, so trips to fee-for-service providers should be minimized."

SHOULD I CARRY HEALTH INSURANCE FOR MY STUDENT?

There are three ways to give your child health care coverage while she is in college:

A: Continue to insure her under your health plan as your dependent.

B: Buy the health insurance that is offered by the college especially for students or buy third-party student insurance plans. (The colleges and universities typically have an arrangement with an insurance carrier to provide low cost insurance.)

C: Don't carry insurance at all and pay out of pocket for any medical services your child uses as he or she uses them.

Salisbury University's Berkman explains that "some student health services provide services for a fee, and insurance is not needed when the student is seen on campus. For most students, this level of care is sufficient."

More and more colleges and universities are requiring some proof of health insurance as a condition of enrollment. Sarah Swager, Vice President for Student Affairs and Dean of Students at Randolph-Macon College, says that the decision about what medical insurance to provide for your student should be informed by:

- The portability of your hometown insurance

- Your student's medical condition/needs

- Cost

- Whether the benefits offered by the college/university plan are adequate for your peace of mind

In evaluating the choices, you're likely to find that Option A—maintaining your family coverage and possibly supplementing it—is the most prudent. Your existing family coverage (Option A) will provide better coverage than most of the college insurance plans offered. Most college care plans are lean and mean, designed to provide basic coverage. They often don't cover things like catastrophic illness or injury, prescription drugs, or mental-health treatment. They will often decline expenses and treatment for pre-existing conditions, and many of these plans are expensive.

Vicki McNeil, Associate Vice President for the Division of Student Affairs at Loyola University—New Orleans suggests that, "If your own insurance can cover your student out of state, then possibly it would be the better option. The schools' insurance is really considered a supplemental insurance and can help those whose coverage will not lend itself to out of state students (or for [those] who have no coverage)."

Thomas A. Smith, PhD, Associate Dean, College of Arts and Sciences at Loyola concludes that, "Generally speaking, your own medical plan will be far better than the plans offered by universities," but he cautions parents to make sure that their insurance will cover your student when away from home and to be aware of any credit-hour requirements needed to maintain student/dependent status.

Swager agrees that "Most insurance plans offered by colleges and universities are not as comprehensive as your employer's medical insurance might be, but these plans are usually relatively inexpensive." The cost is kept down because the benefits are limited and there are significant co-pay and deductible expectations. If your son or daughter has no other medical insurance, she suggests that you purchase a policy through the college or university that he attends.

Remember, too, that your child will be spending holidays and summers away from campus—which can add up to as much as five months of the year. Obviously, you'll need to have medical coverage for the noncampus times as well—another argument for keeping the kids on your family health plan.

If you keep your family plan, you need to weigh your PPO and HMO decision one more time. With an HMO and a local network of doctors, you may not be covered for anything but emergencies when the student is off at college (i.e., out of town). If you're on a PPO plan, you'll have more leeway. You can choose a doctor covered by your plan near the school, though you may pay out of network charges.

Linda Mackenzie, Director of University Health Service at SUNY Binghamton, urges parents to understand how their own insurance companies enforce "out of the area" coverage on their policies. "Do not assume," she says, "that your personal plan will continue to offer the same levels of coverage in the college community that you have experienced at home. Consider the school insurance plan offerings against what you have and do not be too quick to dismiss it as unnecessary. On the other hand, if you can identify what you believe is adequate coverage in your family plan, waiving the school plan could save a few dollars. If the school plan offers worldwide or expansive coverage, it could provide an important supplement to the insurance you already have."

The best way to weigh your options is to first draw up a list of your student's specific health needs. Then, look at the availability of services on campus versus the health insurance company's regulations. If a student is generally healthy, student health services on a pay-as-needed basis can be fine, though it's a bit of a crap shoot since you're depending on your student's continued good health. If you expect care to be more frequent or routine then compare the colleges' student policy against your own and make the best decision. If your child has a preexisting condition that requires regular medical expertise, then look for an off-campus doctor who's willing to stick with your student as a surrogate for a few years. Doctors in college towns are very familiar with this type of request.

TIP: Germ Warfare

There's no happier germ than the germ that lives in a college dorm. In dorms, close-knit living is an understatement. Close-knit also means that germs travel fast and furious, often spreading through the campus in cycles. Clark University administrators say "Germs abound in college settings and it can be easy to go from being sick to being really sick. Then you move into missing classes and getting behind in your work. And, the stress of trying to make up all the work often leads to relapses." Breaking the cycle early is important for your child and for the entire school.

Hand washing, something even a first grader can master, is probably the most important prevention for the spread of disease.

What Does a College Health Plan Cost?

That's like asking, "What does an insurance plan cost?" Annual premiums can range from $300 up to $3,000. Cornell University's health plan, for example, covers all pre-existing conditions and provides $1 million in lifetime coverage for an annual cost of $1,059.

There are a number of new sites on the Internet that allow you to compare various student health policies. The website www.E-healthinsurance.com suggests that you begin by determining whether your family coverage is adequate or you need to get the student a policy by looking at:

1. Whether the insurance plan you have extends coverage to the area around your child's college

2. Your child is nearing the age at which she can no longer be covered under your plan (This is usually around 24 years of age.)

3. The cost savings of removing your child from your insurance plan is greater than the cost of the separate student insurance plan. To determine if this is the case, visit the college your child attends and investigate to get a quote from their plan. Get a quote from third party plan for student health insurance.

4. Compare the cost savings of removing your child from your standard medical plan (you may need to contact your insurance company to determine this amount).

Remember too, that if your child has a preexisting medical condition expenses relating to preexisting conditions will not be covered by the student plan until the policy has been in effect for 12 months.

What's the Best Way to Get a Prescription Filled?

Some campuses, especially the large ones, fill routine prescriptions for things like antibiotics right at the health center; others require that students visit the local pharmacy.

Still others, as Gordon Gee, Chancellor at Vanderbilt University, explains, "will fill prescriptions they have issued, but not those issued by outside entities." That's why he feels that "frequently, the easiest route is for the student to visit student health services for an examination (at which point they can be referred to a specialist if need be) and to begin a new prescription using the school's health center as the source."

Rhodes College Director of Health Services, Patricia Sterba, says that another option is to have the medication mailed directly from to the student. (Check your local pharmacy or prescription plan to determine if this service is available.)

It's good to identify a pharmacy at school well in advance of arrival, and make sure they'll fill prescriptions from your hometown doctor and accept your insurance coverage. Jeannine Reed, Director of Student Health and Counseling Services at Goucher College reminds parents that "if the prescription is for an ongoing medication—like thyroid pills or oral contraception, for example—arrangements can be made to transfer it to a local pharmacy. If the medication is one that your physician needs to monitor more frequently than your son or daughter visits home, your physician will probably recommend that he or she find someone at or near the college to take over the care for that particular medical issue." This is because many hometown doctors will not continue to prescribe a drug if they can't see your student in person, even for minor conditions. For example, even though it doesn't seem like a big deal, a dermatologist may not continue prescribing a skin treatment regimen while your child is away because he feels the condition needs to be monitored.

What Should I Do if My Child Gets Sick?

Sick happens. Don't panic and don't put your keys in the ignition to start driving to campus. (At least not yet.) Kids, even big college ones, get knocked down by colds and the flu. When they arrive, they sweep through the campuses with ferocity. There's nothing worse than a panicky parent on the phone asking them in one breath if they have a fever and in the next breath how in the world they're going to keep up with all of their school work. Undoubtedly, the same thought has already crossed their minds.

So...once you've taken stock of the situation and determined that it's not life threatening, you can always try the "take two aspirins and call me in the morning" remedy. Sometimes a parent who listens with a sympathetic ear to a "woe is me" phone call is enough to put a college student on the road to recovery. For allergies, headaches, and upset stomachs, most kids won't have to go further than another friend's door down the hall to find some instant relief from an over-the-counter medicine. It's also sage advice to encourage your children to show a little TLC to dorm mates who are feeling under the weather. These kindnesses have a reciprocity that they'll depend on.

In general, you needn't be concerned about common colds and even touches of bronchitis, strep, or flu; the college community can usually handle these. But administrators at Clark University's Health Services Center offer that "you do need to be concerned if your son or daughter seems to be perpetually sick; that can be a sign of unhealthy lifestyle choices they are making and may be a sign of a larger problem. Stay on top of [it], consult with people, and don't be afraid to butt in a bit."

Colleges can't be of assistance at all if they don't know your child is sick. So if something is really wrong, urge them to visit Health Services. An hour spent seeing a doctor and getting a prescription can save them days of feeling terrible—and missing classes. Jean Hanson, Director of Administrative Services, Duke University Student Health, RN, MPH says, "My message to parents is that they need to get their child to come in to their school's health clinic or student medical facility. We can't do anything for that student if we don't see them. But it happens a lot. Parents try to diagnose over the phone and then tell us what their child needs. It doesn't work that way. Tell your child to come in and let us at least eyeball them."

That said, Hampshire College mentions that prevention is the best medicine. Before she leaves home make sure that all vaccinations are up to date and that any chronic medical conditions are well-managed and documented.

SHOULD I BRING MY CHILD HOME IF HE GETS SICK?

This, of course, is a question of magnitude. Dorms, no matter how helpful the roommates, are no place to get well if he's really sick. Even making a cup of tea can require an effort, never mind getting a prescription filled. The noise will never be restful and, inside those close quarters, he could be spreading whatever he has. If your child has lingering bronchitis or pneumonia or something infectious, you may need to bring him home to recuperate. While you're thinking that what he needs is a good week of good care, remember that college courses move quickly and just a few absences can make it nearly impossible to catch up. Have your child notify each professor before leaving school and get as many assignments as possible to take home. (There's no sedative like reading *The Political History of Central America 1900–1990* aloud to your bedridden patient, even if it's you who's likely to conk out first.) He should also get the e-mail of one friend in each class so he can stay up to date on notes and assignments.

WILL I BE NOTIFIED IF THERE'S A HEALTH EMERGENCY?

A law restricts hospitals from releasing protected health information. The HIPAA Privacy Rule (Health Insurance Privacy Accountability Act) requires an individual's consent before sharing her health information, even with parents. Therefore, if your daughter is 18 years or older and cannot speak or give consent, the hospital cannot inform you of her illness. Some schools keep HIPAA release forms on file; you sign them when you register for school. If you've signed and filed one then the school can show it to the hospital and they will notify you.

Meningitis: Threat or Not?

According to data available from the Center for Disease Control, the number of deaths on campus from spinal meningitis is relatively small—only about fifteen each year—but this is very avoidable if you get vaccinated. College students are no more likely to get meningitis than other populations, but because they live in such a tight-knit community, a law passed in twenty-five states requires vaccinations for students who live in campus housing. Legislation is pending in the other twenty-five states and national legislation has been proposed. Because there is some controversy over side effects and dangers of the meningitis vaccination, most state laws allow students to waive the vaccination by signing a form stating that they have read information about the disease provided by their college. The article "Five Develop Nerve Disorder After Receiving Meningitis Vaccine," published by *The New York Times* in October of 2005, reported that five teens developed serious neurological disorders within two to four weeks after receiving the vaccine. The meningitis requirements are in flux so check with your college's website.

SHOULD I KEEP OUR HOME DOCTOR OR USE A LOCAL DOCTOR AT THE COLLEGE FOR MY CHILD?

It doesn't matter as much which one you have, but you should have one. It's a bad idea to depend on Health Services for your child's ongoing care. That's not what the student health centers are set up to do.

Many parents opt for a hybrid solution. They have their kids maintain regular doctor and dental appointments over school breaks when they're at home, but they line up a doctor in the college town to help monitor any ongoing conditions or the onset of a sudden illness.

For many parents (and their kids) going away to college means the final break with the pediatrician. Your student is probably ecstatic that they won't need to sit on a pint-sized chair in a waiting room fill of crying babies any longer. Because your child will be home for a large portion of the year, it's good to find a home physician and have the pediatrician forward the medical records to the new doctor.

"Transferring your child's primary care to a physician who is geographically close to the her college is especially important if the student has a preexisting condition or requires specialty care," says Jennifer Berkman, Director, Student Health Services at Salisbury University. Just remember that "the farther away the student goes to college, the more difficult it can be sometimes to identify care providers that your insurance plan will cover."

A Parent's Guide to Parent's Health-isms

Most of us are not going to be mixing potions of lavender and hyssop, but parents all over the country have been relying on a few time-proven remedies and relief worth passing along from generation to generation. While we're not suggesting that these replace a doctor's visit, students may find some temporary relief until they determine whether further medical assistance is needed. Taken with a large grain of salt, here are the household remedies:

Athlete's foot: Wear flip flops in the shower and use an antifungal powder.

Coughs: Use a vaporizer with a drop of eucalyptus oil added; elevate your head to eliminate drip; drink water (it breaks up mucous).

Diarrhea: The BRAT diet (Bananas, Rice, Apples, and Toast)

Food poisoning: It happens. Stay near the bathroom and if it doesn't end in 24 hours see a doctor.

Hangovers: I'll leave this one to the kids to share their favorites, but drinking lots of water before you go to bed is a good idea. Drinking less liquor in the first place is an even better one!

Slight Burns: Run burned area under cold water.

Sore Throat: Gargle with warm salt water.

Stuffed Nose: Eucalyptus oil or create a steam bath by turning the sink water to hot, putting a towel over your head and breathing.

Ticks bites: Remove the tick with a tweezers (be sure you've got the whole insect and try to save it just in case it carries lime disease). Watch for the development of a red rash circling the bite. (Wear socks and long pants near campus woods areas.)

Toothache: Rub a few grains of cayenne pepper into the gum around the tooth or chew on some cloves dipped in honey. These numb the area, but call a dentist in the morning.

Other common sense tips for college student health:

- Sharing things is a part of college dorm life, but remind your child not to share eyeliner or other eye makeup—pinkeye spreads quickly.

- Try not to share cups and drink from same bottle if the other person seems sick.

- Wash hands always, often, and well. Use soap.

- Go easy on the caffeine. There's a sliding scale of caffeine-laced products from coffee on through over the counter medications. Too much can cause a bad case of the jitters and queasy stomach. Teas like Earl Grey have as much caffeine as coffee so don't think you're being virtuous by switching to tea. Colas are high in caffeine too, especially the boutique colas like JOLT. Kids will often buy over the counter Vivarin or NoDoz to stay awake and study—it's equal to about nine cups of coffee. (Amphetamines rely on stronger than caffeine chemicals and can really do a number of kids' mental and physical states.)

CHAPTER 6

Don't Forget About Academics

Somewhere on the list of what to bring to the dorm, which credit card to use, and which meal plan to choose, you ought to save a few brain cells to think about your role in your child's academic life. Yes, least we forget, that is ostensibly why they head off to college in the first place.

As parents, we tend to worry less about academics than the social issues because we believe that the school has an expertise in this area. Not so fast. The school has an expertise in hiring professors, creating curriculum, and scheduling classes; what they do to engage your child in the process varies greatly from school to school. You're going to need to be proactive, especially if your child is intimidated by the smart and the erudite, or not one of those "go out and grab what you need" students.

The pattern I see at most schools is that a majority of the kids do not take anywhere near full advantage of their academic opportunities. What do I mean? They don't take the opportunity to visit a professor during office hours or to use the campus's full suite of resources for academic help. They often flounder silently until they've fallen hopelessly behind, and they are often unable to map out a four-year plan based on anything but serendipity. To put this in perspective, I don't know too many adults who'll look back and say they took full advantage of their college opportunities either. We survived; they will too.

So what is our role in our child's academic life? First, we want to let them do their own thing and make their own mistakes (as long as the mistakes are relatively benign). We want to point them toward resources they may be too "busy" to notice. Most of all, without driving our kids crazy, we want to make sure they're getting the quality education we've paid for and the education they'll need to succeed after they graduate.

This chapter looks at:

- Choosing classes
- Setting grade expectations
- When and how you'll be notified if your child isn't doing well

- How extracurricular activities impact learning

- When to declare a major

- How to think about a four-year plan for graduation

- Transferring schools

- The role of tutors, learning centers, and academic support staff

- Studying abroad

WHERE CAN I FIND A LIST OF REQUIREMENTS FOR GRADUATION?

Short of tattooing these on your forehead, it's good to keep the requirements for graduation close at hand, since it's all too easy for your student and you to lose sight of the endgame when you're caught up in the moment.

At Mount Holyoke College, and this is standard at most schools, you'll find the requirements listed in the university bulletin and course catalog. They are also available in multiple places on the college's website, including an "Especially for Parents" page.

Back in the day, we counted our college credits on our fingers. Today, most colleges have individualized automated degree audits that your student can access by computer. They list all requirements and track your student's ongoing progress. This information is available online with access permitted by student password and user names. So, according to the Mount Holyoke staff "a parent could 'theoretically' have access to this great resource." If your student hasn't granted you access to their personal page, then you might want to encourage them to check the page each semester and make sure that their courses and credits have been properly recorded.

WHAT'S A REASONABLE COURSE LOAD TO TAKE?

Universities and colleges have a number of variations on the course load theme. Generally speaking, a full course load is usually defined as four or five courses per semester. "And that is not just a random number," says Clark University. "It is based on years of experience with regard to how much students can handle and still really learn while still allowing them time to get involved in other activities outside of the classroom."

Karin J. Spencer, PhD, Dean of University Advisement at Hofstra University cautions that there is no hard and fast answer about how many credits to take. She does say, however, that many colleges have a flat full-time tuition rate that encompasses a range of credits. "It is also not uncommon," she says, "for parents to tell their new students: 'Take the maximum—get your/our money's worth!' But depending upon the actual combination of courses and the level of student preparation, that could be a recipe for disaster."

Finally, you and your child should be mindful of other demands on their time. If the student wants—or needs—to have a part-time job, take a realistic look at those constraints. A student cannot work thirty hours a week and still have a clear head to do well with a seventeen or eighteen hour credit load. Also factor in extracurriculars, including the demands of living off campus, commuting, intercollegiate athletics, clubs, going to the gym, and any other time commitments.

WHAT SHOULD MY CHILD BE THINKING ABOUT WHEN IT'S TIME TO CHOOSE CLASSES?

If your child is taking a full course load, he should strive for a balance of different courses. If all of their courses have huge amounts of reading (a typical literature or political science course can ask for as many as 400 pages of reading a week per course), or if all of the classes have time-consuming labs, he should probably try to vary the pattern.

"Any course combinations should ideally be a mix of reading-based and quantitative-based courses," says Hofstra's Spencer, "and taking more than two lab-based sciences in the first semester of college is probably unwise—even for the most enthusiastic premedical student. Help your son or daughter to build a program that works on perceived strengths, so that their first semester will be an affirming one. But don't be afraid to encourage something new—a new language, a new discipline—that may just open some minds and doors and lead to life-long interests."

One of the biggest philosophical differences that schools have is the number of core requirements and what subjects those core requirements demand. Some schools, such as Reed College, have an extremely rigid set of requirements so that every student emerges with a truly well-rounded liberal arts education. Others (like Wesleyan) with no core requirements except for those in the student's major concentration put the onus of a liberal arts education in the hands of their students.

Most schools have some core requirements, often in foreign language, physical education, and core subjects like math, writing, humanities, social and physical sciences, and history. It's the combined wisdom of many colleges that suggest the students should do the following:

A: Get core requirements out of the way early. This lets students concentrate on their major in junior and senior years.

B. Balance the load between easy and tough courses. Most advise not taking more than one doozy course per semester.

WHAT SHOULD I KNOW ABOUT DROPPING, ADDING, AND WITHDRAWING FROM COURSES?

Most schools give students a designated period of time at the beginning of a semester to make adjustments in their schedule. They might find out that a course is not what they thought it would be, that they've chosen too hard a class load (or not hard enough), or that a schedule adjustment might help them out.

Whatever they do, they should do it as quickly as possible. Typically, dropping and adding classes carries no penalty—with the exception of a small fee for processing the papers, but many schools don't allow you to drop or add after the first week of the semester. (And for good reason, since the classes dive right into the syllabus and are in full swing by the end of the first week.) After that period, students only have the option of withdrawing from a class. Often a withdrawal is indicated on a students' permanent record, so the best idea is to get those drops and adds taken care of early on.

> **TIP:** www.pickaprof.com
>
> This website, started by two recent Texas graduates, is now available for more than 50 schools. Students are invited to evaluate their professors according to various attributes including how they grade, their teaching styles, and the homework load they assign. Other students can then use these reviews to chose professors they'll enjoy most.

Dropping a class may affect financial aid or the student's full-time status so they should fully understand the school's requirements before doing so. And remember to sell those books from dropped classes back to the campus book store pronto!

Course Calculator

Hofstra University administrators say that a good rule of thumb is to take an overall look at the number of credits required for the degree, subtract any incoming credits (AP, etc.), and arrive at an approximate number of credits that must be accomplished over the course of the subsequent semesters. This will be a rough estimate at best, since not all transfer credits necessarily help reduce requirements. In addition, if the student changes her major, new requirements may add to the credit count. Chances are, the average number of credits per semester will be in the range of fourteen to sixteen.

How Much Say Should I Have in Which Classes She Takes?

By the time they get to college, you should be well past telling them what courses to take—but you can certainly be an influencer and a good listener. There's a fine line between being a nag and offering suggestions; as a matter of fact, sometimes there's no difference in the delivery, just the perception.

One thing parents have going for them that students do not is some real world experience, that big picture outlook that comes with age, and perhaps a bit practical motivation. Parents, with a longitudinal look, will ask questions like: "Did you decide on your courses for next semester?" or "Don't you think it would be helpful to take a course like statistics or computer science?" These are perfectly acceptable intrusions when the right tone and timing is in place. One of the biggest laments parents of graduates have shared (usually after their kids have tried to find gainful post college employment) is that they wished they'd put a little gentle pressure on the kids to get some more marketable skills.

Associate Dean of Student Affairs/Dean of First-Year Students at Bowdoin College, Margaret L. Hazlettt, says that parents can best assist by asking questions about their student's interests and encouraging them to seek out information about graduation requirements. Parents can also encourage their child to speak with their faculty advisor, other faculty, and the class dean.

Good conversation about classes in general can head their thoughts in the right directions. The highest compliment your children can pay you is to ask your advice about their course of study. Even if your advice is ignored, it is processed. And because it came in the form of advice and not an ultimatum, it's more likely that they'll return for more.

Lots of Class

There are many variations on the types of courses a school, or even a program, offers. Here are some of the major genres students will see as they build each semester's class schedule:

Lab Course: These are usually part of the sciences curriculum; they involve a hands-on, investigative research component that is interspersed with lecture classes. Lab classes are typically worth more credit because they require more class time and double the work. (Sometimes these are called "field courses" if the lab is held out of doors, like it might be for a geology class.)

Lecture Hall: Often reserved for students in their freshman and sophomore years, lecture halls tend to pack a crowd. The professor delivers a set of somewhat prepared remarks, and interaction with the students is typically minimal. The advantage of lecture class can be that you get some phenomenal and inspiring professors. At its best, the lecture is lively and enthralling—not all of them deserve the bad rap they sometimes receive. Lectures often have a seminar component and are sometimes taught by grad students in the field.

Pass/Fail: Students won't be issued a grade for a class they opt to take pass/fail. This option is usually reserved for courses that are not part of a student's major or minor and often encourages students to push themselves to take courses outside of their comfort zones or to simply take an enjoyable "for fun" course without the specter of grades. Most schools limit the number of pass/fail credits that you can take.

Performance: Dance, music, and the arts will often have a performance element of class.

Seminar: Smaller and less formal than a lecture hall, a seminar invites group repartee and discussion.

Studio: These classes often involve art and design classes, and literally denote that class will involve students working on their individual projects in a studio setting.

Survey: An introductory look at a discipline that serves as a good foundation for further study. Surveys of literature, art history, and psychology are common.

Work/Study: In these classes, various combinations of field work may take place off campus in conjunction with the classroom lectures or seminars—often called experiential learning.

The word "prerequisite" will be used often, too. That means that in order to take a course, a student needs to have taken certain other courses first, most likely following a sequence. In lieu of class prerequisites, some classes will let students in if they secure the instructor's permission first—regardless of whether they have taken the prerequisite course(s).

WHAT KIND OF GRADES ARE REASONABLE TO EXPECT FROM MY CHILD?

If your child is planning to continue on to graduate school, then college grades very are important. (Remember too that though he thinks he will never go to grad school right now, a lot can change in the course of four years. If he strives for good grades through college, at least that advanced degree will always be an open option for him.) Generally speaking, however, they are less important than they were in high school—when they would determine where your child would go to college. If he's heading straight out into the real world after college, it's doubtful that too many prospective employees will inquire about his grades.

Grades do count for something though. Words like "summa cum laude" or "honors society" certainly dress up a fresh-out-of-college resume. Grades also determine whether your student will receive scholarship money (which he will need to reapply for each year). They are important for self-esteem because they are a partial indicator of whether your child is truly learning something or just goofing off. Some Greek houses or other organizations also require their members to uphold certain academic standards.

As far as an exact grade? That's a tricky topic. Schools, programs, and even individual professors vary wildly in their grading policies. Some professors adhere to a strict bell curve in which a student's performance is judged relative to other students in the class. Others are more concerned with measuring how well each student mastered the required material. Some will give extra credit, which offers students who've done poorly on exam a second shot. Some even grade the student against themselves, hence the paper that comes back with "I know you can do better." And still other professors seem to quietly believe that if you got to college (especially a highly selective one) then you deserve a decent grade. (For more about the "You must have been smart to get here" theory, check out Ross Douthat's book *Privilege: Harvard and the Education of the Ruling Class*, Hyperion, 2005. Douthat, a recent Harvard graduate, wrote a tell-all memoir of how easy he found it was to get through Harvard once he was in.)

Concerning grades, there are a few commonalities that parents should know about:

1. There's a wise saying that goes: "Half of getting a good grade is showing up." It's true. Kids who go to class, take notes, and participate are almost bound to do well.

2. Putting too much emphasis on grades might force your child to shy away from an important but challenging course or from

taking a course with a demanding professor. When she gets a "C" and you know that she's been working (you can tell by those A's in other classes), salute her for taking on something that wasn't easy. If she tells you that Professor Smith is the toughest professor in the school—and it's the first time she's giving you that line—believe her. Professors, for the most part, expect a great deal more than your child's high school teachers ever did.

3. Your red flag should go up at mid-semester, not during finals. Mid-semester is when you should ask how the grades are going so far. If there's been some poor performance you should, with your child, explore the reasons. Is it that he hated the subject? The professor? Is he having trouble understanding the material? Or, is he just plain slacking off? Once the reason is determined, it's easier to take the proper action. When report cards come, it's too late.

While you should certainly ask your children about their grades, it's important to put the question in a larger context of showing an interest in their academics. The Office of the Registrar at University of Washington encourages parents to have conversations about their children's general academic progress, not just their grades. Talk to them about the courses they are taking and their favorite instructors. What courses are most interesting? Have they been thinking about some possible majors? Is their intended major competitive? These are easy conversation starters for testing the waters and getting comfortable talking about grades.

If that first-semester grade point average is lower than what you saw from your child in high school or lower than what you had hoped, it means she is a normal college student. According to Albertson College, this is not at all unusual. Many students' grades drop slightly while they adjust to the workload and environment of college.

Whatever you decide your expectations for grades are going to be, get them out in the open right from the beginning. Even better is if you have a relationship that allows you and your child to decide on grade expectations together. He would prefer to be successful in college, and good grades help him feel that he is beginning to get the hang of college life in general.

Grade Inflation

Show me a parent who doesn't swell with pride when their college student makes the Dean's List and I'll show you a good candidate for psychiatric analysis. Unfortunately, parents and students need to be aware that there's more and more evidence suggesting that students may be getting higher grades than they really deserve, and parents are part of what's driving the trend.

John Merrow, a reporter who's been involved in numerous studies about today's college education was an executive producer of "Declining by Degrees," a PBS special that looked at four colleges and the education that they were providing.

In an interview with Jim Lehrer, Merrow was asked what his biggest surprise was after creating the special and he said, "Not that students are binge drinking, not that athletics is a business, and not that most students don't seem to have to work very hard to get good grades, because we knew those things. What came as a surprise was what one of our experts calls 'the non-aggression pact' between professors and students. It amounts to an unspoken compact: don't ask too much of me, and I won't expect much from you. This allows the faculty members to concentrate on what their institution values: publications, research, and getting grants. And it means that students get good grades and can float though college with plenty of time for socializing, networking, and other activities. Few complain, even though to an outsider it's pretty clear that the emperor has no clothes. That came as a shock."

In a paper, "Grade Inflation: It's Not Just an Issue for the Ivy League," written by Merrow and published by the Carnegie Foundation in 2004, he listed some proof. He cited a study by the American Academy of Arts and Sciences that showed that in 1950, about 15 percent of the population got a B-plus or better. Today, that number is 70 percent!

Fifteen years ago, students with A averages accounted for 28 percent of SAT test takers. Today, a whopping 42 percent of college-bound high school seniors have A averages. Oddly enough, these students score no better on the college admissions tests than "A" students did a decade earlier.

Numerous newspaper accounts reported a full 50 percent of the students attending Columbia University were on the Dean's List in 2002. Subsequently Columbia revisited it's Dean's List requirements and upped the cut-off list.

The reasons for grade inflation are many and varied—and some are more valid than others. Some say that busy professors simply don't have enough time to grade properly. Others, like Merrow, feel that there's an unspoken pact between professors and students that says, "Don't bother me, and I won't bother you." Some professors are new to academia from other fields and might feel they want their first classes to do well. Other professors want to ensure popularity of their courses, and an easy grader's reputation spreads through campus like wildfire. One theory says the grade inflation began during the Vietnam War when good grades could keep you from being drafted.

Institutions can also put pressure on the academic departments in order to improve their graduation rate. The best way to improve a school's graduation rate is to make sure that everyone passes everything. When everyone graduates with good grades, everyone—the students, their parents, and the school—is happy. And that happy fact perpetuates more admissions and more grade inflation.

Is there ever a good reason to inflate grades? One could argue that giving grades in some classes—creative writing, painting, etc. is difficult and always subjective. One could also argue that if the entire class fails a test there may be a problem with the test or the teacher, so why should the students suffer?

As long as there are grades there will be arguments about what constitutes a fair grade. The pendulum is always swinging. At this moment in time, schools seem to be getting more serious about avoiding the temptation to dole out all A's. That, depending on your feelings about grades, is a good or bad thing.

WILL I BE ABLE TO SEE MY CHILD'S GRADES?

One of the biggest eye openers about being the parent of a college student is that you're not automatically entitled to see anything having to do with them...not their grades, not their medical records, nothing. When you realize that you're paying for the privilege of seeing nothing, it's even stranger.

You will not be getting their grades in your mail. You have no right to see their grades without their explicit permission unless you have a signed authorization or proof that they are your financial dependents.

Jim Van Wingerden, Parent Relations Director of Calvin College says that the rules of the game have changed thanks to the interpretation of FERPA (the Family Educational Rights and Privacy Act) enacted in 1974.

FERPA is a federal law that establishes rules and restrictions as to who does and doesn't have access to a college student's records. "In some cases, parents are ensured access to grade information if the college student is claimed as a legal dependent on the parent's income tax statement," says Wingerden. "In other cases, a student who is over 18 must sign a waiver that authorizes the college to share grades with the parent. Parent-access-to-grades policies are also nuanced by student development theories, which basically take the view that college students will be most successful in their transition towards becoming responsible adults when the college interacts with them (instead of their parents)."

In other words, schools may have different interpretations of FERPA, but most colleges would like to see the students step up as masters of their own grades. All the same, it's a good idea to have your child sign the waiver that allows you to see their grades as a matter pro forma. Most parents whose children have signed waivers have never had to resort to using it in order to see their child's grades. Still, they remain comforted by the fact that the form is on file in the event that their child started to perform uncharacteristically in school.

Again, like that surveillance camera in a 7-11 store, you don't watch it until you need it, but knowing it's there deters crime. Just knowing that her parents could check in on her grades if they wanted to, tends to apply a gentle pressure to your student's desire for good grades.

WILL SOMEONE TELL ME IF MY CHILD ISN'T DOING WELL ACADEMICALLY?

No, as crazy as it seems, they won't. Again, requires universities to respect the privacy rights of adults, and students are considered adults the day they turn 18. Student records, including grades and transcripts, are considered confidential by most colleges and universities and are not released—not even when a student is failing.

The Catholic University of America recommends that parents and students discuss how they will share grade information in depth during the summer prior to the start of the academic year. Your child will be more confident about seeking your help if you are even-keeled and fair-minded about grade performance and if you've both been talking about grades from the beginning. The university also suggests that you have a conversation with your student in which you discuss how you would react—and what subsequent action would be taken—if they were to show a less-than-stellar college performance.

Choosing a major based on what a student wants to do when she leaves school is like chasing a moving target. "It has been said that over 50 percent of the jobs that will exist in 10 years do not even yet exist today," Ron Herron, Vice President of Student Affairs at SUNY Purchase College points out. "And, the data on major choice among college students bears this out: The typical undergraduate changes his or her major three times while in college!"

Herron says that with both the knowledge explosion and the dramatic shifts taking place in the working world it becomes difficult for young people to have a singular clear vision or choice. Today the most popular majors, according to The Princeton Review survey, include Business Administration, Psychology, and Elementary Education. But, in the last few years new majors are emerging to prepare students for some of the next generation's jobs. For example: Video Gaming, Computer Security, Informatics, Substance Abuse/Addiction Counseling, Medical Illustration, Geriatrics, Resort Management, Military Technologies, Athletic Training, and Multicultural Education for teachers who plan to enter bilingual grade school classrooms.

CAN I SPEAK TO HER PROFESSORS?

There's no law prohibiting you from calling a professor to ask a few questions, but it's not likely to win your child any brownie points. In fact, it is likely that they'll talk about you as what Wheaton College administrators often call "the baby boomer-turned parent."

"Resist the temptation" is Wheaton College's advice. Gail Berson, Dean of Admission and Student Aid says, "That first phone call you get, replete with tears about a nasty professor or a devastating grade, can bring out the 'let's make it all better' in any of us. One of the most important lessons you can teach your student is that she can solve her own problems. Yes, you're there to listen, be empathic and offer suggested remedies. But don't fix whatever the problem is for her. It's our nature as parents, particularly those of a certain generation, to be deeply involved in our child's life. But it is neither appropriate when your child is in college nor helpful to her if you intervene. Remember: It's college, not high school."

Kurt Holmes, Dean of Students at The College of Wooster, recognizes that if your child is struggling you're going to want to help, and most professors will want to assist. "But," he says, "it is more helpful to talk with your child about how she can utilize the professor's time or other college resources" than to make the call yourself.

"Communication between professor and student is instrumental in the development of critical thinking and autonomy," adds Bernard Chirico, PhD, Vice President for Student Affairs at University of Mary Washington. He says that one of the defining characteristics of a good school is the accessibility of its faculty.

As Jonathan Green, Dean of the College and Vice President for Academic Affairs at Sweet Briar College points out, faculty plays an active part in campus events, orientation, and family weekends. These are more appropriate times and venues for parents and professors to interact.

Of course, there are exceptions to every rule. If your child is ill and has to leave school, if there's a death in the family, or there are other extenuating circumstances, it may be a good idea to give the professor a heads up either with a note, an e-mail, or a call.

How Many Extracurricular Activities Are Too Many?

Every student should find some way to contribute to the extracurricular life of their school. It's a way to meet people in a non-academic setting and get involved in the school community. While classes are great, many require students to passively sit there; extracurricular activities usually demand rolling up those sleeves or working up a sweat.

Some students go for depth and commit themselves to a single passion, be it theater, sports, student government, or the school paper. Others go for breadth and dabble in a number of different clubs. By their senior year it's always nice if they've risen to a leadership position in some organization or another, but it's certainly not a prerequisite for graduation. Encourage them to find out about the clubs and activities during their freshman year and pick one or two they find interesting. The busier they are the more people they will meet and the less they will have thoughts of homesickness. Besides, you'd be amazed by how much a serious club affiliation can works in their favor during the job search.

Is Playing Sports Going to Hurt My Child's Academics?

Schools differ in all sorts of ways—the food, the dorms, the classes. But one of the most telling ways is in their philosophy about sports. A Division I school that doles out large scholarships and pays its coaches salaries that are based on the team's wins has a different attitude about sports then a Division III school that offers no athletic scholarships and has a considerably more relaxed attitude about competitions. (Division II schools offer athletic scholarships, but don't have as many sports options as Division I).

Coach Mark Mermelstein, from St. Mary's College in Maryland, has coached at both Division I and III schools. He says that the only way a student can know whether she will be able to manage the sports commitment is to visit the campus, meet with the

> **TIP:** Graduation Rate Data
>
> The U.S. Department of Education collects graduation rate information from every degree-granting higher education institution in the United States. You can find the annual Graduation Rate Survey (GRS) on the Department of Education's website, but in a fairly cryptic format. The easiest site to use is www.institutiondata.com. The posting of this information is now required by the federal Student Right to Know Act.

coach, talk to the athletic director, talk to athletes in the program, and ask questions about the school's philosophy and priorities.

"Ask the athletes what they don't like about the team as well as what they do like and it will help you know whether it's right for you," Mermelstein advises high school athletes. Regardless of division status, students on college sports teams will usually wind up practicing six out of seven days a week during their sports season. "That," says Mermelstein "takes a serious commitment and requires a strong sense of priorities." Over all, Mermelstein says that student athletes tend to be disciplined and hence tend to do well in the academic portion of their college experience, despite the time commitment to their sport.

In a recent speech, Dr. Myles Brand, President of the NCAA, reported that student athletes in both Divisions I and II graduate at a higher rate (meaning, they have a lower drop out rate) than the general student body.

WHEN DOES SHE NEED TO CHOOSE A MAJOR?

When it comes to choosing a major, college students fall into two groups: the ones who know what they want and the ones who don't. The second group is by far the larger, with an estimated 80 percent of students entering college with no major in mind. Which, don't panic, is not a problem.

A major can be broadly defined as a specialized cluster of courses that a student must complete in order to graduate. These courses may revolve around a subject (math), a theme (women's studies), or a professional goal (premed). A major requires a certain concentration of course work in a specific area. Not knowing what one wants to major in is not a bad thing, but the longer a student puts it off, the greater the chance that he will have trouble meeting the requirements and won't graduate in four years. This is especially true if the school does not offer every course he needs during every semester.

Universities have different requirements and expectations about majors, but the general consensus is that you should declare a major by the second semester of your sophomore year. While many schools will ask students to list an intended major on their application, they recognize that this is mere speculation. Students are welcome to declare themselves "undecided" on the application, too.

What if She Wants to Change Majors Once She Declares One?

There's nothing wrong with changing majors, but there can be a penalty in terms of graduating on time. There are typically prerequisites and a specific course of study for each major, so if a student switches from English literature to physics for example, she'll need to take quite a different set of prerequisites. Colleges are accustomed to students switching majors, and a student's advisor should be able to help her navigate the process.

Twists on the Theme

Colleges vary greatly in their core course requirements for graduation. The two extremes are schools that have no requirements and schools that have so many requirements that there's barely time for an elective—most lie somewhere in between.

Here's a quick look at some of the course variations you'll see:

Major: A group of classes around a subject or theme that the student agrees to complete before graduation

Minor: Also a group of classes, but with fewer requirements; meant to serve as a supplement to the major field of study

Dual Major: Requires the student to complete two full courses of study before graduation—they may be related or unrelated (though related is more practical and often more encouraged)

Independent Study: A course of study agreed upon by the student and advisor that creates a special project or major.

College of Honors: Typically a college within the college that focuses on a classic liberal arts education combining a rigorous study of classics, natural sciences, and social sciences, along with a thesis as a graduation requirement.

There are also different types of degrees. BA is a Bachelor of Arts, BS is the Bachelor of Science. There are also certification programs like teaching programs.

WHAT CAN I DO TO HELP CHOOSE MY CHILD'S MAJOR?

Purdue University suggests you encourage your student to take advantage of career counseling and aptitude testing programs. They also suggest you do two other things:

First, even if the school has no set requirements, you should urge your student to take a well-rounded roster during freshman year with courses in math, science, language, humanities, and social science. Next, aim for them to have chosen a major by the middle of the sophomore year.

Taking longer than four years to earn a bachelor's degree is not unusual and carries no stigma. But it does add to the total cost, so families should be aware of the potential financial impact. (Students also tend to get impatient if all of their other friends have graduated and they are left to come back for a fifth year to finish up their credits.)

Dr. John Inman, Registrar of Grove City College, suggests that parents keep the college catalogue on hand to refer to when looking at requirements for different majors. (Just make sure it's the one from the year your student entered school.) Inman says, "Official catalogs are specific to the year of matriculation and should be kept as a reference through graduation, as the catalog is the final word on requirements.

TIP: Point Your Child Toward Academic Help on Campus

Schools usually have some version of the following to help students find academic success:

- Learning Center

- Writing Center

- An English Department or Department of Literature-sponsored tutoring lab

- Peer tutoring

- Professors available through office hours, e-mail, and/or phone calls

- Study sessions online

- Informal or formal study group sessions

- Live review sessions with the professor or teaching assistant

SHOULD I EXPECT MY CHILD TO GRADUATE IN FOUR YEARS?

If you are the one paying the bills, it's certainly reasonable to expect a four-year graduation—until you look at the numbers, that is. With a full 40 percent (some estimates say more than 50 percent) of students taking longer than four years to graduate, your expectation may be a bit of an anachronism. That doesn't mean there aren't things that you can do to try and make a four-year graduation a possibility.

For one, some schools have better batting averages than others. Ask the school how many kids fail to graduate in four years and how much attrition they see (how many students they lose from the initial freshman class) in the course of four years. Then, do your best to assess whether it's a weakness in the campus support system or the "child's own doing." While you don't want to use graduation rates as the sole way of judging a campus, it provides a data point that might trigger an alarm. All schools publish their graduation rates and all schools try to balance the line between being a "diploma mill" where every student graduates in four years to a school that has alarmingly high attrition.

Some schools, recognizing the pressure to finish college in four years, have begun programs that offer students a Four-Year Contract. Students must agree to meet with an advisor and map out a realistic four-year plan of study that includes a number of checkpoints along the way. Students on the plan can't transfer schools, they can't fail a class or take incompletes, and they need to carry a certain number of credits each semester. If they keep to their contract, they will graduate in four years. Some of the schools that are offering these include Colorado State, University of Iowa, University of Kentucky, and University of Washington.

Four Years Plus

Parents often have strong financial incentives for wanting their kids to finish college in four years. An extra semester or two is expensive, especially when you tack on room and board. Yet, a growing number of students are taking longer than four years to graduate. Here's a look at some of the reasons:

- They are taking time off from their studies midway through or spending a semester abroad (which doesn't necessarily lengthen the time it takes to graduate, but it has the potential to)

- They decide on their major too late in the process to fulfill the course requirements in four years

- They need to proceed more slowly, limiting credits per semester, due special needs

- They're in a combined five-year program (some programs grant a combined BA/MA; for example, Columbia University has a five-year program in public policy that offers a BA/MIA—Masters of International Affairs)

- They transfer from one program or major to another and not all of the credits get transferred

- They transfer from one college to another and not all of the credits get transferred
- The school does not offer all of the courses they require in the progression they would have needed in order to graduate in four years
- They are work-study students or have jobs that require them to take a lighter class load
- They fail a class
- They have an illness

The numbers are pretty alarming, with four out of ten students taking more than four years to graduate. If having your child graduate in four years is important to you, she needs to decide on a major course of study fairly early on and stick to it. Transferring schools or switching majors makes it less likely to happen on time.

WHAT IF MY CHILD WANTS TO TRANSFER SCHOOLS?

The great thing about making a mistake in choosing a college (or not getting into the first-choice school) is that, if the student wants to, he gets to try again. It's called the transfer process. There are many valid reasons for transferring schools. As students mature, they may find they want a specialized program of study their school doesn't offer or a larger school with more choices, or a smaller school with more faculty contact. They may want to graduate from a more prestigious school, or be closer to home if a family member has fallen ill.

Then, there are less valid reasons. If your student is unhappy and simply thinks she'll be happier somewhere else just by virtue of the fact that it's somewhere else, transferring might be a bad idea. Work with your child to pinpoint the underlying reasons for the unhappiness and make sure she's not in for a repeat performance at the next school.

Transferring schools can be expensive and time consuming, not to mention emotional and exhausting. Even if it ends up being the right option for your child, is not to be taken lightly. It requires new applications, new interviews, and a physical move. New friends, a new town, a new dorm, new requirements for graduation and the discovery that all of the student's credits may not transfer are part of the package, too. The transfer college will expect to see good grades and a compelling essay; they don't want to hear excuses about why it didn't work out the first time.

It's true that credits are often lost in the transfer process. Your child may even need to retake some courses that are similar to those they have just completed. Some schools also have a minimum grade requirement for accepting transfer credits.

Most students transfer after they've completed their sophomore year, and that's when schools believe the reasons for transferring are most compelling. Transfer earlier and risk them thinking that the student may not have given it a fair shot or doesn't have enough of a track record at the current school; transfer later and risk them thinking it's simply too late to accomplish much at the new school.

Most students who transfer and want to begin in the fall semester of their junior year will want to submit their applications in January of their sophomore year.

Under the "Advice" section in the College area of www.princetonreview.com you can also find four articles on transferring schools, which cover choosing a transfer school, the process, pros and cons of transferring, and life after the transfer.

SHOULD I HELP EDIT HER PAPERS?

True confession time: How often did you edit your children's papers in high school? Well, you can put away the red pencil and close down Microsoft Word's tracking mode, because the deans do not want you editing any more. "While you may be very well-intentioned in your efforts, and your son or daughter has no intention of violating strict academic integrity codes, the boundaries between appropriate and inappropriate collaboration may be difficult for the new college students to understand," says Faith Leonard, Vice President and Dean of Students at American University.

"A precise definition of editing is impossible," says Georgia Tech. The university says that everything on the continuum from making suggestions and correcting grammar to completely rewriting can be subject to school review for ethics violations.

Instead of editing and collaborating on homework, parents should be encouraging them to get academic help from on-campus facilities. "This approach will help your student gain the strategies, self-confidence, and independence necessary to solve any problem that may come along—writing papers and otherwise," says Leonard.

> **TIP:** Informal Arrangements
>
> No formal tutoring on your child's campus? Tutoring doesn't work with her schedule? Have your daughter approach one of the class whiz kids and ask if they'd be willing to act as a tutor for an hour a week. It often turns out to be a valuable relationship for both of them and the cost is usually minimal.

Does that mean you shouldn't help them with their work at all? Of course not. Georgia Institute of Technology administrators believe that if "your student needs to pick your brain for ideas for a paper topic, a lively discussion is appropriate and helpful."

And don't give yourself too much credit, either. There are plenty of stories from parents who've edited their kid's papers only to get back some pretty bad news on the grades! Sure, you may have read Oedipus Rex 20-plus years ago, but it's likely that you're a bit hazy and that the professor may have discussed a slightly different interpretation of the plot than the one you recall.

WHAT ABOUT ACTING AS A SOUNDING BOARD FOR A PAPER HE HAS FINISHED WRITING?

While she prefers that the parents don't correct the papers for their children, Lynne Spies, Assistant Professor of English and Director of the Writing Program at Ralph-Macon College, sees a role for parents to help students to become their own best editors as this: If you want to help, "begin with the parent reading the paper aloud to the child or with the child reading the paper to the parent. As the paper is being read aloud, the child may catch obvious errors. Then, after the paper has been read, the parent should ask questions about any part of it that seemed unclear or confusing," says Spies.

Study Tips

Perhaps you should have thought of this earlier, but it's never too late to instill your children with good study habits. Make sure you have these simple bases covered:

- Buy highlighters and index cards and encourage them to write as they read.

- Suggest that they form a study group with others in the class. For many this works incredibly well.

- Remind them not to watch the movie in lieu of reading the book! Movies take artistic liberties that may not show up on the quiz.

- Discourage cramming for a test: It increases anxiety, fatigues the brain, and research shows that it seldom raises scores.

- If they have a huge reading load and do not read quickly, consider using supplemental audio tapes or books on tape. These tend to be available commercially for many classics.

- Nudge them about showing up for class, keeping awake, and taking good notes.

CAN WE HIRE PRIVATE TUTORS TO HELP OUR CHILD?

Before you hire anyone, make sure you've exhausted the on-campus services, which tend to be free and quite good. Bryn Mawr College, as an example, offers faculty who work one-on-one with students; peer tutors who are especially helpful to students in introductory languages, sciences and math; peer mentors who can help students become better studiers in general; and writing tutors who can help with everything from a freshman paper to a senior thesis. Private tutors are available, but at Bryn Mawr, as with most places, "students find the college's support systems do the trick," says Associate Dean, Judy Balthazar.

Much of the formal tutoring on campuses is sought out during freshman year. The University of Colorado at Boulder administration says that some schools also offer specialized tutoring or tutoring beyond the freshman year that may incur an extra charge.

WHERE CAN WE LEARN ABOUT WHAT TUTORING IS OFFERED?

"Today, tutoring is available on virtually 100 percent of college campuses in the United States," says Jane Neuburger, Director of Learning Resource Center at Syracuse University.

But, even though most colleges offer these tutoring services, your student might have to show some initiative before they get help say administrators at Pitzer College. "Tutoring at some colleges is handled on a departmental basis, so if a student was struggling with biology, she would find out about tutoring through the biology department. Language departments have laboratories with audio tapes and other teaching aids, and many academic departments will provide their own tutoring and test-preparation study session."

Some tutoring facilities transcend departments and looks at the gestalt to improve skills. These types of services often include a "Writing Center" to help students improve their narrative writing skills. Others provide services like "language tables" to assist in learning a second language. Information technology departments often provide help sessions to aid in learning new software.

Pitzer also suggests that you encourage your student to get to know professors and visit them during office hours. This is a time when professors are available specifically to talk with and help students. Ursinus College's Deborah Olsen Nolan, Associate Dean and Dean of Students, says that the best way to find about programs for tutoring is through college literature, the website, at orientations, and from their faculty advisors.

ARE THE TUTORS QUALIFIED?

Most universities will have a tutoring or learning center where students can engage tutors. These tutors are most often upper-class students who are trained by the Tutoring Center and are working to make some extra spending money. Tutors are required to have a high grade point average and go through training on how to be an effective tutor. They will guide your student to understand how to think about the subject, finish the homework, manage their time, outline/note-take, and do well on the tests and quizzes.

Syracuse University's Jane Neuberger encourages peer-to-peer tutoring relationships and suggests connecting with an upper class student who has taken the class before. Neuberger believes that some students feel more comfortable working with other students than visiting a professor. And truthfully, the tutor as a student is uniquely situated to bridge the gap between instructor expectations and student understanding.

Professor Power

As a parent of college kids, my mantra of "Go talk to your professor" usually fell on deaf ears. Then I would try, "The professor's going to find out how little you know one way or another, but you'll get more points if you initiate the conversation!" This one seemed to resonate.

Professors report that they could die of loneliness during office hours, since few students take advantage of the opportunity to seek help and clarification. But students whine that professors can be intimidating, or explain the same material again in the same way only to have it not make sense again.

J. Ann Hower, Director of New Student Programs at the University of Michigan, says that the earlier in the project or process that students can talk to their professor or teaching assistants the better. A visit to the professor can help identify the reason why your daughter did not do well on a paper or exam. It can make sure that your son isn't marching down a dead end with his choice of a topic for his paper. They can walk in and ask the professor's opinion on a topic of choice, or simply ask how they could have done better on an exam. (Professors love to talk, so usually all the students need to do is initiate the question.) The hidden benefit? Professors or teaching assistants will appreciate a student's initiative to remedy a problem and will probably be on the lookout for his or her improvements.

Colleges for Students with Learning Disabilities

Whether you call them learning disabilities, challenges, or just learning differently, there are some schools that are better suited to meet the needs of children who are seeking special arrangements. *The K & W Guide to Colleges for Students With Learning Disabilities or A.D.D.* by Marybeth Kravets and Imy F. Wax is an invaluable resource for finding the right school with the right services for your child.

Is It Better to Study in the Library, Her Dorm Room, or Somewhere Else?

Educators have been studying college studiers for years, and the best they can tell us is that everyone studies differently. That said, few students study well with distractions. Marlboro College deans give this simple piece of advice, "Don't study where you sleep."

Susan Lantz, West Virginia University's Parent Advocate says, "It's rare that a student has a good experience studying in a residence hall." She cites stereos, TV, food, roommates, friends, bed, and sleep as just a few of the distractions. "Plenty of light and desk space are important, plus computer access, if needed. Along with that, they should look for plenty of room to spread out," says Lantz.

David Satterlee, Director of First-Year Programs at Susquehanna University agrees, saying that "students who study in their residence hall room can expend all their energy fighting distractions." He suggests students try different locations and then settle on one. "Some student like the library, others use an empty classroom. Colleges usually have many small, quiet study rooms in residence halls and classroom buildings," he says. "Whatever works best for the student is the best choice."

"Some need absolute quiet while others need music and occasional interruptions," says Karla Carney, Cornell College's Associate Dean of Students. Having a consistent place to study that matches his learning style allows the student to focus, which is why the residence hall doesn't always work.

Is It Better to Study Alone, with a Friend, or in School Study Groups?

A Princeton Review survey asked college students how they studied best during exams and almost three-quarters of them answered that they used some form of group studying. Just like there's no one right place to study, "there is no one better way to study," says Daniel Stewart, Dean of Students Services Flagler College, "especially since each student is different. Ultimately the student needs to find the one that works best for him, and that might mean trying all different techniques and using a combination of all of them."

"Ideally, a student ought to study alone, with friends, and in school study groups at various times," say Swarthmore College administrators. They feel that studying with others enhances learning by giving the students the opportunity to be both a teacher and a receiver of others' experience and ideas. They also view it as preparation for real life, as many careers will place them in situations that require collaborative work. Collaborative work has, in fact, become a cornerstone of many schools. At the Franklin W. Olin College of Engineering teamwork and collaboration are considered some of the best preparation for real-world work situations and are integrated into class work wherever possible.

Jacqueline Kiernan MacKay, Assistant Vice Assistant Vice President for Student Services, and Wanda S. Ingram, Associate Dean of Undergraduate Studies, both at Providence College, point out that there are pros and cons to studying in a group, however. "The benefit is that students are able to share ideas and new perspectives and review for exams. But, some groups can be counterproductive if they degenerate to 'gab' sessions, address superficial information, or avoid difficult topics."

Of course, the real answer is "Whatever it takes!" say administrators at Seattle University. The most common pattern is that students will initially profit from exploring the material alone and then working within a study group later to make sure they have it down.

ARE SMALL CLASSES BETTER THAN BIG LECTURES?

There are advantages to both. Small classes offer an intimacy and exchange between students and the instructor. Large lectures tend to be well-prepared, well-presented discourse. A good lecture can be fascinating (even if students are staring down at a professor from afar). Oftentimes there is more information in contained in a lecture than there might be when there's an open dialogue. Freshmen and sophomores in larger schools will often find their introductory classes take the form of large lectures. Seminars and smaller classes are often the domain of upperclassman. It's important that your child realize the benefits of both and make sure she shows up at those large lectures even if attendance isn't taken. "Getting the notes" is never the same as hearing it first-hand, either.

SHOULD SHE SPEND A SEMESTER ABROAD? IF SO, HOW WILL THE COSTS COMPARE TO HAVING SPENT THE SEMESTER AT HER OWN SCHOOL?

As the world shrinks and business becomes more global and as diversity plays a larger part in the economy, studying abroad becomes more than just "a fun change" for the semester. It becomes an invaluable experience that contributes heavily to a student's preparedness for the today's world.

Almost every school offers some form of international travel or semester abroad, but schools vary greatly on the degree to which they encourage and facilitate the experience. Judy Balthazar, Associate Dean at Bryn Mawr, points out that "many students choose not to study abroad in order to delve deeper into their majors, to take on leadership roles in the residence halls, or in other realms." Some schools, because of intense course requirements within a program, make it difficult to find the time to study abroad. But many institutions encourage and even make travel a part of the mission of the college.

If your student is thinking of studying abroad, you'll want to be the one who thinks of any major repercussions. (That's your job isn't?) While they may be ecstatic about studying the culinary arts in Italy, you're going to need to determine whether they'll lose financial aid for the semester, whether you can afford the trip, and whether it will hamper your student's ability to graduate in four years. Many colleges like Wabash

College will put financial aid toward study in a foreign university, which makes it affordable if you choose a program in one of the less expensive countries. Even better, Rochester Institute of Technology doesn't charge university tuition for study abroad programs, so what you pay depends entirely on the cost of the international program. Some programs, such as those in Japan, are quite expensive, whereas a study abroad program in Mexico is much less expensive. Some foreign programs are not only more expensive, they are more dangerous because of economic or political situations, and some programs are more immersive in the country's culture and language than others.

Most educators echo Chuck Lamb's, Director of Residence Life at Rochester Institute of Technology, sentiments: "If the opportunity presents itself in a cost reasonable manner that doesn't interfere with the positive advancement of the student's academic program, for goodness sake, do it!"

Students who want to travel, but can't afford it, or who don't have time have other alternatives as well. At Wabash College, for example, they offer "immersion learning courses" that tie international travel to on-campus courses. Each year, about ten classes have significant travel components—typically over spring break or just before or just after the end of the term. With these types of programs, students aren't forced to leave their home campus for an entire semester, yet enjoy the benefits of being immersed in a foreign culture. And students who are varsity athletes, club presidents, or involved in student government can take advantage of off-campus study, but on a limited scale. The best news is that these programs are often free of an extra charge.

In addition to the costs of studying abroad, you'll need to be mindful of the academic credits. Some schools allow students to go to international programs sponsored by other schools, but they won't always accept the full credit toward your child's major for courses taken abroad. University of Washington's International Programs and Exchanges Office advises discussion and research to ascertain how many credits you'll receive for your study.

WHY STUDY ABROAD?

"Studying abroad helps prepare students for lives in an increasingly global society," say administrators at Gustavus Adolphus College. The experiences they'll be exposed to will help them:

- Become more adaptable, independent, and self-confident
- Acquire a fuller awareness of their abilities, career interests and personal values
- Gain insights into their own culture and that of the host country
- Understand the way other cultures view the U.S.
- Become more sensitive to the differences and needs of other peoples
- Gain an in-depth knowledge of the history, language, and contemporary issues of another part of the world
- Bring experiences and knowledge back to campus, creating a community where diversity is valued

WHO ARE MY CHILD'S ACADEMIC SUPPORT HELP ON CAMPUS?

There are many people who become part of the student's support team. Cynthia Cherrey, Vice President of Student Affairs at Tulane University begins with the RA who becomes an important peer support person for academic as well as residence life issues. RAs will be able to offer opinions about scheduling, courses, and planning the four years because they better understand the requirements.

Other important supporters include the full-time professional staff in the residence hall and your student's invaluable academic advisor, who will help your child chart a path toward graduation and make sure he stays on track. Their professors are also important. In fact, getting to know one or two faculty members well can be invaluable—especially when it comes to writing those letters of recommendation if your child decides to apply to graduate school.

Many schools are taking novel approaches to ease the transition from high school to college. Robin Jones, Associate Dean of Residential Education at West Virginia University, oversees the Resident Faculty Leaders (RFLs), a program initiated in 1995 as part of Operation Jump-Start. RFLs often invite students to dinner, arrange field trips, and host other social and academic activities throughout the semester to help them meet new people and feel included as they adjust to life at school.

The Sims

Simulation may be just the thing to stimulate your family's discussion about academics. Electronic Arts recently added a new game, Sims 2 University, to their collection of SIM games. The Sims is the popular simulation series where you imbue electronic characters onscreen with certain attributes (jealousy, brains, brawn, kindness) and let them meet in various environments to see what happens. As you play Sims 2 University, you can pick majors, decide where you'll live, figure out how to pay your tuition, play sports, or join a club and work through all of the drinking and partying issues.

Surviving the Liberal Arts

A liberal arts education is designed to prepare students to think and theoretically, serves as a solid foundation on which to build any number of careers in the real world. Yet, in truth, many liberal arts students graduate feeling aimless and without skills. Here's a recipe your child might consider for surviving a liberal arts education and coming out on top:

- Pursue a passion. Choose a major that excites you, one that you could see yourself working in.

- Take career-enhancing courses. Learn to write and communicate well. Take statistics if you're studying economics or psychology, for example. That will help differentiate you from the pack. If you're studying philosophy, take some political science, anthropology and math or computer skills to round out your marketability. Take a few computer courses and learn a bit about Web design, too.

- Learn a foreign language. It's a global economy and if you can converse in a second language, you are more likely to stand out in the job pool.

- Keep your computer skills current. It doesn't matter if HTML is replaced with the next new thing or if JAVA fades from fashion. Computer skills translate well and elevate you in the eyes of a prospective employer.

- Investigate internships. There's no better way to experience a taste of the work force than to get out there and get your hands dirty. Experiential learning programs have become increasingly popular on campuses.

- Do a thesis. At many colleges and universities, senior-year students are offered the choice to either continue to take classes or do a research project of their own design. Doing a project makes you an active contributor to academia and not just a passive listener. A good thesis can even be your ticket to a landing a good job.

CHAPTER 7

Your Kids, Your Money

When I was growing up, there were two taboo subjects in our home: money and sex. We did manage to eek out a few uncomfortable conversations about the mechanics of sex, but our dad told us very little about how he brought money into the house and what he did with it when it got there. I suspect he was proud of the fact that he was taking care of things and didn't ever want us to worry.

I know my family was not alone. Many of us, and now many of our children, head off to college without a clue about what it means to live on a budget, shop for a bargain, make do without, balance a checkbook, or figure out a tax return.

While students may head off blissfully ignorant, many parents find themselves in a financial no-man's land because, essentially, these kids aren't out on their own quite yet. They're still financially dependent (in varying degrees). Only now they're out of sight and far away from the watchful eye of fiscal prudence—with spending money in their bank account to boot.

Parents are always surprised when kids haven't learned about finance through osmosis, and they're even more surprised when a child makes a major money mistake like loses their rent deposit because they didn't sign a formal lease, or winds up with a ghastly amount of credit card debt and a tarnished credit rating.

College students' financial inexperience is only amplified these days as plenty of college campuses become more temptation-filled. Some of the campuses I've visited make being a kid in a candy shop seem not at all tempting by comparison. There are on-campus masseuses, room cleaning, and laundry services. The school coffee shops sell lattes that cost more than those found in Starbucks. In town, the latest rock bands show up for weekend gigs routinely and the Moroccan restaurant where you sit in little tents lures students away from their meal plan with the campus cafeteria.

The worst of it is that students can do these things without ever taking a dollar bill out of their wallets. For the "Swipe-It" generation, the student ID card, credit card, and debit card have created a nearly cashless campus. They can have their fun without the pain of watching the cash wad dwindle.

If there's a shining light in all of this, it's that today's students are more savvy about money, credit, and finance than most previous generations have been. Sure, they buy more things, but at the same time they're more used to having and managing their money than any generation before them. The Internet has helped them research purchases and buy things online for a better price than in the stores. They've held jobs, and they've been exposed to the language of finance through the many news and other shows on television. (We may all be thanking *The Apprentice* one day.) The Federal Trade Commission reported in 2003 that according to the most recent study by Nellie Mae, a national student loan financing organization, 83 percent of undergrads have at least one credit card, and the average credit card balance for college students is $2,327. Nellie Mae also reports that students double their average credit card debt—and triple their number of cards—by graduation. And here's some news in regards to getting them a card for "emergencies only." According to a recent study conducted by the U.S. Public Interest Research Group (PIRG), of the 79 percent of surveyed students who use credit cards for multiple purposes, only 13 percent reported limiting credit card use to emergencies.

This chapter focuses heavily on the kinds of financial decisions you'll need to make during your child's freshman year although it's a wise idea to revisit these decisions annually in light of the rapidly changing economy. I can't guarantee that this information will actually save you money, but at least you'll get an idea of where the money's being spent and what alternatives you have to curb the damage.

We'll cover:

- How much money is the right amount to be spending
- The best way to raise fiscally responsible students
- How to make smart choices on credit, debit, and checking programs
- How to manage the new stored-value Student IDs

- How to control ATM-itis

- The best way to control in-town spending

HOW MUCH DOES THE AVERAGE STUDENT SPEND EACH MONTH?

How much can laundry, a little shopping spree now and then, a few movies and DVDs, and some snacks cost? More than you'd think! Incidentals are big bucks. (Isn't that true for our own spending as well?) The weekend stash you take out of the ATM on Friday after work can easily wind up as a few crumpled George Washingtons by Monday morning. Parents and students agree that there's more incidental spending on urban campuses in places like Ann Arbor, Boston, or New York than on rural campuses. But whether they are city mice or country mice, according to Student Monitor, LLC, a market research firm, students spend on average $205 a month on incidentals.

The breakdown goes something like this:

A Typical College Student Budget

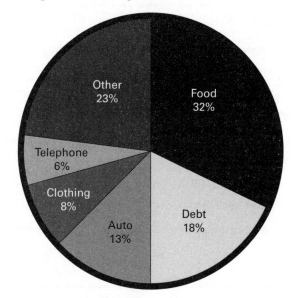

Source: Student Monitor, LLC (a market research firm specializing in the college market)

Should They Have Their Own Money or Depend on Me for Incidentals?

A combination of their earned money augmented by your generosity is the ideal way to go. The money students spend typically comes from a variety of sources. Some of it comes from their own wages, some from a parental allowance, and some from a loan or scholarship. Traditionally, most students are still supported, at least in part, by their parents. Most also work part-time, either during the summer and holiday breaks, or during the school year.

According to Student Monitor, LLC students earn an average of $4,500 per year. But a Harris Interactive Poll conducted in 2003 found that college students control $122 billion in spending power; $24 billion of that in discretionary spending. Do the math and it's pretty clear that they spend much more than they make. That money has to come from someone!

TIP: Where the Money Comes From

- Three quarters (75 percent) of students maintain jobs, earning $645 per month on average.

- A fifth (20 percent) have an on-campus job and four in ten (42 percent) are spending school breaks working.

- Mom and Dad kick in, contributing another $154 to a student's monthly income.

- All told, a student spends more than $13,000 per year, 19 percent of which is discretionary.

Source: Harris Interactive. "College Students Spend $200 Billion Per Year."

http://www.harrisinteractive.com/news/allnewsbydate.asp?NewsID=480

How Do We Create a College Budget?

"You should sit down with your student and talk through expenses he or she might have prior to going to college," says Karla Carney, Cornell College's Associate Dean of Students. Expect them to spend money on:

- Entertainment (movies, sporting events, clubs, dining out)
- Laundry (and possibly the occasional dry cleaning)
- Automobile expenses
- Haircuts, books/magazines/newspapers (academic and casual reading)
- School supplies/photocopying/computer supplies

"After he has completed a semester, sit down again and review how the spending has gone. More important than establishing an exact amount per week is helping the student understand the process of budgeting, prioritizing how they spend their money, and managing the money they have effectively."

How Much Can I Expect My Child to Spend?

"That depends," says Carney. She reminds parents to consider several factors: whether the student is living on or off campus, has a meal plan, is involved in campus organizations that require a fee, has a car, has an off-campus job requiring gas, the cost of living in that particular town, etc. The typical range is somewhere around $250 a month, with some margin to accommodate individual needs.

Parents of freshmen feel obliged to pull a number out of a hat but—provided your child doesn't undergo a major personality change and inflation stays constant—your best gauge of college spending is your student's high school spending profile.

Cynthia Cherrey, Vice President of Student Affairs of Tulane University suggests starting modestly. "Remember," she says, "you can always adjust the amount later...and it is easier to increase!"

While it's easier to increase their spending allowance, it's not easier to tighten parental control once it's lax. At Catholic University of America the deans suggest an inverse corollary. "Start with a higher level of parental control until the student demonstrates financial maturity."

WHAT SORT OF SPENDER IS MY CHILD?

Here are some telltale high school clues. Did she hit the coffee shop with friends for an after-school snack each day? Did she sip Perrier or tap water? Did she have a hard time making it through the weekend without a trip to the mall? Were her sports and hobbies expensive? Was she always going to a concert or did she prefer hikes in the park? Designer jeans or Army/Navy? You get the idea. If there's a history of indulgence, then you should be prepared to do a little behavior modification or expect more of the same.

By the same token, if you give her a set amount that needs to last all semester, that might help them to curb those decadent ways.

Where's Your Child's Consumer Compass?

Freshman year can pose some tough fiscal choices, and it's tough for you too—wondering if your child's inner consumer compass will be strong enough to point to "no" when it most needs to.

Can he turn down an invitation to join the "every-weekend-is-ski-weekend" crowd or to book his Spring Break in Cancun? Can she set the limit at one restaurant dinner every two weeks and infrequent trips to the mall? If your child is easily influenced, you may need to build a stricter budget than you would for those who are disposed to being frugal.

In the midst of this, it's good to know that thriftiness has a place on campus. Even the most pampered of college kids seem to enjoy the "making do" attitude of college life. Here are a few things about college life that contribute to the "I'm just a poor college student" mentality:

Diversity. Thank goodness for economic diversity. With a few exceptions, schools aim for all kinds of diversity including economic. Your child will get to meet others from every socio-economic stratum. There's a bonding, even a bit of pride, in being a poor college student for a few years. Without sounding corny, most students seem to recognize the sacrifice their parents have made the past 18 years and try to keep limits on the spending. (Parents, a little guilt here is a good thing.)

Shabby chic. In general, it's hip to live the shabby, but stylin' life. Used furniture, second hand clothes, and ramen noodles have a campus cachet—at least on some campuses. Trash treasure furniture, www.craigslist.com bargains, and consignment shop finds are all status elevators. Parents can use this to their advantage.

The frugal roommate prayer. The only thing worse than having a roommate who thinks nothing of dialing for a sushi delivery every evening is the one who wants you to chip in for the Weber Grill and hand-woven rug so that you can throw the perfect dorm party. A roommate with no budget is scary; pray your child gets a practical, frugal one, or at least that his practical, frugal side will rub off on his loves-to-spend, AmEx-toting roommate.

TIP: Add at least $1,000 to whatever the college quotes as the estimated total cost of a year: Colleges will often give you a suggested discretionary amount of money to allot, but they are notorious for under-representing the true cost of college. The fees and project supplies, the trips home, the phone calls, and other minutiae add up. Adding about $1,000 to the total they estimate will bring it closer to the real, end-of-the-year figure.

How Much Cash Should Be in My Child's Wallet?

The consensus amongst educators is that students rarely need cash on campus, but that's not the same as saying they rarely need money. Roughly speaking, it seems that most students on meal plans and living in dorms spend $30 to $50 a week, with some weeks higher than others. If you figure that school is in session for about 8 months, and you budget $250 a month which includes a little padding, you won't be too far off.

A survey at Saint Anselm College found students reporting that they spend, on average, $50 a week for incidentals including pizza, a movie, gas for their car, shampoo, etc. Deans at Wabash College and The University of the Pacific felt that $20 to $40 of pocket money per week was all students would need—though the students might tell you otherwise.

"Always check the school's website," suggest administrators at Pitzer College. "A school will typically suggest an amount (that your kids will always argue is too low) for living and miscellaneous expenses." They also suggest not using your child's first weeks in school as a gauge of what is a normal budget because students are buying books and supplies, as well as going out and getting to know each other.

> **TIP:** Make a list of wallet contents.
>
> Students and their wallets often seem to part ways. Since some of their monthly bills—the hot little credit card, for example—may be sent to their permanent address, it's a good idea for them to have the important information they'll need to get replacement credit cards, student ID cards, driver's license, etc. on hand. Have them make a written list (a list stored on the computer is good, too) of all card details and squirrel it away someplace safe.

> **FACT:** Students spend an average of $68.50 monthly with their university ID stored-value card. The $68.50 monthly figure went up 100 percent from 2003 and 2004, meaning these cards are quickly growing more popular. (Student Monitor, LLC)

WHAT IS A ONE-CARD SYSTEM?

The biggest change between the college campus you fondly remember and the one your child will be attending (other than the price of tuition and coed bathrooms) is probably the advent of the cashless campus. Most student ID cards now contain the "smarts" to track campus spending, debiting your child's account as she goes. Each campus has a cute little name for their debit system like the mascot-based Huskey Card or Penguin Card or the rather high-tech sounding Free-Roam or Universal Access card. Alan Levy, from the University of Michigan, defines the trend as "Debit cards with a declining cash balance option that can be encoded on a student ID card." Basically it's money at hand in a convenient, easy-come-easy-go format.

Now, the same ID that lets students into the dining hall buys their sporting event tickets, shower gel, T-shirts, and snacks—anything that's sold on campus can be theirs with the swipe of the card. The good news? Students can walk around without a dime in their pockets and pay for everything from Xerox copies to textbooks, from loads of laundry to an extra-large latte. The schools can directly deposit student loans and campus paychecks right into the account. At most schools, parents can add money to their child's accounts online or by telephone. Sometimes these debit cards are connected to a the campus ATM machine, making it far to easy for students to swipe their card and have the machine spit out more cash whenever they need it. Local businesses often accept the university's one-card making the temptation to swipe even greater.

WHY DO COLLEGES LOVE THESE NEW ID CARDS?

University of Michigan's Levy, says, "They are good for parents because the billing is part of the standard student account with the institution and because transactions are generally limited to such staples as food, textbooks, and supplies. It's good for students because they need to carry only their ID card to do almost everything they want to do or buy around campus."

Some card programs take the idea one step further. Pitzer College's "flex-dollar" program lets students use the card at any campus eatery, but they can also add "Claremont Cash" to the card (Claremont is the local town), so it can be used to buy books, food at some local restaurants, and goods at the nearby shopping plaza.

At The Franklin W. Olin School of Engineering, students and their parents may deposit funds to the account for use in residence hall laundry machines or Coca-Cola vending machines. Off campus, "Dining Dollars" can be used at neighboring colleges: Babson, Wellesley, and selected Domino's Pizza stores.

For the most part, students love the cashless arrangement. Parents, as you might guess, may not be quite as enthusiastic. Suddenly your child, the one with little or no previous "plastic" experience, is rather free to go "swipe" wild. Forking over a wad of bills makes a strong impression of "when it's gone, it's gone"—one that swiping a card just doesn't. Thankfully, these cards are debit cards so they'll be cut off when the well runs dry. (Well, technically the user can go a bit over, as all of the cards have a modest amount of overdraft protection). A statement of the card's charges is frequently sent out with tuition bills. You may be shell-shocked at how fast a college student can run through the money. At least the statement will allow you to discuss the line items that seem suspect, before it's time to pay the piper, and pump more money onto the card.

And do make a point of looking at those statements. Things like late charges for library books, exorbitant Xerox charges, daily boutique coffees and teas might be areas in which they can cut back next semester, as are any other avoidable expenses. A general guideline might be to keep no more than $150 on the card at a time.

WHAT IF MY CHILD LOSES THE ID CARD?

Now that the student ID card has money attached to it, losing it takes on new meaning. Sharon Kompalla, Apartments Area Director at the Rochester Institute of Technology's Center for Residence Life, offers this suggestion: "Contact your son or daughter's college and inquire about a pin-protected account on their Student ID. If the card is lost or stolen, the money can't be accessed without the pin. (Of course, the Golden Rule here is NOT to share your pin-code with your friends.)"

> **TIP:** Opening a checking or savings account can usually be done on the spot; credit card applications take time to process.

ARE THERE ATMS ON CAMPUS?

Oh yes there are. In addition to ID cards, the other big source of swiping power on campus is the cash machine or ATM. ATMs have become as common a site on campuses as school-logo sweatshirts. On some campuses, the student's stored-value ID card is linked to the ATM. That means that they can get cash from their card just as easily as they get their textbooks or snacks. It's just one more item on the list that gets debited from a single account, and that can be a problem. In addition, the campus ATM is usually provided by a local bank, which poses another problem. If it's a local bank, you'll need to devise a system to deposit money into your child's account. The easiest way is to establish an electronic transfer from your bank to theirs.

Remember too, that with ATM machines on campus, unless your child has free privileges with that bank, she will pay a transaction fee each time the ATM is used to withdraw money. Kids can shell out a few dollars a week in transaction fees, especially if they're only taking out small amounts of money at a time. If your child is going to rely on the ATM, then she might want to think seriously about opening an account its associated bank and setting up ways for you to electronically move money into that account.

How Monthly Spending Gets Done

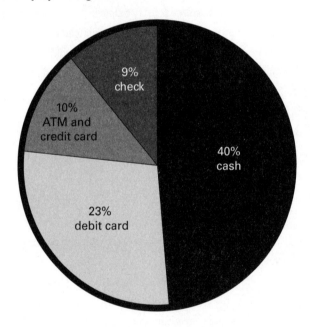

Source: Student Monitor, LLC 2004

TIP: Credit Card Survival Tips

Your children will be getting some amazing direct mail or online offers for low or no interest credit cards. The advice from Chase Bank Student Services is to tell them not to get lured into the trap of applying for multiple cards because they like the prizes or the zero interest introductory rates. Getting cards and then canceling them, which some students do just to take advantage of the introductory offers, will hurt their credit standing.

Incurring late charges will also hurt their credit standing. Encourage them to use their personal calendaring program on their computers to set up ticklers to remind them to pay the bill on time. Remind them to change their mailing address over the summer so they don't get a statement mailed to school when they're not there.

How Will We Know What Banks Are in Town and What They Offer to Students?

When you go to freshman orientation, sandwiched in between the tables with information about meal plans, the clubs and activities, and the health center are folks (or at least literature from) the local financial institutions. The representatives who want to open accounts for your children love this time of year and they love the sight of parents. They know that not only will they win your child's account, but they take comfort that you're there to bail the kids out of any financial troubles they might get into.

Of course, they've got you cornered at a weak moment. You'll arrive on campus bleary-eyed from packing and driving and in no mood to discuss banking options. If you haven't thought about credit versus debit cards before this moment, it's going to be like going food shopping when you're famished: You'll pick up costly extras that you don't need. The moral of the story? Do your banking homework before you get to orientation.

First, if there is one, read the parenting portion of your school's website. Most schools list the branches of the local bank or credit union that you'll find on campus along with local banks in the area, too. A phone call or a visit to the bank website will show you their student offerings—and come to campus knowing exactly what you need and how you plan to get it. That way you can go ahead and take the free pens and the coffee mugs having already read the literature and weighed your options. You'll co-sign on the dotted line with confidence that you haven't—in your tired state—missed any important fine print.

> **TIP:** Your kids have a lifetime of credit ratings ahead of them. When they leave college and apply for other forms of credit and loans, their credit rating will be checked. If they've been authorized to use your account as opposed to opening their own, they are not building a FICO credit rating, which is the standard rating that is checked when applying for a loan or credit card. They will, however, receive a Bureau of Credit Rating, so it's important that they not incur interest payments. To do this they must pay the amount they owe each month, on time and in full. To get a FICO rating—which will help them earn more credit down the road, they need to have a card in their own name.

WHAT'S BEST: CREDIT, CHECKING, OR DEBIT?

There is no perfect answer to this one, but whatever you decide, you'll probably want to reevaluate it during the course of their college years and make sure they are still using the type of account(s) that works best for them. Credit cards are a great way to start them on getting a credit rating which they'll need should they ever want a life of their own. And, even though frequent flier miles aren't as powerful as they used to be, your child might qualify for a free flight at least once during their college years if they have a card that rewards them in miles for every dollar they spend.

The biggest question about credit cards is whether you should get your child a card in her own name or let her latch on to your account. The advantage of a debit card is that your child is limited to a finite amount of spending. When whatever you'd deposited in the account is gone, it's gone. There's never that fear of running up a line of credit and it teaches them to live within their means (provided you don't just keep refilling the empty cup). Checking accounts are great for that tactile sensation of sitting down at regular intervals and "paying the bills." The downside is that their not as immediate as electronic transactions. Today, most checking accounts come bundled with a debit card.

> **TIP:** A *Newsweek* article, "Money Guide: A Cash Course for Kids" (Sept. 12, 2005), suggested showing your kids your own credit report (now available for free at www.annualcreditreport.com). Robert Manning, author of *Credit Card Nation*, interviewed in the same article, says that when he lectures to students, he tells them that upon graduation their credit score will be even more important than their grade point average.

How Popular Are Credit Cards on Campus?

Even administrators at colleges with campus-wide cards like the University of Washington's Husky Card (a pre-paid campus card) find that 50 percent of college freshmen come to campus with additional credit cards in hand. By the time they're seniors, an estimated 96 percent of students have credit cards.

> **TIP:** Parents may want to investigate some form of student access checking accounts. With these accounts, students will be able to share a checking account with their parents. The statement is mailed to the parents, who also have access to the account. Designed specifically for families with kids in college, these accounts typically have low monthly maintenance fees.

According to the Student Monitor, just under half of college students they surveyed, 46 percent, have some form of credit card.

If He's Going to Have a Credit Card, Should My Son Get His Own or Be Authorized on My Card?

"College is a great time to learn about fiscal responsibility but the lessons learned from that can come at a cost (in the form of extremely high interest rates!)," says the staff at The University of Puget Sound. (And that's not to mention a tarnished credit rating if the spending gets so out of control that payments are late or missed.) The type of credit card you choose should be based on how much parental oversight your child will need.

If you authorize your child to use your card, he will receive his own card, with his name on it and his identification number—but all the bills will be sent to you. You will be paying for his expenditures based on your credit card interest rates, which are typically higher than student interest rates. If you're conscientious about paying your bills on time and in full, at least you won't be charged interest. Despite the slightly higher rate, some parents prefer this arrangement because they can monitor all purchases, and they don't have to worry about whether their child has paid the credit card bill on time—or at all. They also like it because they can take advantage of the perks that come with some credit cards, such as rewards or frequent flier miles.

If students get a card in their own name, they will be paying their own bills and establishing their own credit. There's a good chance that they'll also be paying a lower interest rate (at least initially), since many credit card companies advertise low-interest cards that are especially created for students. (In late 2005, student interest charges were about 9.9 percent, while adults typically paid 15 to 18 percent.)

At Puget Sound University, the administration feels that your choice of card, "Boils down to how much you trust your son or daughter" to be responsible with this newfound financial freedom. If you trust that your child can manage her own finances, then having a card in her own name is good.

At Wabash College, the deans suggest looking for a card that offers:

- A low rate of interest
- No annual fee or a small annual fee
- A minimal penalty for late payment
- A low credit line (look for a card that caps the credit at somewhere between $300 and $1,000)

Do I Need to Cosign a Credit Card?

You need to cosign a credit card only if your student is under 18 years of age.

What's a Checking/Debit Account?

We all know what a checking account looks like, but to most of our kids, these books of paper where you scratch in some numbers and a signature with your pen are an anachronism. After all, you can't swipe a check!

There's no doubt that paying by check can be imprecise and uncertain. It's hard to know when a check will arrive and when it will be cashed. It can be annoying to keep track of them, and many stores and markets will no longer accept them. The modern mate to the checkbook is the debit card. It looks like a credit card but it links to the user's checking account. Instead of using a revolving line of credit to pay for purchases, the funds are withdrawn straight from the checking account. Most stores now accept debit cards and many bills can be paid online using a debit card as well.

The benefit of a checking/debit account versus a credit card is that the user cannot spend more than they have. (Although, like Student ID cards, most debit accounts do feature some degree of overdraft protection.) This is a rather straightforward way to live on a fixed budget. Debit cards offer the convenience of not having to carry cash, with the safety of not living beyond one's means. Plus, the student doesn't have to qualify for a checking/debit card the way they would for a credit card. If your child runs short of funds or has an emergency, you can always add or transfer money to his account either by setting an electronic payment directly into his account or the old fashioned "wiring" him money. Finally, debit cards can instantly access cash from any ATM.

HOW POPULAR ARE CHECKING/DEBIT ACCOUNTS ON CAMPUS?

Debit cards continue to grow in popularity. According to the Student Monitor, in 2004 68 percent of students surveyed used a debit card. Checking accounts were still the most popular choice compared with credit cards on campus—82 percent of students surveyed had a checking account in their own name and were averaging four checks monthly.

	Checking	Debit Card	Credit Card	Smart ID	Cash
Good on campus	Probably	Yes	Yes	Yes	Yes
Good off campus	Difficult unless local	Yes	Yes	Limited	Yes
Good online	Not usually	Usually	Yes	Very Limited	No
Required to	Open account with a mimimum balance	Open account with a mimimum balance	Apply, credit check	Doubles as school ID and meal card	None
Fees	Modest or free	Modest or free	Varies. Try for no annual fee, and a low interest rate. Pay on time and in full.	Included in tuition	None

Will They Cash My Checks at the Local Stores?

We've all seen the signs at the register that say "Sorry, we cannot cash checks." College town shopkeepers, weary of bounced checks, will often put the kibosh on cashing checks sent from home. At Purdue University, they suggest that most merchants near the university campus are accustomed to out-of-town checks, but having a bank account with a local bank will eliminate some delays. Horace J. Amaral, director of Enrollment Services at the University of Rhode Island agrees, recommending that students open an account at "A national financial institution with a local branch near the campus."

Should My Child Have a Savings Account at College?

Parents who find themselves heaving a deep sigh when they look at their dwindling funds during the college tuition years will probably share the sentiment, "College is no time to be saving money." And the banks are nodding in agreement. Plenty of banks offer special savings account programs for kids ages 8 to17, but college seems to be a dead spot in the savings map.

Don't count on your students socking cash away while they're at school, says Elon University's Scott Nelson, Assistant Dean of Students, and Smith Jackson, Vice President and Dean of Student Life. "Savings accounts for students are an oxymoron. Savings accounts are good for the 'back home' bank, so the money students save during summers and breaks will be out of sight and, hopefully, out of mind." Most students take their earnings and loan monies and deposit them directly into their checking accounts.

How Popular Are Savings Accounts on Campus?

A surprising 64 percent of students surveyed have a savings account in their own names, according to the Student Monitor. At the moment, the most popular investment on campus is savings bonds.

What Are Student Savings Clubs and Should We Join?

One way for students to save a few dollars while they're in school is by joining one of the many student savings clubs that are offered by/through various private groups. These clubs offer discounts to students who purchase their affiliated products and services.

The Student Advantage is the nation's largest student discount program. Users save somewhere between 10 to 50 percent at more than 15,000 locations around campus, online, and across the country. The card can be purchased for $20 for one year. It offers discount travel, discount tickets to events, movies, clothing, rental cars, school supplies, and more. In part, this is a marketing ploy to get students to consume one brand over another. Instead of spending marketing dollars, companies align themselves with groups like this and offer discounts. If your student is already a fan of the companies and services affiliated with this and other cards, student discount cards may make sense. "But do exercise caution," say administrators at Seattle University. "Know your child's ability to budget wisely, and understand the fine print. Also, give some thought as to whether you want to patronize some of the business and products offered through these discount cards."

Flager College's Daniel Stewart, Dean of Student Services, suggests looking carefully at the types of programs there are out there. "Any discount card which allows the discount to be applied immediately is a good card. Cards which accumulate points or discounts later do not work very well."

What Is Fiscal Tough Love?

You've heard of tough love, right? Well, fiscal tough love is the type policy you're going to need to enforce. There are some great stories in the world of college parenting. And it can be a hard thing to do. *Money* magazine in September 2005 reported on a story about a mother who's son racked up a $380 phone bill one month because he was breaking up with his girlfriend—actually two girlfriends. The mother made him pay the bill, and despite the fact that she sympathized, told him: "Next time, break up after 7:00 P.M."

It's not easy being tough about money, especially if you're fortunate to have enough to do a bit of padding in your bank account. But fiscal tough love says "It's because I love you that I'm not going to put any more money into your account if you overspend!" This should be your mantra throughout the college years.

Credit Card Addiction

According to *Money* magazine in September 2005, 35 percent of students consider themselves to be in debt, and 23 percent of college students owe more than $3,000 on their credit cards. Bob Manning, a professor at Rochester Institute of Technology, is an expert in the use of credit cards and the author of *Credit Card Nation*, which offers a sobering look at the use and abuse of credit cards on campus.

Manning says that there was a time when any child who was under 18 years old needed their parent's approval and signature to get an authorized credit card. In the early 1990s, the credit card companies eliminated this requirement. At the same time, they began to offer higher lines of credit.

The credit card companies see students as low risk and potentially high income customers, says Manning—low risk because the card companies know that parents will bail their kids out if they get into serious debt trouble. Whether it's college students or adults, Manning says the credit card companies are aware of the fact that it's trivially easy for Americans to live beyond their means.

Manning's advice to parents is to take it slow. He recommends starting off with a debit card—at least for the first semester of freshman year—and then moving up to a credit card if it seems appropriate. The debit cards look like a credit card, he says, so the kids won't feel out of sync with their plastic-flashing friends. While they won't build credit using it, they won't damage their credit either, since the money is taken directly from their bank account. He also recommends that rather than one lump sum, you send them money monthly. For more information, see http://www.creditcardnation.com.

Nine Steps Toward More Frugal College Students

1. If you haven't done it since they sat in the shopping cart, take them on a shopping trip to a supermarket. Do a little real world math review by seeing if they're savvy enough to figure out whether 16 oz. at $1.50 is better or worse than 8oz. at 95 cents. Have them create a budget for several meals then do the shopping for them. They'll probably roll their eyes at the thought. But when they're strolling the grocery aisles at school, they'll have some newfound confidence.

2. Teach them to ask for student discounts and frequent stores that offer them. College towns appreciate students' business and many offer student discounts. Students should always carry their School ID and not to be afraid to ask. Plenty of cultural spots (museums, theaters, sports events) and even transportation and travel offer discounted tickets for college students as well. (And if they're using public transportation, make sure they figure out the best deals—single ride versus monthly pass, for example.)

3. Teach them to plan ahead: The supermarket or warehouse store is typically cheaper than the local deli for snack foods. Try to get them to buy in bulk when they can and then ration. Encourage them to shop with friends when stores are offering two-for-one type sales or bulk purchases.

4. Talk about how you'll deal with service items like haircuts and whether you are going to pay or it's up to them. Most kids wait until they come home on break, but they may find a budding stylist on campus.

5. If they have it in their area, consider using www.craigslist.com to buy items and services. Whether they need a pair of skis, a chemistry tutor, or someone to help haul their sofa home from the Salvation Army, this is

the place. If you're not in a booming Craigslist metropolis, eBay works for good deals on certain items as well.

6. Watch photocopying, laser printing, and late charges at the library. You wouldn't think kids could go over budget in the library, but they manage.

7. If they like late night snacks, it's cheaper to keep bread and cold cuts in the dorm than to run out to a fast food joint or buy a ready-made deli sandwich.

8. If they get textbook lists early enough, they'll have time to check the prices online on sites such as www.Half.com. If they're lucky enough to find the books they need, they'll likely pay a fraction of what they'd pay in the campus bookstore.

9. Encourage them to find friends who also need to be frugal. It's more fun to see how little you can spend on a Friday night and still have a good time when you have a few pals who are on the same mission.

SPECIAL SECTION: KIDS & EARNING MONEY

FACT: Working Girls

When *The Chronicle of Higher Education* surveyed the incoming class of 2004–2005 they found that more than half of the women thought there was a very good chance that they'd have to get a job during college while only 40 percent of guys shared the sentiment.

Parents are perennially torn between wanting their children to earn a portion of their own money to pay for school and the gift of giving them four years of uninterrupted study. Sometimes having a job while going to school is an absolute necessity; other times it's an option that becomes the subject for debate.

Having a job during school undoubtedly gives kids a chance to learn to budget their time, earn their own spending money, and possibly get some real world experience.

Some things to consider are...

- The advantages and disadvantages of students who work part-time
- Working on campus vs. off campus
- Picking a summer job that makes sense
- The ramifications of earning money as a student
- What it takes to be an entrepreneurial student

DOES MY STUDENT HAVE ENOUGH TIME TO HAVE A JOB DURING THE SEMESTER?

The transition from high school to college leaves a lot of discretionary time for most students. At Susquehanna College, Helen Nunn, Director of Financial Aid, did a little math for us to point out that "Students who are used to attending classes for six or seven hours each day in high school

> **TIP:** Work Study
>
> Most campuses in the U.S. support special initiatives for Federal Work Study students (FWS). Some of these initiatives include off-campus programs. Typically these are programs that are focused on community service, tutoring, or helping community service agencies. Often students who are part of off-campus work study programs work in teams—for instance teams of tutors that travel to schools or after-school program sites together by bus or the school may provide a van. This is a special case of a work study program and Katherine Stahl, Executive Director of American University's Career Center, suggests looking into the availability of programs like this at your child's school.

(30 to 35 hours/week), find that now they're only obligated to be present in class, on average, from 16 to 20 hours per week (not including labs or music lessons). In addition to early morning hours, evening, and weekend hours, this leaves another 10 to 20 hours just during the workday. For most students, time management becomes critical to academic success and fitting a part-time job into the student's scheduled contributes to a good outcome. Who hasn't heard about students who nap or who become engrossed in video games or soap operas instead of using their time productively?"

Time management is critical to academic success, agrees Kurt Holmes, the Dean of Students at the College of Wooster. "On average, students do better in college when they are engaged in campus life and busy. One of the best ways to accomplish both goals is a campus job."

Is It Okay to Work During Freshman Year?

If at all possible, freshmen should delay working until they assess their academic workloads. Freshmen have not yet established how much time studying for college classes actually takes. That's why Katherine Stahl, the Executive Director of American University's Career Center cautions that first-year college students find that the demands of fewer classes per week but more assigned reading, research, and papers are difficult to manage. "Freshmen," she feels, "may need a term or even a year under their belt before they feel they understand these demands."

Bob Kent, Director of the Career Services Center at West Virginia University also interjects a cautionary note for first-year students." Juggling classes, a part-time job, and other activities can be a challenge," he says. Even if a job seems like a good idea for your child, you might consider having them wait until sophomore year, when he's learned how to tackle college life a little better. Kent suggests that "If the student needs financial help, exploring scholarship and internship possibilities may be the way to go."

SHOULD A STUDENT WORK ON CAMPUS OR OFF CAMPUS?

Not everyone is eligible for an on-campus job, but if your child can get one, she should take it. She might make more money off campus, but Marlboro College's Elena Sharnoff, Public Affairs Officer, and Nancy Pike, Dean of Students, say that "A job on campus is a good way for the student to get to know the college community and to get plugged into college resources. Plus, on-campus job supervisors are often aware of and sympathetic to student schedules—especially around exam times."

Kent Holmes from The College of Wooster points out that the extra money is a fringe benefit of the job; the real benefit is that you will meet staff who can be great resources and role models. He offers this checklist to help determine work/study priorities:

- How badly does the student need money?

- How many hours a week will she work?

- Does your student thrive on having a well-planned day, or would she be overwhelmed by an extra commitment?

- How tempted would the student be to concentrate more on work and less on school?

FACT: Hours Spent Studying

Lynda J. O'Malley, Dean of Students at Hofstra University, says that for each hour spent in the classroom, three hours should be devoted to studying outside of the classroom. With that logic, it's probably reasonable to work no more than 8 to 15 hours per week depending on the student's workload and his time-management skills. She also notes that having a job gives a student structure to their schedule, a chance to meet more people, and a resume booster, in addition to the extra cash. For students who have a proven track record of balancing multiple commitments, a part-time job can be a good idea on many levels.

Another thing to consider is whether he has held a job before. Prior job experience would at least mean that he or she has an idea of what to expect by taking one on.

At Randolph-Macon Woman's College, Connie Gores, Vice President for Enrollment, points to research that shows that students who work on campus—but no more than an average of 12 hours per week—are usually more successful academically than students who work off campus and those who work more than 12 hours per week. "On-campus, students manage their time better and know whom to go to when they need assistance," she says.

TIP: There are plenty of less time-consuming jobs that let kids pick up a bit of extra cash when they need it.

Take surveys online: Websites like www.pointsincase.com and www.studentcenter.org recruit college-aged panelists for participating in surveys. Sometimes they receive cash for participating and sometimes they receive merchandize. Other companies like www.paid-online-surveys.com and www.surveyscout.com recruit from a wider audience including college students and will pay, on average, $25 to $50 a survey, but charge you $35 to join their survey pool. If you join a survey group, do not expect to get rich quick. My experience is that the surveys offered for your participation are never offered as plentifully as they initially claim, but you can make some pocket money. If you join a survey group, make sure that you do it by creating a separate e-mail account on Hotmail, Gmail, Yahoo! or any other free service so that you don't compromise your main e-mail address. You should also read the privacy section of their online terms carefully and make certain their names will not be passed around to countless others.

Look for piece work: Schools often hire students just for special events like graduation, theatrical performances, or campus-wide theme days. Check with the Career Office or the part of the administration that handles events.

Cater: If students are willing to work weekends then catering halls in the area are usually happy to hire for their larger events.

Getting a job on campus usually requires applying for a work-study or merit scholarship and filling out the FAFSA form. If that precludes your student you'll need to consider off campus employment, but a visit to the Career Office to discuss the possibilities of both is always a good idea.

WHAT IF SHE GETS AN OFF-CAMPUS JOB?

Every college kid who works wants their job to sound as cool as possible. Ads looking for waitresses at a hot new restaurant, bartenders who can potentially make hundreds a night, or someone to take the night shift answering phones at a local radio station often sound more appealing than afternoons spent reshelving biology tomes in the dusty stacks of the school's library. But when a student's grades start to plummet because she can't stay awake in class, that off-campus "golden opportunity" might quickly start to lose its luster and shine.

TIP: Enjoyable Jobs

Students with a specific passion or talent might want to look at jobs off campus that better match their interests and abilities. Having a high-tech skill like Web design makes it feasible to find clients and do freelance work. If a student is an avid ice-skater, a job teaching at a rink makes sense. Ditto for the music major who plays at weddings, or the history buff who doubles as a local tour guide. Students should consider using the local newspapers or the Internet to advertise their services, or going to the local Craigslist website to advertise or find jobs.

From a kid's point of view, working off campus is seductive. The jobs they can find around town typically pay more than campus jobs and it gives them a chance to get away from campus and see "real people."

The negatives can be considerable, however. They need to find a means of transportation from campus to the job and back again. Then they need to factor the hours spent commuting into the equation, as well. Off-campus employers may have little sympathy for exam week, other academic concerns, or even the need to go home for holiday breaks. Plus, the jobs typically involve more menial labor, which doesn't look as good on a resume.

Of course, there are exceptions. For example, "Students who have positions at home with nationally recognized stores and restaurants may be able to explore transferring their position to another location close to campus," says Lynda J. O'Malley, Associate Dean of Students at Hofstra University.

American University's Katherine Stahl says that "off-campus jobs become far more interesting and accessible to second-year and older students who already have some work experience and wish to build their resume with work that more closely aligns with their academic studies. These jobs or internships are more easily accessible in urban areas, but are increasingly facilitated by colleges across the country.

WHERE SHOULD STUDENTS GO IF THEY'RE INTERESTED IN FINDING A JOB?

Visit the Career Services Center on campus, suggests Bob Kent, Director of the Career Services Center at West Virginia University. "The staff can offer valuable tips and strategies for landing that first part-time job" as they often have both on- and off-campus job listings. Check bulletin boards on campus, too—local businesses often post jobs on these boards. If students become friendly with their advisor or professors, it never hurts for students to mention that they're looking and what they're looking for.

WHAT IF MY CHILD WANTS TO START A BUSINESS?

Students today have grown up much more cognizant of the business world than their predecessors. Stories of students who have become on-campus entrepreneurs are increasingly common. Many have heard about the two young Harvard students who started www.thefacebook.com, a website that lets students socialize and share personal information. Michael Dell, another college dorm startup, is the founder of Dell Computers, one of the largest computer manufacturers. He began his computer fiefdom in his college dorm by assembling and selling his computers to classmates, and has become one of the worlds' most powerful businessmen. Student-run businesses go beyond high-tech services and have ranged from successful moving companies to helping other students file their tax returns. Students have become tailors, cooks, cleaners, hairstylists, tutors, T-shirt designers, personal trainers, website designers, and more.

Some colleges do everything they can to foster this entrepreneurial environment; others prefer that their students to stick to their studies. At Babson College, the Center for Entrepreneurship provides a natural way for students to create and implement businesses while at school. In part their success is based on an interdisciplinary approach that introduces students to entrepreneurship. At Clark University, on the other hand, administrators feel that "a student business really requires a full-time commitment, and students can rarely afford to do this without sacrificing their academics. We have seen some get a good start, but then falter either because of time commitment, the fluidity of student workers, or burn-out."

"Many residential campuses discourage or prohibit student-run, on-campus businesses" say administrators at Hendrix College, "because residence halls are not designed to accommodate a business. Rooms are typically small and storage space is limited. In addition, access to the residence halls is restricted to occupants and accompanied guests. Increased traffic into and out of the hall would generate noise and security concerns."

Many students, driven by an entrepreneurial spirit and an unwavering need for cash, simply run campus businesses that fly under the administration's radar. When Worcester Polytechnic Institute was launching an organization for students interested in entrepreneurship a few years ago, they asked the 50-plus students who showed up to the first meeting if any of them already had a business. "To our surprise," the school reports, "over 30 raised their hands." The school's Collaborative for Entrepreneurship & Innovation at WPI offers programs to help students with their business problems and issues. "Running a business while in college requires the same level of organization and dedication as any other activity in which a student becomes immersed—whether it is sports, theater, student government, or working for someone else," WPI's administrators say. "Is it easy? No. Is it done? Yes, everyday."

The chances of your child becoming the next Michael Dell may be slim, but if his grades don't suffer, he's got the right to try.

Budding Entrepreneurs

At Worcester Polytechnic Institute, Stephen Marcus began a business to build cell phone towers as part of an entrepreneurship course at school. As the business grew, his company invested in other WPI students and is now a successful two-way communications company managing million-dollar projects. Another fine example is Eric Tapley, who began a Web design company in his junior year at WPI. Four years later, he has 65 clients and 5 employees.

At the University of Tulsa you'll find one student who's in popular demand when he moonlights as a disc jockey at campus parties, another who sells real estate, and a junior with a successful consulting and risk analysis firm.

Ohio Northern University makes student-run businesses an integral part of the school experience. Students are in charge of running the athletic concessions for sporting events. As another example, the school began a student investment group back in 1989 with a $35,000 scholarship endowment from the Robert E. Hillier Family Charitable Trust. The scholarship was created for the specific purpose of allowing Ohio Northern business students the experience of investing. As of January 1995, that portfolio was valued at $102,412.

Should My Child Work a Summer Job for the Experience or for the Cash?

It's the old question of balance. If your child can make $2,000 to $2,500 a year, she can cover a good part of her school expenses beyond room and board. This will—ideally!—give her an adult-in-training sense of responsibility and accomplishment. Hopefully, it will be harder for her to let those dollars go once she's at school, remembering how hard she worked for them all summer. On the other hand, if she is selected to intern in the senate for the summer or on the set of a documentary film in Central America, she may want to skip the paid job. Money can pay for a great many things, but it can't buy experience. The people students meet and the things they do in "jobs" like these will pay off in the long run, both on the resume and in character enrichment.

If she plans to rake in a paycheck during those summer months, though, get them thinking about summer jobs when they're home on winter break. Seriously! The best jobs are often gone by February.

What Are the Tax Ramifications for Working College Students?

Most kids will pay taxes through their employer and get a refund at the end of the year because they earn so little. But, just like their parents, students can be penalized for making too much money. Once you've established financial aid at school, you must reapply each year by refiling your FAFSA (www.FAFSA.org). If you work and earn money over the summer you must enter that amount into your new FAFSA filing. It is possible that, by having a summer job that pays well, your student may alter your expected family contribution (EFC) equation and will be offered less scholarship money than had he not worked. The Federal Student Aid Hotline won't shed much light on the implications of a working student; they just say it will affect the overall formula just like other changes in your financial situation effect the overall formula. If you suspect your child might be in this category, you should check with your accountant or a college financial counselor who could best anticipate the effects of your student's salary on your overall contribution. Perhaps your child might consider volunteer work or unpaid internships instead. These are often prestigious and look great on resumes even if there is no cash remuneration.

CHAPTER 8

Gearing Up for School

Freshmen parking? Straight ahead.

As American consumers, "We are our stuff." Stuff defines us. Nowhere is this more true than on the college campus. What a student brings to college says a lot about who they are. It also says a lot about a person's ability to think ahead and be prepared, or about their desire to surround themselves with a pile of things they may never use simply because they feel better for having them around.

Packing for college is not like packing for vacation. The campus is where your child will be living and studying, year after year, for about seven months at a stretch. They'll need clothing and gear for every season, occasion, and weather. They'll need cleaning, office, and beauty supplies and lots of plastic containers to hold things. They'll need a boatload of electronics with a lock or two to keep it all safe. For many kids, college is the first opportunity they've had to exhibit their own sense of style and design, especially if they've had to share a bedroom at home. It's also the first time that many of them will have to take care of and keep track of everything they have to their name—and replace it (once they realize it's missing) in the case that they don't.

It's an endearing time to be a parent—watching as they find ways to put their imprimatur on the dorm's rather impersonal spaces and hearing about the experiences of learning to do a load of laundry that doesn't leave them dressed in pink. Visiting them will be like harking back to those first back-to-school nights in elementary school where their drawings hung on the bulletin told you a bit about the sense of art and life they were cultivating very well without you. Sure, they'll lose things and destroy things, but they'll learn as they do so. From the computers to the wall posters, they will be their own installers and interior designers.

While their gear and their spaces reflect their distinct personalities, they also reflect a common set of stuff. You've seen it in the malls and in the miles of aisles at Wal-Mart: The posters, the magnetic wipe-off boards, the extra-long flannel sheets, the tacky gobs of blue goo to secure those posters to the wall, the bathroom buckets, and the batik-print bedspreads—these are, more or less, the makings of a dorm starter kit. The

"Back to School" sales may be nothing more than a manufacturer-created season aimed at making you buy all sorts of things you never thought you needed. But your student does need some of them and part of your job will be to distinguish the needs from the wants.

Entire books have been written on how to pack for college, but we'll provide a quick recap along with tackling some of the issues that kids face during their years on campus.

In this chapter you'll learn:

- About the basic essentials for dorm living
- What high-tech equipment your child really needs
- How to prepare him for self-sufficient laundry duty
- Decorating tips on the cheap
- What your responsibilities are for dorm property
- The do's and don'ts of cooking in the dorm

How Do I Know Whether My Child Is Packing Too Much?

You know she's packing too much when you have to rent a U-Haul to get your child to and from college each semester. In most cases, that is totally unnecessary and she should think about scaling back. College students fall into three general categories when it comes to packing, and their packing personalities are often inherited from you-know-who:

Type I: The Monk who packs as if he's heading into a monastery. He plans to—and will if you let him—wear the same pair of pants and one of three shirts for the next four years at school.

Type II: The Practical Researcher who brings a reasonable amount of stuff, balancing her load with a few frivolities thrown into a mostly functional list of items.

Type III: The Pack Rat who can't bear to part with any possession he has ever owned and now feels a need to drag it all down to school with him, where he will accumulate even more stuff and insist on bringing back an even bigger load of stuff by the year's end.

Nowhere is it written that students entering the dorm must carry only new items, of course. But many students do just that, as if they're shedding their old lives and taking on a new one that was purchased at a string of August "Off to College" sales. Set a budget with your child and draw some lines (and lists) about what they can take from around the house and make do with and what you're going to need to buy. There are at least few key items that might be worth investing in that because they'll be using throughout the next four years. Here are just a few examples of where it may pay to spend:

A sturdy trunk for storage: Put a nice runner on top of the trunk and it doubles as a low end table while storing bulky items or off-season clothing.

A small form factor music system: He may have a gigantic wall of sound for his stereo system, but at college, space is at a premium. While not absolutely mandatory for basic human functioning, every kid loves having her own music collection and a good way to listen to it. As she packs for school, this might just be a good time to junk the childhood stereo system with the tall-as-you speakers. An Apple iPod or other MP3 player along with a docking station (see the Altec Lansing IM3) make great dorm systems. Many kids who have good speakers on their PCs will simply use their computer, doing double duty with it as their stereo. If you had already planned on getting her a new computer, think about getting one with nice speakers and a DVD player so she can watch movies and listen to music. Some of the new PCs even come with television tuners built in.

A nice rug: With a few exceptions, the majority of dorm rooms still have sweepable, but really cold, harsh floors. A rug can be used again and again and it'll do wonders towards warming up the dorm. Choose rugs that can be swept clean and easily carted outside for a good beating. Stay away from shag and light colors and they should be fine.

Any Suggestions for the Best Way to Decide What to Bring? What about for Moving It to and from School?

Here's advice from administrators at schools across the country who, in terms of packing, have literally seen it all...

Balance Sentimentalism

Moving is always stressful, and trying to decide what to leave and what to take can be heartbreaking for an already emotional soon-to-be college freshman. Lots of nervous students want to hold onto as many of the comforts of home as will fit in the car. However, it is always best to pack light! Remind your students that their knick-knacks will all be waiting for them when they come home over the holidays and summer break.

—Pitzer College

Edit that Wardrobe

Have your son go through his closet and assess what he actually likes to wear and what's just chilling out on a hanger because he's been too lazy to get rid of it. Once he has cleaned out his closet, then he can start thinking about packing for school, taking into account any climate changes. If your child is moving from Maine to Southern California, he can probably skip the down jacket and sherpa-lined boots. On the other hand, if he is moving from California to Maine, you might have a hard time trying to find the kind of winter gear he will need at a store near you. Consider buying those things at a store near school, or online—where most things a student will need can be purchased from any state at any time of year and shipped right to their new address.

—Pitzer College

Think about Future Activities

If she wants to join an outdoor activities club or a dance team, she should bring along those hiking boots or flamenco skirt. (If not, leave them home.) Thinking about these things before she leaves is exciting for the student and helps her to be more practical as well. Encourage your child to surf their future alma mater's website and publications and research what activities are available around campus so she can pack accordingly.

—Pitzer College

Consider School Location

Other items to consider are furniture and bedding. This will vary from school to school. Some of the dorms do not have air conditioning, so a small room fan is recommended. However, these items can be easily bought at the local Target or Ikea. Other items that you can buy after you arrive at the college are bedding, desk lamps, and laundry hampers and detergent, provided you leave yourself the time to do it. Your student will usually have at least a couple of days to settle in before classes start anyway. If you feel like that's too last-minute, plan to arrive one day ahead of the scheduled first day. Though you won't be able to get into the dorm before it's opened, you will be able to do some local shopping that's more leisurely.

—Pitzer College

Plan for Summer Storage

You might want to look into a local storage place, where your student can store all of those college-specific items that you'd prefer not come home for the summer. They can even share the cost of storage with their roommate or friends, as one storage unit will likely accommodate more than just one person's items.

—Pitzer College

Try to find a storage company that will deliver to the following year's residence.

— Syracuse University

Dorm Decorations

There are usually poster and art sales around the first few weeks of school, so your student might want to take advantage of those instead of bringing all of his or her favorite posters from home. Posters are notorious for getting permanently bent or ripped in the moving process. Also, make sure you look into the dorm room policies regarding decorating and room size. You don't want to buy something especially for her wall only to learn it's too big for the wall or won't be able to hang from the cinder-block wall material at school.

—Pitzer College

Wheelie Suitcases

A suitcase with wheels that can expand or shrink by zipping certain compartments is a great option for college packing. If students go home for a long weekend or for spring break, they can make their bag smaller, and then expand it for their return home during the summer.

—Pitzer College

A pop-out wheeled carrier is worth the investment if a student is going to be carrying his bags a quarter of a mile from his parking spot to the fourth floor of his residence hall. And if he is flying off to school, buy a whole set of luggage that stacks on top of the largest case with wheels!

—University of the Pacific

Consolidate

It's key to think creatively about how to keep the number of items your student is traveling with to a minimum. Instead of taking several boxes of keepsakes, photos, and special mementoes think about having your child put together an abbreviated "best of" scrapbook or album of just the favorites to take to college.

—Pitzer College

Identify Your Local Discount Store

Target, K-Mart, Wal-Mart? Remind supporters of your new college student that gift certificates don't take up any room at all. After the clothes are dropped off, take a general survey of the room. Then enjoy the final few hours with your student leisurely picking up what you were worried about forgetting at a local discount store.

—University of the Pacific

Check the Lists and Pack What You Can Carry

The rule of thumb in my house when we traveled was only pack what you are able to carry by yourself! Most students can't imagine parting with any one treasure and the temptation is to bring everything. As the parent, you must assume your role as "the voice of reason." Check websites and resource guides for "what to bring" checklists and, more importantly, suggestions of what not to bring. Some institutions have rules on items including halogen lamps, wattage on the microwave, and full-sized versus residence hall-sized refrigerators. Know before you go.

—Syracuse University

Call the Roommate

Your child should call before school starts to say hello and have a discussion about items each person is bringing in order to maximize the space available in the room and avoid duplication of effort.

Check to see if some of the larger items of interest might be available for rent on campus; i.e. microwave, fridge, or computers. Not only will you save yourself the trouble of moving it to and from school, but it work out to be less expensive.

—Syracuse University

Ship It

Ask your housing office if your college has an agreement with UPS or another company to "ship your stuff" ahead of you. This will alleviate having to travel to campus with all your belongings with you. Wouldn't it be nice if all of your boxes were there awaiting your arrival?

—Syracuse University

The Hand Cart

If you don't ship the items, invest in a small hand cart to bring with you for move-in day. While some schools provide such amenities, you will not have to wait around for one to become available.

—Syracuse University

Plastic Storage

Invest in some plastic storage containers with lids—preferably the size that will slide under your bed and stack easily into the back seat of the car. I recommend the clear containers so you can easily see their contents. They will also come in handy during semester breaks to store the "non-essentials" that are usually placed in your home's basement or garage for safe-keeping.

—Syracuse University

Seasonal Packing

Pack for the season if you have the ability to "reload" during a fall break or a Parents' Weekend visit. For example, if traveling to upstate New York, you probably won't need heavy/wool items until late October.

—Syracuse University

In the "Older Is Better" Category

Not everything needs to brand new and color-coordinated. At the risk of sounding selfish, it's a good time for parents to pawn their rattier towels off on the kids who will lose them anyway. Parents: Buy a new set for yourselves this time!

Here, a list of things that kids enjoy taking from home without buying them new:

- Their favorite pillow
- A few carefully selected items like posters and photos
- Towels—a few washcloths, hand towels, and large bath towels (The bath towels are the one area you might want to splurge and make them

big and cuddly. When she gets up to shower before an 8:00 A.M. class, at least she'll be using a nice big towel at the crack of dawn.)

On the Desktop

Remember desk blotters? They're out. . . . The PC takes main stage on the desk these days with the printer—if he has one—often placed on a book shelf above the computer. But do get a pencil holder (though it's likely the pencils may never find their home), highlighting markers, a calendar (even if he has one on the computer, a wall calendar is an "in your face" reminder of due dates), a stapler and staples, paper clips, and folders, folders, folders! If you can get your student to learn to file their papers in folders by course, they'll have a decided advantage.

WHAT'S THE ONE THING FAMILIES FORGET TO BRING?

The Residence Life staff at University of Puget Sound points out that often what parents and students forget to bring are the intangibles:

Personal responsibility: This is not camp (or home) where others will pick up after your child and fix all of his mistakes.

Ability to budget: That includes time and money. Too many students have had their lives programmed and organized for them and don't have the skills or experience to do it themselves.

Ability to amicably share a room with another person: Too few of kids heading to college have ever shared a room and have a tough time suddenly negotiating space, time, and respecting boundaries with a roommate.

Sentimentality: In the rush to get away from family, students forget to bring framed pictures of their loved ones. She should pack the scrapbook and bring some extra blank pages.

As for the tangibles, Puget Sound mentions...

Vintage things: Amidst all their chasing after the latest trends, students should remember to stick with what they know and bring the old comfortable stuff: old work boots, a favorite sweatshirt and your mom's old afghan.

Health records: For many students, college is the first time they have to be their own health advocates and many don't have the knowledge, experience, or skill to do that well. Bring medical IDs, insurance numbers, and records of the student's heath history. Marlboro College's Elena Sharnoff, Public Affairs Officer and Nancy Pike, Dean of Students also suggest packing important documents like a copy of the student's birth certificate and his eye glasses prescription.

Geeky things: Students shouldn't try to hide or reinvent themselves the first weeks of school: Haul all those Dungeons and Dragons books with you. RPG's (role playing games) are a great way to break the monotonous reality of college social life.

As for the dorm room essentials, Marlboro College says families often forget pillows, lamps, light bulbs, a hammer, dishes, eating utensils and drinking glasses. The College of Charleston adds cleaning supplies, surge protectors/power strips, and computer cables to the list. Xavier University says families forget to bring extension cords, and Hofstra University's Associate Dean of Students Lynda J. O'Malley, mentions a caddy for all their bathroom supplies and a pair of flip-flops for walking back and forth between their bathroom and their residence hall room. For move-in days, West Virginia's parent advocate, Susan Lantz, says it's helpful to remember a dolly, rain wear, patience, and a sense of humor.

TIP: A Parent-to-Parent List of Forgotten Essentials

Battery charger and rechargeable batteries: The number of battery-powered items in a dorm room is staggering!

Cork board or bulletin board and a calendar for room: It may sound old fashioned, but having things hung up in front of his nose and being able to see a month at a time for deadlines is superior to computer-based calendars that tend to give you a birds' eye view of what's due when. (While PC calendars can show you a month or so at a time, in those larger views they tend to just indicate that "something's going on" but not what it is.)

Extra ink cartridges and printer paper: If your family has a printer you know that the more you buy, the cheaper it gets. Keep spare ink cartridges and paper around so your child won't be begging for a sheet of printer paper from a dorm-mate in the middle of the night; if ink cartridges run out they usually do it after the bookstore is closed for the day.

Flip-flops: Must-have item for the shower. These might feel squishy and strange but it beats the old "fungus among us" line.

Good reading lamp (or a book light for the bed): Roommates will appreciate it if your child avoid using the overhead light while they're trying to sleep.

Label all power cords and chargers: The computer, the iPod, the digital camera…each has its own set of accompanying cords. Taking a few minutes to put a tape label on these with your child's name and which device the cord belongs with is an investment against future headaches.

Laundry bag: One of the best laundry bags is a collapsible mesh bag that has wire stays in it. You can fold it flat to store it, but it pops open to a stand-up bag. It's the only chance for getting the clothes somewhat wrinkle free.

Mesh sock bag: By putting socks in a mesh bag and laundering them all together means less chance of the classic sock disappearing act. (Now they just need to hang onto that bag!)

Milk crates: Milk crates are the LEGOs of dorm room decor. Stack them, fill them, and they serve as bookshelves, storage, tables and more.

Shoe rack: Unless they are doing field work in dust balls, a shoe rack is recommended to keep the floor of the closet much cleaner and tidier.

Specialized hangers: In addition to basic hangers, bring along ones made just for pants, skirt, and hanging multiple items.

Stamps, envelopes, and stationery: Even if they don't get used very often, you're doubling the odds that you might get at least one letter in the four years she's gone.

Two weeks worth of underwear: They can skimp on other things but they need enough underwear to get them from one laundry day until the next. If not there's the risk that they'll stop wearing them, start recycling them or wear them inside out. College students are notorious for cutting corners!

A welcome mat: Helps keep the mud and dirt outside the room.

A working camera: Did you ever notice that practically no one has pictures of their years at college? Giving your kids a camera significantly ups the chances you'll get to see more of their four years at school and they'll have memories they can literally hold onto.

Write-on-wipe-off board to hang on door: These never go out of fashion and are always well used.

WHAT'S THE ONE THING MOST STUDENTS BRING BUT NEVER END UP USING?

The flip side of forgetting something is bringing everything your child owns, just in case he might ever need it. David Satterlee, Director of First-Year Programs at Susquehanna University, says clothes are the biggest offenders in the "excessive category." "They'll probably bring twice as many clothes as they need, and end up fighting with roommates over storage. Very quickly students find themselves wearing the same favorite pieces of clothing over and over again," says Satterlee. "Dress-up clothes are seldom used. Students will fill a closet with fancy things and then forget to bring raingear. Sooner or later, students will need to walk across campus in a downpour and they'll need either a large umbrella or a good raincoat. A long class can seem even longer when you are sitting in wet clothes."

At Tulane University, Cynthia Cherrey, Vice President of Student Affairs, conducted a small survey and confirmed that clothing was number one on the list of unused things, but number two (no surprise here) was an iron. At Saint Anslem College students said they never ended up using those emergency phone numbers they were made to bring, but since they take up very little room it's probably worth bringing them. And Swarthmore College suggested a moratorium on knick-knacks, stuffed animals, books, photos, and CDs saying that in moderation they were fine, but that many of these simply take up space.

> **TIP:** A Dorm-Room Toolbox
>
> If you want your child to be instantly valued in the dorm hierarchy, send her to school with a toolbox. Include a hammer and nails, a tape measure, screwdriver, gaffer tape, sticky tack (for hanging things up on walls that won't allow nails), an extension cord, and pliers. You can even add a small level, a wrench, or a glue gun. It makes a great going away gift for any college-bound student.

The Combined Wisdom of Many Parents Packing List

Some advice on what to bring from a parents survey done at Centre College (http://web.centre.edu/parentprograms/advice.htm from the parent's portion of their website).

FOR THE ROOM

A rug

A three-tiered plastic "cabinet" to hold things

Under-the-bed plastic storage boxes, stackable crates

Extra-long bedding

Other bedding: blankets, bed-spread, etc.

Reading light

Laundry bag

Basket/bucket for the bathroom

Towels

Shoes for the shower

Extra hangers and over-the-door hanger

Something to put computer or sound system on

Safe or lock box

Small fan

Mirrors

Portable seating—like a bean-bag chair

Pictures of siblings/pets

A "desk box" (stapler, hole punch, tape, scissors, ruler, white-out, sharpies)

GENERAL ROOM SUPPLIES

Laundry supplies

Small flashlight

Hot/cold packs

Thermometer

Basic first aid and over-the-counter medications

All kinds of tape (including duct tape and "sticky tack")

Large and small 3M Command adhesive squares

3M Command adhesive strips

3M Command adhesive hooks

All sizes screwdrivers, hammer (these can be checked out for quick use at the parent info tents during freshman move-in)

Paper towels, general cleaner, dust cloth or rags for cleaning the room during the year

Electronics and appliances

Computer (some parents specified a laptop)

Internet connection hardware

Network card for your computer

Telephone

Phone and answering machine

Cell phone

CD/DVD player

Power strip

Extension cords

Surge protector

Extra-long phone cord/computer line

Headphones

Small refrigerator

Microwave

MISCELLANEOUS

An umbrella

Quarters in rolls! It's a laundry thing, unless your school has gone electronic.

A sense of adventure and humor

Money for Wal-Mart [or other chain discount store]

Directions to Ace Hardware/Wal-Mart

A fall jacket if it gets cool before Family Weekend!

PLEASE KEEP IN MIND THAT CENTRE COLLEGE [LIKE MANY COLLEGES] PROHIBITS BRINGING:

Candles

Frying pans

Hot plates

George Foreman grills

Halogen lamps

Toaster ovens

Waffle irons

Portable heaters

Ceiling fans

How Can I Get Everything to School if He's Flying?

If your child is flying to school, plan ahead and ship a box or two to the dorm. Check with the college to make sure you've got the right mailing address for packages, and find out the earliest date the school can receive them. Will there be someone to sign for packages on the student's behalf before they arrive? Where should he pick them up once he does?

Boxes are charged by weight so you might consider carrying the stereo on the plane and shipping the clothes! With UPS, FedEx, and other services you should be fine if you mail things one week before your student is expected to arrive. That gives you some padding without the boxes hanging around on campus for too long. Get the tracking number and purchase insurance just in case.

If you're sending a box of books, CDs, DVDs, and the like, look into sending it "Media Mail" through the U.S. Postal Service. It takes longer— sometimes around ten days—but the rates are very reasonable, even for heavy boxes.

Seasonal clothing

There's your comfort zone and then there's your climate zone. If you live in a warm climate but your child is going to school in a cold one, the best way to get the more severe weather-ware is to go to a store near campus, or shop at online stores and have them delivered right to school. Here are several good options:

www.REI.com

www.EMS.com

www.LLBean.com

www.LandsEnd.com

www.SierraTradingPost.com (closeouts and bargains)

What Are Some Good Places to Shop for College Stuff?

Stores like Bed, Bath & Beyond make it easy to shop for school—and just as easy to go overboard on college shopping. They supply college check-off lists and offer things like "bedding in a bag" with nifty names like "Joe College" along with coordinated room schemes and all the furniture and accessories to go with. Most every college in the country will have a Target, Kmart, or Wal-Mart nearby. (In small towns where there's a lack of things to do, students treat visits to these stores as a highlight activity.)

> **TIP:** The Indelible Pen
>
> They may be too old to be sewing labels in their clothing, but labeling a few special items with indelible ink is always a good idea.

Shopping for college gear is easy online, too: www.CollegeGear.com is an online bookstore, athletic store, and school merchandizing store. Enter the name of your school and you'll find things you didn't even know existed like the collegiate bird house, golf balls, and more. Hard to find T-shirts and athletic gear are all here, including Greek wear. For travel, entertainment, and special deals just for students check out www.studentadvantage.com.

> **TIP:** Products that Go a Long Way
>
> **Electric pencil sharper:** An essential for math majors but helpful for all who write or sketch freehand
>
> **Gaffer or duct tape:** One of the best multipurpose tapes for heavy duty as well as light projects
>
> **Room freshener:** A little spray goes a long way in the dorms
>
> **Small sewing kit:** They will have to learn how to use a needle and thread once enough buttons fall off or pants need mending.
>
> **Super glue:** Can fix just about anything

> **TIP:** Comparative Shopping on the Web
>
> Use comparative shopping sites like www.shopzilla.com or www.price-grabbber.com for looking at the best price across a number of stores. Make sure you factor shipping and handling into the final prices. The surplus site www.overstock.com stocks housewares, books, music, and sporting goods and often offers $1 shipping. That can make for a substantial savings when you're buying something big, heavy, or expensive.

How Can I Save Money Buying Books?

Books and supplies are fairly constant costs, and they're not inexpensive. You should expect to spend around $400 to $600 each semester on books, and if your child chooses to study the sciences or another specialized field, you'll spend even more. Some colleges can give you a school-specific textbook costs estimate. Students at schools on a quarter system need to buy books three times a year instead of just two, for example. But there are ways to save.

"Most universities make every effort to procure a large percentage of used textbooks, as well as a good quantity of new textbooks," says Donald "Buz" Moser, Director of University Stores at Wake Forest University. "However, used textbooks are always in high demand across the country, so there is not an unlimited quantity." Some students actually prefer new textbooks, but if you're buying used, buy early. You should be able to find one in decent condition at the beginning of the book-buying rush. Also know that in some cases, courses require recently published textbooks that are only available new.

As an additional cost savings, most campus bookstores will buy back your child's used textbooks (which they then resell). He will make back only a fraction of what these books cost new so he shouldn't expect much income from this (though every little bit helps, right?). Some students want to keep the books they buy in their major subject area since knowledge tends to be cumulative and they'll use old books as reference. It will depend on the student, his major, and the book. You know that the instant he sells a book is the instant he'll need it, of course!

Colleen Rich who works in the public relations at George Mason University says she and her college-aged son save money by shopping online for his textbooks. On www.half.com she and her son were able to replace a pricey Spanish book he lost for $20. In the bookstore the same book bundled with workbooks sold for $110.

The problem with buying used books is that you need to be an early bird. You'll need to get the book list for the courses you're taking early enough to order and have the books delivered in time for class. Sometimes this just isn't possible. In addition to www.half.com, which specializes in used books, www.barnesandnoble.com and www.amazon.com have large textbook selections for both new and used books. Another popular online bookstore is www.varsitybooks.com. Make sure you check out what they charge to ship them, as that can add to the costs and chip away at the savings.

Administrators at Baylor University recommend that students shop all of the area bookstores to compare prices and that they go to class before purchasing their books. "Professors may indicate a book is not going to be used after all, that a book is recommended but not required, or that a book will be used late in the semester—enabling them to postpone some of their purchases and ease the crunch at the beginning of the semester."

Both students and professors have gotten creative to try other ways of reducing textbook bills as well. Some professors go so far as to write their own books and have them bound at a copy place. Students then are simply instructed to purchase one of these books from the copy store—at a price much lower than that of a traditional textbook. Some students have tried sharing a textbook, which rarely works for obvious reasons—though occasionally it's a make-due arrangement. Others have attempted to borrow the book from the library. This plan is usually foiled by limited copies of one title, due dates, and late fees.

Is There a Limit to the Number of Outlet Extenders That Should Be Added to a Room?

Hendrix College says that sometimes the number of extenders permitted varies with the age and type of the construction in the dorm. Macalester College, like most others, limits students to one outlet extender per student.

Mark Light, Director of Facilities and Technology at Ohio Northern University, says that the concern is not only the number of extenders but how safely they are used. "The key is to NOT plug them in end-to-end, NOT to drape them across the room, and NOT to hide them under rugs."

Where Can We Store Her Belongings During the Summer and on Breaks?

Wheaton College feels your pain. Gail Berson, Dean of Admission and Student Aid, says, "You've barely moved your student onto campus when it's time to pack up for the long holiday break or summer vacation! What barely fit in the car on move-in day now has multiplied."

What to do? Wheaton suggests that you check your Parent Handbook to see if storage is available through the college. If not, find a storage company near the campus that will store the goods securely. Often, these companies will provide the person-power to do the actual packing too. (Don't forget about the option of her sharing that space with a friend.)

Last resort? Make the trek to campus yourself, enlist the help of your child and a few able-bodied friends, and jam it all back into the minivan. Again.

> **TIP:** Hug a Janitor Today
>
> When it comes to moving furniture or a quick-fix if you have the right tool, there's always the school's maintenance staff. While they're technically not supposed to do individual "favors," it's always a good idea to make friends with the campus staff.

"Your proximity to the school makes a difference," says Bernard Chirico, PhD, Vice President for Student Affairs at University of Mary Washington. "If you're within a day or two driving distance, you will probably consider making the drive and taking everything home. If your trip is longer than that, summer storage may be the answer, along with shipping those few things that your student couldn't carry but can't do without."

WHERE CAN I STORE SKIS AND BICYCLES AND OTHER LARGER THINGS DURING THE SEMESTER?

Schools vary in their ability to offer storage for bicycles and skis. Sometimes it's a matter of where the school is located. Those schools located near recreational areas will often make arrangements for storage of everything from kayaks to mountain bikes and snowboards. Once again, it's good to check ahead of time if this is important to you and your child.

DOES MY CHILD NEED HIS OWN COMPUTER?

According to one student at Union College, "You could get by without one, but it would be a royal pain in the butt." Even though it's often not mandatory, most students do have their own computers. Laptops are becoming the preferred choice, especially with the increase of wireless Internet connections on campus. And it's not just for the academics. Ron Herron, Vice President of Student Affairs at Purchase College, says computers play as much a part in campus social life. "Students study, write, create, chat, research, shop—you name it—at all hours of the day and time, not just when computer labs are opened or staffed." He says to consider a computer as one more item in the "cost of education of your child." You should plan to replace it at least once in the four years too, as technology advances rapidly.

That said, it is certainly possible to get by without a computer since, according to Sarah Cardwell, Director of Residential Life at Sarah Lawrence College, most colleges have a sufficient number of computer labs/facilities to accommodate student needs. "It's the convenience factor of being able to work whenever a student wants," she says.

Fairfield University is a good case in point. According to Don Adams, Assistant Vice President of Computing and Network Services, the school provides over 300 computers for its 3,550 students accessible in public labs and common areas. Still, over 90 percent of the freshmen have their own PC or Macintosh. Of those who bring computers, 70 percent bring laptops and the other 30 percent are desktop devices.

Some schools are so pro-computer—with a desire that their professors have the option of developing coursework that involves computers and a desire that their students keep up to date with technology—that they distribute free laptop computers to all of their incoming students. (Or rather, they hide it in the general tuition costs, but in any case...) At these schools, all students then start their college career on equal footing with a brand new, shiny laptop!

SHOULD WE BRING A DESKTOP OR LAPTOP PC TO CAMPUS?

This is a question that has been plaguing parents since notebook (or laptops as many now call them) computers came onto the scene. These days, more and more students are bringing laptop computers because they are so versatile and not as expensive as they once were. Plus, students can pack it up and tote it to study sessions, the library, or a coffee shop where they can work—often with the use of Internet in many of the places they go around campus.

Salisbury University's Jerome Waldron notes that costs have dropped in recent years and the features and capabilities of notebooks easily match the desktop models. The rapid growth of wireless networks on campuses and in communities has made mobile computing more rich and attractive.

TIP: Wireless Mayhem

If the mere mention of the word "wireless" makes your eyes roll back in your head think of it this way: There are four ways the word "wireless" gets used (and abused).

802.11 or WIFI: This type of wireless allows your PC to talk to a wireless router that connects to the Internet via your standard Internet connections (at home this would be your cable modem or DSL; at college or the office it's often a connection via a high speed data line).

Bluetooth: You've probably seen Bluetooth headsets for cell phones—Bluetooth users can keep the phone in their pocket or pocketbook and just wear the headpiece. Bluetooth sets up a wireless personal network which typically operates in a pretty small space. Bluetooth is good for things like moving data from a PDA or Smartphone to your computer.

Infrared: This type of wireless requires line of sight. You actually beam data between two things. Typical infrared wireless devices include a mouse or a joystick.

The cell phone network: Yes it's wireless too, but in a very different way. It relies on cell towers that transmit back and forth to your phone.

And just to complicate things, many devices, especially handheld computers can have Bluetooth, 802.11, and infrared all in the same device.

"One of biggest concerns with laptops, however," says Waldron, "is security." Laptops can easily be stolen, so common sense precautions include lock down pads, cables, and other security devices to make sure the laptop does not wander off. Also make sure your homeowners' policy will cover laptop theft.

If you opt to buy a laptop, it should include the basics: an easy-to-read color screen, a roomy hard disk, a usable keyboard, and WIFI wireless networking. Next, be sure to add other options that you might find included on a traditional desktop computer. For example, a CD burner or combo CD burner/DVD drive which is a great way for students to create everything from back-up copies of their work, to shared class notes, to multimedia projects. Make sure that the laptop has two or three USB ports for peripherals like a printer, a flash drive, or a digital camera. Also, make sure that, in addition to built in WIFI (wireless connectivity), your laptop has a traditional 56k modem for those times you might need to connect to the Internet over a phone line and a network port for hard wired Ethernet connections. Lastly, an extra battery is a good idea to help students through long classes or study sessions, or on days when you don't have time to recharge your battery. Less important, some new laptops might offer Bluetooth connectivity (a way for the computer to "talk" to peripherals like handhelds or printers in what's often called "a personal area network"). Also remember that laptops tend to use touch pads and buttons instead of a mouse for navigating on screen. If your child prefers a mouse you can add an external one, or even a wireless one.

"If the student knows they prefer to work in their own room then they can use a desktop PC which will most likely have a more comfortable keyboard and larger monitor" says College of the Atlantic's Andrew Campbell, PhD, Associate Dean of Student Life. Desktops also make sense if you are price sensitive; typically you can save nearly $500 to $800 that you'd spend on an equivalent laptop. Desktops also make it easier and less expensive to add things to like CD burners or a new flat panel monitor. Finally, students who like to use their computers to watch movies and listen to music prefer desktops because the screen is bigger and the speakers are better quality than with notebooks. They are also less fragile and breakable and don't get lost or stolen nearly as often.

Consider though, that if the school has standardized on Macs you might want to follow suit. Mac schools can make PC user's lives difficult by not having ample PC support. (The same is true for PC schools and Mac users.)

> **TIP:** Flash Drives—For the Ultra-Portable Student
>
> The next best thing to a notebook computer (sometimes better) is a USB flash drive. These devices are about the size of pack of chewing gum with a little connector that slips into a PC's USB port. The computer recognizes them as an external or removable drive. Students can store their work on the USB drive and then take it to class, the library, and home for the weekend to work on it there. Any computer with a USB drive will be able to read the contents.
>
> Another trick many students use is to store their files on the campus server which allows them to access their files from any computer on campus. If they're going away for the weekend, they can learn to access the campus computer remotely or alternatively e-mail their files to their account and pick up their e-mail and their work on another computer.

If you are in the market for a new PC first check with the local bookstore on campus. They often have special deals with the manufacturers, but don't automatically assume that this is the best deal you can get. Shop around. Refurbished PCs that have been returned and made ready for resale can be very good deals, with good guarantees and warranties, and all of the major online outlets have attractive back-to-school pricing.

DO WE NEED TO HAVE WIRELESS COMPUTER EQUIPMENT?

Perhaps the biggest change in on-campus computing in the last few years is the installation of wireless networks. It used to be a big deal that every dorm room had a wired Ethernet connection, but now many campuses are already shedding the wires in favor of wireless network hubs.

Jerome Waldron, CIO at Salisbury University, says that in 2004, according to the research firm, Campus Computing, 77.2 percent of campuses surveyed reported that they have wireless networks in place. The creation of "hot spots" (where students can access a wireless connection to the Internet or e-mail or campus intranet) in libraries, dining facilities, classrooms, coffee shops, and lounges is on the rise. Most laptop computers purchased today come equipped with a 802.11g wireless card already built in, so students can connect as soon as soon as they arrive on campus. If you buy a new notebook make sure that it has wireless capabilities.

Do Schools Provide Computer Software?

Most schools offer students a suite of basic tools for e-mail, Web browsing, and antivirus protection. But, with those exceptions, students are expected to have their own software packages running on their machines. There are student versions of software packages like word processors and spreadsheets available for a fraction of the price the rest of us pay. Some courses require certain software packages in the same way that they require textbooks, but professors will tell students where to get them and what they can expect to pay. Currently, 802.11g is the latest standard on the market, with 802.11n, a tester connection, almost ready to go.

What Happens to Her College E-mail Account Once She Has Graduated?

College students become tremendously spoiled by their high-tech life on campus and the silver spoon is the free broadband connection, the free e-mail address, and the free space to store e-mails and files on the school's servers. But since our modern age makes it almost as difficult to change e-mail addresses as it does physical addresses or phone numbers, you have to be prepared for what happens to that .edu address once your student graduates.

What happens varies from campus to campus. At Baylor University, a student's school-based e-mail account belongs to them for life, according to Lisa Steed, Training and Support Specialist for Information Technology Services at the school. "Once a Baylor Bear, always a Baylor Bear means that recent graduates keep their Exchange e-mail accounts with Web access for approximately one year. After that the mail is moved to a special e-mail server for alums." Their address remains the same; the only thing that changes is how they access that account.

Wake Forest University provides "E-mail-Forwarding-for-Life, but not lifetime e-mail accounts," says Tim Snyder. While not actual e-mail accounts, they will forward e-mails sent to an @alumni.wfu.edu account. Synder says that an alumni account lets alums have an easy address to use for their friends or to include on job applications, etc. As they move through life, and change from one e-mail provider to another, WFU alums can simply log into their account and change the e-mail address to which the school forwards their e-mail. "It also has some vanity appeal, like a vanity license plate," says Synder.

At other colleges, like Stephens College, a student's e-mail account is only active while enrolled at the college. Lou Ann Gilchrist, Dean of Student Affairs at Truman State University, suggests checking with the institution's information technology department. (Not high on the list of priorities for freshman perhaps, but they should check into it before they graduate.)

SHOULD I GIVE HER A TELEVISION TO TAKE WITH HER TO SCHOOL?

To bring a TV or not is a complicated question, agree Jody Terhaar and Jason Laker, Deans of Students at College of Saint Benedict/Saint John's University. "Obviously, we want students to focus on their studies. But, if your son or daughter did well in high school and still kept up with the latest reality show, then the TV might be a fine thing to bring. This is especially true if spending time watching TV has been something that your family does together—it may be a piece of home."

Many schools have public TV-watching areas, and many educators believe this is the best answer. At University of California, Irvine, Leslie Millerd Rogers, Office of the Vice Chancellor Student Affairs, suggests that lounge areas where TV becomes a collective experience lets students "get out, meet new people and use all the areas of student housing."

Consider your child's temperament and study habits as well as the demands of her college courses. It's also important to coordinate with her new roommate, say Terharr and Laker. "Forgetting to do that will probably result in a residence hall room that looks like an appliance store."

WHY DO ALL COLLEGES USE EXTRA-LONG SHEETS ON THE BED?

> **TIP:** Don't Make Unilateral Decisions
>
> Carolyn E. Lloyd, Assistant Director of Residential Life at Bryn Mawr College advises a roommate consultation before tackling a major dorm decorating job. "Many roommate conflicts are created because one roommate makes aesthetic decisions about the room and doesn't involve the others. Remember that shared space should be a place where everyone feels at home."

If you think you're going to strip your child's bed at home and pack the sheets for school, think again. Colleges have standardized on the extra-long sheet, though the reasons are a bit murky. Charles Colby, Assistant Vice President for Enrollment and Student Services Housing at The University of Tulsa, attributes it to a matter of comfort. "In the past, longer bed frames were moved all over campus to accommodate taller students. Because students change rooms frequently, staff had to move beds up and down stairwells sometimes resulting in work-related injuries. Conforming to the longer beds resulted in labor savings and the reduction of those work related injuries. The bonus is that everyone gets to sleep in a longer bed."

Clark University demonstrates a bit more cynicism, admitting that it's a great racket for the bedding companies, since colleges are just about the only place that use these sheets. "But," they add, "the reality is that schools...accommodate tall people." Rippon Collese says, "It's a matter of accommodating everyone from the 6 foot 8 inch basketball player to the 5-foot-tall flutist with the least amount of effort." Some schools have begun offering double-width beds in an effort to lose the institutional quality of the dorms, but there are still relatively few of these.

What Piece of Furniture Is Great for Decorating?

There are always students who swear by cinder blocks and have used them create everything from table legs to bookshelves. Cinder blocks are hard to come by and heavy to transport, but there's usually a group of them that live on campus and get shuffled from year to year. Plastic milk crates are another basic building block of dorm furniture, and they can be found at some supermarkets for free, but many linen stores now sell commercial versions of these. You can also look for smart storage choices, such as a collapsible book shelf that folds flat for transporting.

Union College administrators say that while posters and other decorative items are top-of-mind for students, a high-quality desk chair is probably the thing that will make the biggest difference. "Students spend a great deal of time in these chairs both studying and socializing. If you really want to go top of the line, two words: massage function."

Do Any Dorms Allow Pets? What Kind?

Think goldfish! Christine Porter, Director of Residence Life and Housing, and Raymond Tuttle, PhD, Director of Judicial Affairs and Community Responsibility, both at University of Mary Washington, note that kids miss their pets. "Friends and family can be accessed by phone, e-mail, and webchat, but you can't reach out through cyberspace and stroke your cat or play fetch with your dog."

"Though students pine for the companionship of an animal in the residence hall, very few institutions permit anything other than fish," says

Porter. "Issues of noise, safety, hygiene, allergies, college breaks, and limited space all play into these policies." Combine these things with the busy lifestyle of most college students and it becomes clear that disallowing pets is the fairest possible course of action for both animals and humans.

The University of Mary Washington cites cautionary tales where students—especially those living off campus—will adopt an animal from the local shelter with little thought as to what is going to happen to the pet during breaks or during the summer (especially if the student's family members do not want that animal returning home). It is simply not right to adopt a pet in September and "un-adopt" it in May, they say.

At Sweet Briar College the staff concurs with the "fish only" policy and suggests encouraging your pet loving student to be creative adding turtles, hermit crabs, and other aquariums or terrarium dwelling species to the "creative pets" list.

Believe it or not, however, there are some animal-loving schools that allow smaller critters such as hamsters, turtles, lizards, frogs, and fish. (The University of Florida even welcomes guinea pigs, dwarf rabbits, non-poisonous salamanders, chinchillas, and non-predatory domesticated birds not to exceed one-half pound!) Check with individual schools on their rules about pets, but don't count your chickens before they're hatched. Schools with a liberal pet policy are rare.

DOES SHE NEED TO BRING CURTAINS FOR THE WINDOWS?

Most college dorm windows come with some form of institutional pull down shade or blind. Alberston College says that curtains can be a great way to add personality to a dorm room and make it feel a little more like home. Again, roommate buy-in is critical. Coordinate who will bring curtains and find out what type of window coverings are included with the room, how many windows there are, and what the measurements are.

SHOULD WE BUILD OR BUY A LOFT FOR HER BED? IF SO, WHERE DO WE GET ONE?

Give students two beds and they'll often get busy designing a loft system. At Gustavus Adolphus College, the deans say that lofts are a popular way to create more floor space and a unique, home-like feel. The two most popular loft arrangements are for students to raise a single bed to the height of top bunk bed and put their desk and drawers under the bed, or for students to create bunk beds on one side and use another wall for their dressers and desk.

Not every school allows them, however. Colleges tend to get a bit apoplectic about student as carpenters and novice interior decorators. They see loft systems as safety issues and worry about the damage they might cause to the rooms. Some schools have decided to placate the students by offering modular dorm furniture. University of Denver's Jo Calhoun, Associate Provost of their Student Life Division, says that their campus provides bunkable beds in their housing facilities. In addition, in many residence halls, the beds can be elevated to accommodate a dresser and other items to be stored below. All furniture is movable, so students are able to configure their rooms to their liking.

Other schools offer specific guidelines for building lofts, which comply with State Fire Marshall directives. Some even supply information for contracted suppliers of tubular, metal lofts that are available for rent or purchase. At St. Mary's College in Maryland, students can even get lofting kits provided by the college.

Schools like Wabash College won't recommend lofts because in many states there are strict laws about fire safety. "Lofts that are too close to the ceiling could block the work of sprinkler systems. And lofts often damage the walls and floors of the rooms in which they are installed," say Wabash administrators. At Rochester Institute of Technology, home to so many future engineers, Chuck Lamb, Director of Residence Life says that all lofts need to be approved by Housing Operations to insure safety. Nothing can be built that modifies or attaches to the existing building structure.

What Will Be Allowed in the Dorm Room for Cooking? Hot Pots, Hot Plates, Microwaves?

There's nothing like breaking bread together for developing relationships, but, primarily for safety, most schools prefer these relationships bloom in the dining hall and not in the residence hall. Connie Carson, Director of Residence Life and Housing at Wake Forest University, says that "the key to residence hall cooking is to think in terms of warming items rather than actually cooking."

Again, there's a wide variation from school to school and even dorm to dorm. At Baylor University, Terri Garrett, Associate Director of Campus Living & Learning has a list of sanctioned cooking appliances that is limited to hot pots, coffee makers, pop-up toasters, and popcorn poppers. Microwaves, electric skillets, grills (in door/out door), deep fryers, toaster ovens, and other cooking appliances with exposed heating elements are not allowed. On the up side, fully-equipped kitchens are located in each residence hall, and microwaves are available for student use in the floor lounges and other public areas.

At Truman State University, only automatic iced tea makers, bread machines, crock pots, coffee makers, hot air popcorn poppers, and small refrigerators are allowed. A recently popular item, according to Leslie Millerd Rogers, Office of the Vice Chancellor Student Affairs at UC, is a "Micro-fridge" (a combination microwave and refrigerator) and the school includes contracts for renting them with your move-in packet. These combination units are popular at many schools.

The cooking situation normally changes as the student progresses through school. Many campuses have apartment complexes with full kitchens, but typically these become available in student's junior or senior years. Or students choose to live off campus as upperclassmen, in which case they have an apartment with a standard kitchen.

Should We Bring a Mini-Refrigerator for Her Dorm Room?

Refrigerators are a nice addition because students have some flexibility over their eating and are not slaves to the cafeteria's menu offerings and hours of operation. They can also help students save money since buying drinks and snacks at a supermarket is more cost-effective than buying them at the vending machine.

However, you probably shouldn't buy a refrigerator until you get to campus. Hampshire College says that most campuses have fairly specific requirements about the size and safety of mini-refrigerators in the dorm rooms. Because of that, most schools have arrangements in place giving students the option to buy or rent them easily at a reasonable price at the beginning of the academic year. Look for information about mini-refrigerators in the materials sent to your student prior to matriculation, or ask the housing staff.

Joe Gonzalez, Associate Dean for Residential Life at Duke University, calculates that about 95 percent of Duke students have a mini-fridge in their room. Gonzalez says that you may be able to find a used one on campus after arriving since they tend to get passed along.

Schools are pretty exacting about what a "small refrigerator" means. And each one has its own definition. To University of California—Irvine, for example, small refrigerators are 3.7 cubic feet or less. For parents with multiple children in school, here's your fair warning: Don't assume that the chilling unit that worked for your first kid heading off to school will work for the second or third.

The Science Experiment in the Fridge

The biggest problem with in-room refrigerators is the stuff that gets left in them to mold and fester. Remind your child to keep a box of baking soda in their fridge to absorb odors. Have him remember to clean the fridge with soapy water every now and then. Buying small containers of milk instead of large ones is usually a good idea since there's nothing worse than the smell of spoiled milk. Finally, the freezers in small refrigerators are notorious for either not freezing or over freezing. They should keep freezer purchases to a minimum and use them quickly.

The Spice Rack

A little spice can add a touch of home to some otherwise bland-tasting food. Students can keep a few items like powdered garlic, salt and pepper, some soy sauce, honey (tell them to wash the jar after using or the bugs will have a field day), and a bit of oregano or Italian spice mix handy. These will come in handy for doctoring up some otherwise bland soups and snack foods—even pizzas that need some pizzazz. While the dining halls may have some spices on hand, who says a student with a taste for Tabasco can't bring a bottle of his own?

Freshman Snack Survival Gear

Most freshmen will be just fine with the following: plate, fork, knife, spoon, bowl, cup, coffee mug, coffee pot, and some plastic food storage containers. Plastic plates and cups won't break, though they do tend to wear out faster and absorb the tastes (and colors) of anything warmed in them. Remind your child that ants, roaches, and other bugs love crumbs and food left unopened. If she's going to eat in her room, she needs to be careful about cleaning.

ARE THERE LAUNDRY FACILITIES IN THE DORM? WHAT DO THEY COST ON AVERAGE?

Laundry is an important part of the college ritual. Students will quickly join the ranks of those of us who regularly trade tips on fabric softeners and stain removal. Just about every college has laundry facilities for students to "do their own." Some schools also offer laundry services, giving busy (or pampered) students the option of sending out their dirty clothes to be laundered for them. If that isn't enough, some campus now have dry cleaning on the premises as well. Even with all of the new services, the student who doesn't do his own laundry is missing an important rite of passage.

Laundry on campus is usually a bargain. At Bradley University, for example, residence halls have coin-operated or university debit card washing machines and dryers for the residents. The cost to wash or dry each is 75 cents a load. At Union College, costs are similar, with an average load of wash costing around $2 total to wash and dry.

Early laundry machines took coins and students would trade the shirts off their backs (dirty as they were) for a coveted roll of quarters. Coin-operated machines have been largely replaced at many schools with new debit card systems. At SUNY Purchase College, a state-of-the-art system now includes unlimited washing/drying in the basic room charge. (Now you'll want them doing laundry just to get their tuition's worth.) The best part of the Purchase laundry system is that it can be electronically monitored from the students' dorm rooms. They can actually check on their PC to see if their laundry is ready to be rotated or whether there are any available machines. Incredible!

College Tips For Clean Clothes

Don't overload the machine: Frugal kids always make the mistake of over-stuffing the machine; nothing ends up clean and frequently the washing machine complains of an imbalance.

Cheap clothes often equals bad dye: When your new red shirt is ready for its first wash, do it in the sink by hand, not with a full load of laundry.

Clean out pockets: Nothing like some wadded up tissues to create a laundry-load full of lint! Coins, pocket knives, and lipsticks can also do a number on laundry.

Disappearing socks: Knowing their tendency to part ways, it's good to put socks inside a mesh bag and wash them that way.

Read the labels: Why is it that all the clothing kids really like have labels that basically say, "Wash with like colors, in gentle cycle, and never put this item near any color that's not identical to it. Remove from wash immediately, have an iron ready, or lay flat to dry"? If you're shopping for college clothes, you might want to try clothing that requires a little less maintenance. Could it be that the reason those belly-button baring shirts are so popular is because they've all shrunk in the college wash?

Turn clothes right-side in: Inside-out washes are never as clean.

Wash the grimy ones separately: Mud, sap, chocolate...they can migrate from the dirty clothes to the clean ones.

SHOULD MY STUDENT HAVE A CAR ON CAMPUS?

Each institution has their own policy about students' cars and its own costs associated with parking permits. A large number of colleges won't allow first-year students to bring a vehicle to campus period, simply because there aren't enough parking spaces. Make sure you know the car and parking policies before she drives off to campus.

Jody Terhaar and Jason Laker, both Deans of Students at the College of Saint Benedict/Saint John's University, think it's important to find out what sort of transportation is provided by the college before deciding to bring a car. "Many colleges provide some type of bus service to grocery stores, malls, and social locations," they say. Colleges often run shuttle buses, help with connections to public transportation, and provide ride boards. Usually there is little or no cost associated with this kind of transportation if you have a student ID.

Some campuses have state of the art transportation, like West Virginia University's PRT, or Personal Rapid Transit—an electronic people-mover, connecting the campuses to the downtown area. At holiday time, the Mountaineer Parents Club at the University of West Virginia coordinates low-cost bus service to the Pittsburgh airport and other heavily-populated student areas.

At Franklin W. Olin College of Engineering each student can register one car on campus. Rod Crafts, Dean of Student Life, reports that about one-third of Olin students have cars, a figure that is pretty similar to other suburban campuses. Crafts says that even without a car, it's easy to find transportation into the closest metropolitan area for cultural events and entertainment.

On most any college campus, students with cars often give other students rides to public transportation or rides home on weekends in exchange for some gas money.

"In general it is not a good idea for new students to have a car on campus," says Providence College's Jacqueline Kiernan MacKay, Assistant Vice President for Student Services, and Wanda S. Ingram, Associate Dean of Undergraduate Studies. They feel that having a car can be an expensive and dangerous distraction. It gives students a freedom to leave campus and explore, and some kids aren't ready for that. "Students need to become involved in the life of the campus and make those important connections between themselves and their new institution," they say.

Furthermore, having a car can make your student the designated driver when there's a party of concert off campus, and that's a responsibility, too. If they are in the car-owning minority then they might be the school's "taxi driver" spending all their free time ferrying their friends.

Sabrina Cave, director of West Virginia University's Mountaineer Parents Club, tells students and their parents to ask these questions before making a decision about the car: Is parking available? What does it cost? Is parking close to where the student will be living? Is there adequate public transportation available for students to get to a grocery store, a mall, or a movie theater? Will she (or you) mind that they may end up shuttling friends around? Does she want the added responsibility and cost of car maintenance?

Indiana University of Pennsylvania adds some additional questions to assess need: How much will it cost to have the car on campus (parking fees, gasoline, and maintenance)? Does she need the car for academic reasons—such as traveling to a practicum or internship? Does she need it to travel to off campus employment? Can she find a local mechanic to service her car? ("We have known students whose entire paycheck was used to maintain their car," says the Indiana University staff.) What has her driving history been? Do you want her to use the car for social reasons?

And from the Deans of Marlboro College: "Let the student settle into his or her new environment before making a decision—Fall Break might be a good time to access the situation."

Should My Child Have His Own Car Insurance?

Call your agent and find out where it makes more sense to insure the car and in whose name. Students typically pay high insurance rates. Some insurance agencies will allow you to register the car in the state the college is in, if that's where the car stays most of the year. (You'll have to supply proof of residence, however.) Many insurers remove teenage driver surcharges when they are more than 100 miles away at school.

Now for some facts: Auto insurance is the number-one type of insurance held by college students according to the Student Monitor, a market research firm. They report that 38 percent of college students own at least one type of insurance. Automobile insurance is 26 percent of the total, ahead of health at 19 percent, and life at 8 percent. More than half of students (58 percent) with automobile insurance personally made the purchase decision, compared to 38 percent who made the purchase decision for health insurance.

The Ride Board

At some point, students without cars will look for transportation using bulletin boards, both in the real world and online. These ride boards match a driver and car with riders willing to share the expense. Usually these are harmless—except when they're not. If your child uses a ride board to look for transportation, it's probably best to use the campus board and only take a ride from another student—preferably one she can meet in person ahead of time. Many students use ride boards on websites like Craigslist, but there's no telling who is advertising their services on these public bulletin boards.

Parking Problems

Charlotte G. Burgess, Vice President/Dean of Student Life at the University of Redlands, urges students to pay attention to the options for parking if they decide to bring a car onto campus. It is rare for a campus to have garage facilities. Most often there are numerous parking lots around campus and town. Students should survey them with an eye toward safety. If a lot is well lit and not completely fenced in, a student can be fairly sure it's a safe place. If lots show evidence of significant fencing and all sorts of entry requirements, it would be wise to ask questions about how many car thefts or break-ins have occurred on campus.

GreenBike Programs

Pitzer College, like many others, has a "green bike program" that allows students to borrow a bike for the semester. Some campuses have a number of school-owned bikes that students can borrow, ride somewhere, and leave for the next student to use.

Traveling Gear

Students are nomadic. They'll often take a weekend trip to visit a friend at another school or visit a friends' home, so make sure that they take the essential tools of the road to school with them. Think about packing up a good sleeping bag and backpack at minimum.

SHOULD SHE USE HER CELL PHONE OR THE WIRED PHONE IN THE DORM?

Refer to Chapter 9, "Long-Distance Parenting" and staying in touch for an in-depth discussion of this topic.

ANY ADVICE FOR MOVE-IN DAY?

On move-in day, everything comes to a head. All of the anxiety that you and your child have been feeling creeps closer and closer toward the surface with a danger of blowing up at anyone's slightest misstep.

First, get some sleep the night before—it's going to be a long day for everyone. Second, remember that patience is one of the most crucial tools to bring along for a smooth move-in day, yet plenty of parents seem to have left it back at home.

Tracy Tyree, Dean of Student Life at Susquehanna University has this to say: "Taking children to college is very emotional for parents. They want everything to go perfectly so they can have an idyllic picture as they drive away from campus. The students are experiencing their own sets of emotions as they meet roommates for the first time, begin to negotiate and compromise in that relationship, and prepare to say goodbye to their families, all in a fairly short amount of time." Hard as it may be to do, parents need to step back and let their children take control in this situation, allow them some space to work through decisions with their roommates, and empower them to communicate directly with RAs or others if something goes wrong.

Like a vacation or a wedding, there's no foolproof way to guarantee that nothing will go wrong on move-in day. Having some patience and enough humor left to laugh will go a long way toward parting with your student on friendly terms, knowing that she has everything she needs until you see her next.

CHAPTER 9

Long-Distance Parenting

Honey, time to wake up!

One of my favorite college legends involves a letter that is presumably sent home by a college student with a gift for putting things into perspective.

Dear Mum and Dad,

It has now been three months since I left for college. I have been remiss in writing and I am sorry for my thoughtlessness. I will bring you up to date, but before you read, please sit down.

I am getting along pretty well now. The skull fracture and the concussion I got when I jumped out of the window of my dormitory when it caught fire are pretty well healed. I only get those sick headaches once a day.

Fortunately, the fire in the dormitory and my jump were witnessed by an attendant at the gas station near the dorm, and he was the one who called the fire department. He also visited me at the hospital and since I had nowhere to live, he was kind enough to invite me to share his apartment. He is a very fine boy and we have fallen deeply in love and are planning to marry before my pregnancy begins to show.

I know you are looking forward to being grandparents and I know you will welcome the baby and give it the love you gave me when I was a child. The reason for the delay in our marriage is that my boyfriend has some minor infection which prevents us from passing our pre-marital blood tests and I carelessly caught it from him. This will soon clear up with the penicillin injections.

I know you will welcome him into our family with open arms. He is kind and, although not well educated, he is ambitious. Although he is of a different race and religion than ours, I know you are tolerant and will not be bothered by the fact that his skin color is different than ours.

Now that I have brought you up to date, I want to tell you that there was no dormitory fire, I did not have a concussion or a skull fracture. I was not in the hospital, I am not pregnant, I am not engaged. I do not have syphilis and there is no man (of any color) in my life.

However, I am getting a 'D' in History and an 'F' in Science and I wanted you to see those marks in the proper perspective.

All the best,

Your Loving Daughter

You are now the parent of a college student. Congratulations and good luck…

The strangest part about the kids going off to college is that you need to develop a new style of interaction. The familiar litany of "not while you're under my roof" and "not as long as you're in this house" don't hold much weight anymore. You can't "accidentally" fall asleep on the couch while waiting up to see if they've made curfew; you can't thumb through that copy of *Othello* to make sure that at least something is underlined or highlighted.

Suddenly left without these day-to-day physical encounters, you're going to need to develop a knack for long-distance parenting. Unless your kids go the "revolving door" route and show up at home again after graduation (say it isn't so!), the skills you hone now are likely to be the same ones you'll fall back on throughout their adulthood. As I tell my kids, "I can smell trouble through the phone lines!" Since they left the nest, I've become a master at meaningful phone relationships.

At the same time you're developing your radar, you'll want to be careful not to go to the other extreme and become what's commonly known as a "helicopter parent." Helicopter parents are the ones that just won't go away. They hover and swoop over their offspring's lives—and, at the first sign of trouble, they drop in to fight their kids' battles for them.

Where can you find the right balance? It lies in the delicate task of walking that line between trusting them and worrying about them, between being there and stepping back so they can live their lives, make their mistakes, and learn along the way. High-tech tools like cell phones, e-mail, and the Internet give parents the unique opportunity of staying in constant contact. But just because technology makes it possible, doesn't mean it makes it right or good.

Here's my own cautionary tale: One year, early in the semester, we thought our son had disappeared from the face of the earth when he didn't answer his cell phone for a few days. Turns out the phone was lost, but he'd never given us his land line number because, to be quite honest, he'd never even plugged in his land line phone. Don't make that mistake. Get both the high- and low-tech numbers and make sure they agree to use both.

Speaking of technology, don't think that these high-tech kids are above receiving a good low-tech message. College administrators across the board tell us a box or a letter in the mailroom can be the highlight of a student's day. Without getting too maudlin about it, I can tell you that I was recently at a memorial service where a son made us all cry as he read a letter his mother had written him in college. I doubt the e-mail would have been as well-thought.

For treats you can send homemade cookies, a favorite DVD, or enough toothpaste and shampoo to get them through the end of the semester. I'm notorious for sending "surprise" curiosities that leave my kids' scratching their heads in bemusement. One of the most treasured items has become seashells that I picked up on a trip. I printed a special note of love and encouragement and rolled it up inside the shell. It still sits on my daughter's shelf, long after she's graduated.

Today's parents display a pretty wide spectrum of behaviors. I know moms who call their kids multiple times every day and I know others who call literally once a semester. Some parents will edit their son's papers each evening; others don't even know their daughter's list of classes until it's time to see the report card. I know dads who've written *War and Peace*-length e-mails to their kid off at college and dads who've written little more than their signature on the check. Some parents love "popping onto campus" any weekend that their social schedule falls a bit short. Meanwhile, others show up once for orientation and once for graduation, if that. Where do you fit in? Where *should* you fit in?

This chapter looks at the "how-tos" and "how oftens" of parent/child communications and how to best forge these new relationships. We'll look at how often you should:

- Visit

- Write

- E-mail

- Call

- Send packages and goodies

Along with:

- Planning for e-mail and phone accounts

- Planning for summer and holiday breaks

What's the Best Way to Stay in Touch with My Child at School?

Leslie Millerd Rogers, of the Office of the Vice Chancellor Student Affairs at the University of California—Irvine, reports that UCI parents have told the school that there are three best ways to stay in touch:

1. E-mail: The advantage being that both parties can write and respond when convenient. (That may be 2:00 A.M. for students, but at least they're responding.)

2. A pre-set calling time: This allows families to establish a day and time each week that they'll connect for a chat. It alleviates any worries about when on earth you'll ever track them down.

3. Good old-fashioned snail mail: Never underestimate the power of a handwritten card or letter. In the world of high-speed communications, the written word and postmarked letter receive high scores from students. As Kurt Holmes, Dean of Students at The College of Wooster, says, "No one pulls their cell phone out of their pocket to show the most recent call they received, but they do show off (and keep) their letters."

UC—Irvine administrators found it interesting that parents did not actually recommend buying the student a cell phone with which to keep in touch. They speculate that perhaps parents don't recommend something they don't plan on funding.

Kids tell us that e-mail is more and more something that they reserve for use with their parents and teachers. If they're talking to their friends, it's all about instant messaging, in which the message appears instantly on the recipients computer (if they're online) or SMS text messaging, in which it appears instantly over their cell phones. Parents who want to be really "in" with the latest messaging techniques will find that it's a fun way to converse instantly with your child. But use it sparingly or your child may start to instantly press "delete."

The benefits of instant messaging and SMS messaging are that you can get them anytime, even if their cell phone is out of service or the ring is turned off because they are economical. They are not very personal and it's pretty hard to type anything to lengthy when you're typing with your thumbs on a cell phone.

TIP: The Conversation

Getting beyond "how are you?" and "fine thank you how are you?" is an art form. Sometimes it's best if you make a little mental note to yourself (or, if you're super organized, keep a list) of things you want to talk about. Try these:

- Think of a funny incident that happened to you today.
- Describe the local seasonal changes (which flowers are blooming).
- Share a piece of local news, as in "Remember the stationary store on the corner?"
- Share family news.
- To get them to talk, go for "tell me one thing you learned today" in class.

Also encourage your extended family to send e-mails or letters. For some reason, many families consider the four-year college stint as "out of sight, out of mind."

"One more tip: Be careful in your excitement to learn how they are doing not to let your calls become an interrogation. Be actively curious about them and their experiences instead of over-focusing on whether they are taking care of business," says William and Mary's R. Kelly Crace.

IS IT PREFERABLE TO CALL, E-MAIL, OR WRITE AND HOW OFTEN?

"Whatever you do, it will be wrong," jokes Kurt Holmes, Dean of Students at The College of Wooster. "You will write too often, or not enough. Your e-mail will be considered meddling, or you will be accused of not caring. But whatever you do, stay in contact anyway. No matter what they say, your children still want to know you care about them."

Regular communications, but not too often, was the consensus of most college administrators. Margaret L. Hazlett, Associate Dean of Student Affairs/Dean of First-Year Students at Bowdoin College, says, "A reasonable rate of phone/e-mail contact is once a week, and a visit once a semester or once a year is fine." Painful as it is for parents to accept, most administrators air on the side of less not more communications. In general they feel that the new communications tools actually cause kids to be overly dependent on their families and friends and not integrated enough into the campus community.

R. Kelly Crace, PhD, Director of the William and Mary Counseling Center, suggests that rather than taking a guess, it makes sense to ask the kids how and how often they prefer their communications with you.

TIP: Say It with Photos

Digital photos are a fabulous way to send a quick hello. You can snap a photo, upload it to your PC, then either e-mail it directly or post it to a site like Kodakgallery.com or Snapfish.com and invite your student to log in and view it. The immediacy of digital photos makes it fun and easy. Just don't send too many photos or you'll fill the poor kid's whole hard-drive If your kids have a digital camera or access to one, encourage them to share a few photos of campus life with you. And if you each have cell phones with nifty little cameras, the gratification of a friendly face can be instantaneous!

HOW CAN I KEEP UP WITH WHAT'S HAPPENING ON CAMPUS?

Don't depend too heavily on your student. Instead, think of the college's website as your main line for information. Of course, your child will be the first to tell you that a college's website is full of only the controlled information they want you to see. Even so, there's a vast amount of useful information and plenty of fodder to give you an idea about day-to-day campus life. "More and more universities are creating offices, programs, and websites that can keep parents informed," says Ryan Lombardi, Assistant Dean of Students and Director of Orientation and Parent and Family Programs at Duke University. Ann Hanson from Middlebury College suggests that parents subscribe to the campus newspaper as another way to know what's happening around campus without being a nosy pest.

Many schools create e-mail newsletters for parents and maintain e-mail list-serves and chat rooms where parents can communicate with other parents. Other schools have created parent advisory councils that offer input into school policy and issues. As a matter of fact, since 1999, the number of schools with parent programs have multiplied from a dozen or so to 300, according to Jim Boyle, President of College Parents of America, an Arlington, VA-based advocacy group ("Millennia's Go to College." *Philadelphia Inquirer*, Jan. 24, 2004). In an effort to field the steady flow of queries from parents, new positions like Parents Liaison, Parent Coordinator, and Director of Parent Activities are becoming more common on college campuses.

Parenting Websites Worth Noting

Centre College's www.web.centre.edu/parentprograms/advice.htm includes insightful parent-to-parent advice.

Wesleyan's www.wesleyan.edu/parents shows how many ways parents can volunteer and get otherwise involved.

UC—Davis's www.aggiefamilypack.ucdavis.edu, designed for families of UC students, includes an electronic newsletter and a Q&A column by Mom Marion.

IS ATTENDING PARENTS' (SOMETIMES CALLED FAMILY) WEEKEND NECESSARY? MUST WE DO IT EVERY YEAR?

Nothing except paying tuition is a necessity. However, if you miss Parents' Weekend, you will miss an important opportunity to share a slice of college life with your student. Unless it's a terrible hardship, someone from your family should be there, every year.

Parents' Weekend, which is now often called "Family Weekend," is the college of equivalent of kindergarten's show-and-tell—both in terms of your child showing you the school and showing you to their friends. Usually held in the middle of the fall semester, it provides the family a chance to get together with lots of scheduled entertainment and activity. It's the payoff after the hectic move-in weekend your family survived just a couple months prior. (Some schools plan a second Family Weekend for the spring.)

The administrators at Georgia Tech say that "when you drop your student off at college, there is an abundance of things to accomplish in a short amount of time. You're probably dividing your time between orientation, moving into the residence hall, and of course, shopping for everything you forgot."

As a nice contrast Parents' Weekend, say the administrators at Bradley University, is more relaxed, a chance to share a social calendar with your kids. "During these scheduled weekends, student theater, fashion shows, art exhibits, Greek functions, and sporting events are planned for parents. Parents also have an opportunity to meet faculty and administration."

> **TIP:** Make Those Parents' Weekend Reservations Today
>
> Many college towns burst at the seams during Parents' or Family Weekends. Meaning? The early bird catches the worm. It's never too soon to book for these weekends. Some parents look at the school's calendar as soon as their child chooses a college and makes the reservation before the school year even starts! It's not a bad idea. On weekends like move-in weekend, Parents' Weekend, Homecoming, move-out weekend, and graduation, local hotel rooms often sell out earlier than you can believe. Book both hotel and restaurant reservations as early as you can. Don't forget to check the school's activities calendar for these weekends. Some school-sponsored activities require advanced tickets or registration.

"It's a great time to take stock of your changing relationship, and have fun taking part in the activities that are planned to satisfy both students and their families," says American University's Faith Leonard, Assistant Vice President and Dean of Students.

Two things to remember: This is a staged event. It has very little to do with a normal college weekend. Second, it's meant to provide you and your child with a full plate of activities, so that you'll have at least some shared experience connected to her college. Your kids may forget Parents' Weekend the minute you leave on Sunday, but guaranteed, it will be one of your treasured memories.

TIP: Adopt a Student

Most college students will tell you that nearly every parent finds their way to campus for Parents' or Family Weekend during the student's freshman year. But by sophomore year, there's a dramatic drop off. Faith Leonard of American University suggests that you ask your child what is going on in their lives at the time of Family Weekend. If they have midterms coming up, for example, or a lengthy research paper to complete, your visit may add more trauma and stress than enjoyment. Gauge the situation and consider postponing the visit in cases like these.

If life events are going to prevent you from making it to campus for Parents' Weekend, plan to pay extra attention to your student, even if it's long-distance attention. "Students may feel a twinge of loneliness at your absence if other families are on campus," says Leonard. "And at least you can be assured that housing staff and others are acutely aware of those feelings among students and respond accordingly." You should, too. A care package could be in order.

Finally, if you are attending Parents' Weekend and you can afford it, "adopt a student" whose parents couldn't make it, at least for one meal. If ever there was a time a student would miss his parents, it's on Parents' Weekend when the campus fills with the sounds of reunited families.

Should I Visit at Other Times During the Year?

Parents' Weekend has as much in common with day-to-day college life as the tooth fairy has with dentistry. "To get the feel for the real deal, visit on a weekday to feel the pulse of the campus," says Ron Herron, Vice President of Student Affairs at Purchase College—State University of New York. That said, he discourages unannounced, pop-in visits. There is a strong possibility that you won't even be able to track down your busy kid once you arrive. But more importantly, says Herron, "Surprise visits may turn into shock visits. For a variety of reasons, they should be avoided."

Sally Swager, Vice President for Student Affairs and Dean of Students at Randolph-Macon College, reminds parents to keep the visits infrequent. "It's important," she says, for "your son or daughter to have a chance to develop independence and establish social relationships at college. If you are around every weekend, he or she may miss out on some fun social events and activities."

> **TIP:** Know the mailing address of the school. Some schools have a post office box for letters but then a different street address for packages.

Parents' Weekend Survival Guide

Parents' Weekend is a marathon for both you and your student. Most colleges overstuff the weekend like a deli sandwich, filling it with a near unapproachable number of receptions, sports activities, lectures, music, theater, art exhibits, dances, and more. If you have a couple of kids and a few years worth of Parents' Weekends, you might find yourself with a list of activities that includes going caving with the geology department, rowing with the crew team, listening to famous professors wax poetic, attending a staged version of *The Vagina Monologues* (with the grandparents, no less), taking Irish step dancing, and sitting in on drawing classes in the school of art. After countless receptions that all serve the identical food, you'll perform super-market sweeps and shopping mall blitzes. All this with brothers, sisters, grandparents, girlfriends, boyfriends, or even the dog along for the ride.

Advice for survival?

Save some time for shopping. You may want to hear the lectures and talks, but guaranteed most kids have heard enough lectures by now. On the other hand, they're having mall withdrawal and ran out of toilet paper two days ago. Plan to do some damage to your credit card and get them off campus for awhile.

Give yourself a 10:00 P.M. curfew. They like you, but not that much. Students will appreciate the chance to hang out with friends and you'll appreciate a good night's sleep.

Leave early on Sunday. It's been a great weekend, but sadly, the professors haven't stopped assigning work because it's Family Weekend. If they've got a lot of schoolwork to catch up on, the longer you stay, the more stressed they'll be, and the later they'll burn the midnight oil.

Don't micromanage their education. It's okay to go in and meet their advisor; it's not okay to sit down with the advisor and attempt to plan her four-year class schedule. That's still her job.

WHOSE TELEPHONE NUMBERS SHOULD I HAVE IN MY ROLODEX?

Besides your own child's dorm room phone number (and cell, if they have one), you should have the numbers for at least one local hotel, any local doctors, and the general campus information number. Some schools even have a "hotline" just for parents.

Rice University suggests that the parents' contacts should include the number for Offices of the Dean of Students, the Residential College coordinator, and the Residential College master.

TIP: Care Package Websites

A number of websites specialize in getting a care package to your child. If you want to send a birthday cake or flowers, it's the easiest way to go. Many sites use local bakeries and florists to fulfill the order, so freshness is guaranteed. (You can even visit these sites to "borrow" some clever care package ideas, then recreate them yourself to save money or make the package more personal.) For these sorts of care packages, be prepared to spend about $50 with shipping and delivery costs and to order at least five days in advance of delivery to avoid rush delivery fees.

> www.thesmilebox.com: Design your own custom care package and they'll put it in a bright yellow box. Add toys, hot and cold food, snacks, and balloons, but count on them adding at least $10 to the price of the box to cover delivery.

> www.carepackages.com: Custom packages with great ideas for final exam time. Prepare to spend at least $32 plus shipping.

> www.care4college.com: Free priority shipping, though the care package costs a bit more than on other websites. These can include school supplies like Post-its and highlighters as well as snack foods.

Your own school is likely to offer care packages as well. You may save on shipping, but the cost of the package will likely be similar.

WHAT IF I NEED TO MAKE EMERGENCY CONTACT?

If there's an emergency at home and you aren't able to get in touch with your child, contact the school's Student Life Office. They should be able to locate her and have her call home. If it's after regular business hours, you many need to call Campus Security instead. Having one of her friends' phone numbers for emergencies doesn't hurt, either.

Should I Send Care Packages?

"Even in this age of electronic madness with instant messaging and real-time connections, college students thrive on mail," say Wheaton College's administrators. "The parade of students marching to their mailboxes has not diminished despite e-mail. Add the excitement of a package from home, and you can turn a bad day sunny for any college student."

As for what to send, University of Mary Washington Barbara Wagar, PsyD, Director of Psychological Services, suggests healthy snacks that keep well, especially those that come individually packaged or that store easily. Other winners are toiletries and self-care products like deodorant, adhesive bandages, ibuprofen, batteries, a pack of their favorite pens, and almost any homemade snacks. Here are some other ideas of what to send your student from college administrators from all over the country:

> Be sure to pack those homemade items well, because there's nothing as disappointing as opening the box to find that those special chocolate chip cookies arrived as crumbs.
>
> —University of Mary Washington

> Check with the food service provider on campus. Often, they offer deals throughout the school year featuring goodies for study breaks, stress-buster packages for exam time, and special birthday events.
>
> —Wheaton College

> Recognize that your child's friends call these "share packages." You may want to include enough of whatever you are sending for his or her friends to try some, too.
>
> —Sweet Briar College

> "Nothing is sadder than an empty mailbox. Send notes of encouragement, funny cards, and clippings from your local newspaper that let them know what's going on at home. You can also send things like gas cards, Wal-Mart cards, or Baskin Robbins coupons.
>
> —Centre College.

SHOULD WE USE HER .EDU E-MAIL ACCOUNT FROM SCHOOL OR SHOULD WE USE AN E-MAIL SERVICE LIKE AOL OR YAHOO! TO E-MAIL HER WHILE SHE'S IN SCHOOL?

Remember that changing e-mail addresses is like changing real world addresses: It can disrupt routine and you're bound to lose a few communications in the process. You'll want to talk to your kids about their e-mail preferences, but, if he or she already has an off-campus e-mail account, keeping it active will come handy. Students often use their AOL, Yahoo!, Hotmail, or Gmail accounts to keep up with family and high school friends and use their .edu accounts strictly for campus business, but each student has their own ideas about what works best. A recent study by Yahoo! found that most people have multiple mailboxes and tend to use them to keep personal use, business use, and shopping separate.

Some of the reasoning behind the dual account strategy is historical. Not that many years ago, university e-mail systems were not as robust as the commercial ones. The user might not have been able to view graphics, listen to sound, or use chat features, but today that picture has changed; campus e-mail systems are high-speed and high-bandwidth. As a matter of fact, at University of California—Irvine, where they can now can surf, blog, and instant message 24/7 at many locations all over the campus, students are finding that the reason to keep a non-campus e-mail account is not a tech motivated one but a social one.

There's something nice about keeping the .edu account pristine—free from spam and junk. So it's a good idea to use the non-edu account for shopping online, taking surveys, emerging Web services (like video conferencing or peer to peer networks) that may be blocked from campus systems. Remember, too, that your child's .edu address is not forever. Schools have different policies about how long after graduation a student can keep his e-mail address. Having a noncampus-related e-mail address means it will work before, during, and after college.

As far as the administration is concerned you have only one e-mail account that they need to know about and that is the .edu account. "It's very common for students to come with another e-mail account or even multiple ones," says Ryan Lombardi, Assistant Dean of Students and Director of Orientation and Parent and Family Programs at Duke. "But the student and her parents need to understand that the university will use her university-provided e-mail account for all official communications. That includes any e-mails registering for classes, billing questions, safety issues and so on. A personal e-mail account is fine, but it cannot be a substitute for a university e-mail account."

At Union College officials agree and expect that campus e-mail addresses will be monitored for important information (class updates, campus-wide announcements, etc.). Across the board, campus business is increasingly done on e-mail. At some colleges, professors use e-mail to send announcements, grade papers, offer help, and continue discussions outside of class all via e-mail. At Sarah Lawrence, Director of Residential Life Sarah Cardwell says that e-mail is considered a primary means of communication and that the school holds the student responsible for information conveyed via e-mail.

TIP: Need to Use vs. Want to Use: Phones and E-mail

When it comes to e-mail, most schools require students to use a school-affiliated e-mail account (that ends in .edu) for school communication. If the student wants to use an e-mail service like Yahoo! or Gmail for personal e-mail as a second e-mail account, they certainly can.

The same goes for phone service. Schools will list dorm room land line numbers in the campus directory and will use those phones for any school-related calls about billing, class registration, etc. If the student chooses to use a cell phone for personal calls in addition to the school-affiliated land line, they are, of course, welcome to do so.

Should She Use a Cell Phone or a Landline as Her Telephone?

The Student Monitor reports that 89 percent of college students now own a cell phone. Students have come to expect their communications to be instantaneous and 'round the clock. But while it's tempting to pack their cell phones and let that be the end of it, it's a good idea for them to have a landline phone, too. Not only can cell phones can be intrusive and over-used, reception on some campuses may be spotty and usually the phone's number won't be registered with the campus phone directory.

Cell Phone

Advantages

> Family Plans allow low cost communications
>
> Know you can always reach student
>
> Phone can have phone book and calendar info
>
> Can send text messages
>
> Never miss an important call

Disadvantages

> Intrusive ringing; tend to be overused
>
> Spotty reception
>
> Campus has no record of number
>
> Could have roaming charges
>
> Kids tend to overspend plan using text messaging
>
> Phones get lost

LANDLINE

Advantages

School provides free local calling

School provides answering system

Number listed with campus directory

Good quality phone line is a given

Disadvantages

Long distance calls require additional service

Line is often shared with roommates

Not often in dorm room to receive calls

"In general, students prefer to have their residence hall numbers, not their cellular numbers, listed in the campus directory and with the Registrar's Office," says Marcia Moore of College of Charleston. Reasons for this are obvious, but it can also create a communications problem.

"Unless a student reports his or her cell phone number to the university, the wired phone is one of the primary ways we can use to contact him or her," says the Student Affairs staff at University of Puget Sound. "Even if the student chooses to use a cell phone for primary communication, Puget Sounds encourages them to use the wired phone and answering service (either an answering machine or system-provided voice-mail) to regularly check messages that may come from campus community members, like faculty, staff, or other students."

Cell phones also get lost or stolen. Have all of their phone numbers stored in a safe place so if you can't reach them on their cell, you can try their room. In turn, encourage your child to have all of the phone numbers that are in the cell phone also stored somewhere else in written form. Even if he loses the phone, he will still have your work number, his classmates' and professors' numbers, and so on.

Most colleges fault the cell phone for being a distraction and a tether that can prevent kids from making their own decisions. "If students dial home to report every event on campus, then who are they talking to on campus?" asks the University of Puget Sound Student Affairs staff. "Cell phones need to be used like phones—not like lifelines."

Valparaiso University administration suggests asking these questions while you make your decision:

- Will she be charged excessive roaming charges for calls to areas not covered by your plan's minutes?

- If she's moving to a new geographic area, will her cell phone have the signal strength to work as well on campus and inside campus buildings, as it does in her home area? Will she need to make all calls out of doors?

- If calls to her cell phone number from other phones on campus results in a long-distance toll for the caller, will it discourage other students on campus from calling her?

Most families opt for the hybrid solution. At the University of Illinois—Urbana-Champaign, like many others, there is no charge for on-campus or local calls from a landline phone, so the school suggests that students use the wired phone in their residence hall rooms. Students may also purchase a long-distance calling plan through the university, although cell phone plans may be more convenient for long-distance service, especially if a student has a local cell phone number from her hometown, rather than from campus.

Linda Tyler, Associate Dean of Student Development at Earlham College, reminds us many colleges have cell-free zones such as classrooms and libraries.

Family Plans vs. Pre-Pay

The two most common types of cell phone payment plans for students are the family plan and the pre-paid phone card plan. Family Plans are terrific if you can manage them well. Basically, you buy a certain amount of minutes per month to share amongst your plan users. You'll find that you typically get unlimited "mobile-to-mobile" calls between all phones on the plan, and free calls on nights and weekends; just pay attention to whether you'll be charged for roaming out of your area, sending text messages, and exactly which hours are considered "nights" and which are "weekends." It's been found that most families go over there allotted minutes on their plan each month, precisely because of hidden charges.

The pre-paid phone card (available from vendors like T-Mobile and Virgin) encourage your student to live within a fixed phone budget. They buy a certain number of minutes, then use them to talk or to send text messages. When they've used up the minutes they can buy more online or buy another pre-paid phone card. There are no contracts to sign and no hidden charges, a real plus. However, if they make a lot of calls, these plans can be expensive because the per-minute charge is high. Some phone cards also dock you extra minutes if calls are made from a pay phone.

The Next Wave: VOIP or Digital Phones

If you haven't already, you might want to look into using VOiP (Voice Over Internet Protocol) for your long-distance calls. VOiP allows you to use the Internet as your digital phone service instead of your traditional analog phone line. Internet companies like Vonage.com and Skype.com offer the service, and now the larger service providers like Verizon and T-Mobile are offering versions, too. There are different rates, plans, and equipment depending on your needs, but a call will average around 2-cents a minute in the states and 7-cents per minute outside the U.S. The fidelity is excellent and there are lots of special features you can use on a digital system like this to make it far more sophisticated than your traditional phone. By the time you read this, VOiP should be growing more and more common. (If you're intimidated by the high-tech aspect—many people are—it's pretty safe to assume that your college student is not. Have him do the research!)

TIP: Here's how Ohio Northern University tells their students to cope with homesickness:

- Talk to someone about your feelings. RAs are great resources and are available to you.

- Keep in contact with the people you have left at home. You are allowed to feel the way you do. You are also allowed to enjoy yourself—it is not being disloyal to those you miss!

- Try to balance your academic and social commitments.

- Remember to get enough food and rest.

- Allow yourself the time you need to adjust to college life.

- Get involved in campus life! Make the most of your experience.

- If you are unable to do normal social and academic things, seek professional help from either your doctor or the counseling center.

WHAT IF MY CHILD SAYS SHE'S HOMESICK?

For starters, remember that your children tend to call you when things are less than optimal. Few kids remember to get on the phone to let you know that things are going fabulously. That's human nature.

"Homesickness is one of the most common, and least admitted, challenges for new students," says University of Washington's staff. "It's a normal feeling, indicating that they have very important ties to friends and family." Your job is to take the "egocentric" focus off of homesickness and remind your kids that other kids are probably lonesome too. Being away from home for so long is a big adjustment for any student, and freshman year is always the hardest.

Macalester College deans suggest encouraging your child to do something simple like asking a floormate to go to dinner, joining an on-campus club, or going to a religious service. It's fine to offer common antidotes to homesickness, but just remember not to take it personally if you're rebuffed for having the "dumbest idea ever."

Calvin College's Parent Relations Director, Jim Van Wingerden, says, "Whatever you do, don't ask your first-year student if she or he is homesick. The power of suggestion is, well, powerful." Taking that a step further, parents should control their own emotions and not carry on about how much they miss their kids. Feel free to chirp, "Bye—we miss you!" but don't wax poetic about how empty your house feels or how you don't know how you'll live without them. Instead of "We sure miss you," Ven Wingerden says, try to send empowering and encouraging messages such as, "We are so proud of you."

Remember, too, that homesickness can be on time-delay. "Sometimes it gets worse when the activities and bustle of a new semester wane and there are fewer activities designed especially for new students," say administrators at Hendrix College.

If homesick calls persist and there are other symptoms accompanying it, like losing weight or sleeplessness, you may need to contact the school and see if there's a way to address the problem together.

How Can I Encourage My Child to Keep Practicing Our Religion while at School?

Clearly the best assurance is to choose a college with a religious orientation built in. A 2005 survey done by The Princeton Review found Reed College, Bard College, Eugene Lang College of the New School University in New York City, Hampshire College, and Lewis and Clark College ranked at the top of their "Students Ignore God on a Regular Basis" list. Contrast that with Brigham Young University, Wheaton College, Grove City College, the University of Notre Dame, and Samford University where, according to the survey, "Students Pray on a Regular Basis."

Just because your child goes to a more secular institution doesn't mean he'll leave their religious training behind. It's common that students will miss their religious traditions once they are away from home, and at least some of them will attempt to recreate those experiences at college. Most campuses have some sort of services available on campus, and/or they will have relationships with the faith organizations in town. Mount Holyoke and MIT have both built interfaith chapels where many different religions can be observed in a shared space. Many local churches, synagogues, temples, and mosques are sensitive to the needs of students on campuses nearby and have programs set up to take a student in for a religious holiday if they live far from their homes. Campus groups like Christian Youth and Hillel House are often funded by their schools to offer services to students who wish to partake. At Colorado College, for example, religious groups include: Baptist Student Union, Campus Crusade for Christ, Campus Pagan Association, CC Catholic Community, CC Prayer Warriors, Chaverim/Hillel, Fellowship of Christian Athletes, Faculty and Faith, Intervarsity Christian Fellowship, Latter Day Saints Institute of Religion, The Mill (affiliated with New Life Church), Navigators, Shove Council, Seekers (at First Presbyterian Church), Spiritual Classics (reading group), Society of Friends, Unitarian Universalists, Young Life, Zen Buddhist Sangha—an eclectic and diverse offering. Check your child's college website to find out what they offer and check churches and temples in the college town, too.

What Should I Expect from My Student Over Summer Vacation?

Summer vacations from college give new meaning to the "can't live with them, can't live without them" adage. For all the hoopla about going off to college, it only lasts somewhere between seven and eight months of the year. That means that for a full quarter of the year, your kids will need alternative plans.

January 1st, believe it or not, is an excellent day to start thinking about summer. The beginning of the new year is when you should begin encouraging (make that berating, in extreme cases) the kids to look for jobs, apply for internships, or make their travel plans. By April, they should have a good idea of what they're doing. By May 1st you should have an exit strategy in place for the summer, including when your child is leaving school and exactly where you are going to put all of that stuff you feel like you just dragged down to school last month. Some campuses provide summer storage, others have storage rooms for rent nearby. At others, most parents and kids simply opt to move everything back and forth with them each year.

If they move back to spend the summer with you, remember to be tolerant of their new personae. They won't be used to the curfews and the questions. On the other hand, it's fine to lay down certain rules of behavior that will be observed. Indulge them for a day or two—favorite foods, no alarm clock, and no making of the bed required. Then it's time to get them back on a productive routine. Asking for a bit of payback (a fresh coat of paint in the room, the cleaning out an old closet, a bit of weeding in the garden) is perfectly permissible.

Naturally, make some time over the summer to discuss their grades from the past year, the courses they've signed up for in the year coming, and how college, in general, is going.

An entire book could be written about the college summer vacation alone, but suffice it to say both you and your children will get to test drive your new relationship.

WHAT SHOULD I EXPECT DURING WINTER AND SPRING BREAKS?

Winter and spring breaks are just long enough to drag on and just short enough to make it tough for the kids to do anything really substantial. If your child has connections through his pre-college summer job, they might be able to sign on for a month's work in the winter. Retailers, ski areas, and restaurants all need seasonal workers as well. For students at schools that use the quarter system, they may find themselves with right around six weeks off of school between Thanksgiving and New Year's. This should be enough time to get a seasonal job; some students even do short-term mini internships.

There's also a good likelihood the kids will ask to do some traveling at some point, too. Do your best to steer them away from those Spring Break meccas (Daytona, Cancun, and others). Some colleges offer special trips and courses over the break, and there's always a family vacation. Be clear on what you will pay for and what they should pay for during break times, too.

As for the schools, some schools that do winter and spring break sessions will ask that your child empty their room out and store the contents just as they would for the summer. But the vast majority just leave the rooms as is.

CHAPTER 10

Words From the Wisest

I spent some time with two young moms a few weeks ago who were about to send their children off to kindergarten. They were anything but joyful; words like "terror," "despondent," and a pervasive sense of "sadness" come to mind. They did not want their children leaving them, not even for a half-day program in their local town. I wanted to say, "Wait until your kids head off to college; you'll feel the same way, but worse!" but I bit my tongue. I wanted to lecture them on the importance of "letting go," but again I bit my tongue. I finally decided to let them revel in their sadness and offered only practical advice instead. "Don't forget to keep that spare set of clothes complete at all times. Velcro is a great invention. Label everything!"

I hope that reading this book has been the college equivalent of Velcro and name labels. Focusing on the practical always helps tame the emotions.

I like to think that some of the best advice we get comes from the practical experience of those who have been there before us. Throughout this book we've heard from deans and administrations of colleges and universities. They've generously shared their best ideas about how parents can make the most of their children's college years. It's only fitting that we now end with even more poignant words of experience—first from college students who try as they might to "tame the parent monster," and then from parents who have already sent their kids to college—and have lived to tell about their experience.

TAMING THE PARENT MONSTER

I asked students and a few recent graduates around the country to share their most helpful advice to parents, and they didn't hold back! Their responses are here for the taking...

On Academics
Don't underestimate my class load.

—Soren Packer, Indiana University

On the College Experience

Know the amount of culture shock that could happen to your child during the first year. I grew up in a pretty diverse metropolitan area and left for a small liberal arts college with a rather homogeneous population in the middle of nowhere. I spent a lot of my first year trying to entertain myself and find things to do.

—Vi Ha, Pomona College

Kids in college drink, and it's okay.

—Elizabeth Daley, Bard College

Graduation is for you guys, the parents.

—Soren Packer, Indiana University

MTV spring break is not how most students party.

—Dieu Ha, Pomona College

I know better than to leave my drink unattended. (Note to Parents: This is a reference to spiking party drinks with date rape drugs.)

—Dieu Ha, Pomona College

On Visiting

Visit your kids at least once between the first day of college and graduation.

—Soren Parker, Indiana University

If you want to see what actually goes on at school, don't come during Parents' Weekend.

—Elizabeth Daley, Bard College

When you come to visit, rent a hotel room.

—Elizabeth Daley, Bard College

Don't embarrass us on Parents' Weekend.

—Arli Christian, Wesleyan University

Don't visit too much.

—Tamara Cacchioni, Vassar College

Call before you stop by my dorm; don't make unexpected visits.

—Jessica Brand, SUNY—Buffalo

When you have to come pick your kid up on the last day of the semester, please be on time. It's not cool not to. If you don't come, we get kicked out, and then we are basically homeless. Also, they stop feeding us if our parents don't come.

—Elizabeth Daley, Bard College

On Finances

Discuss financial issues with your child, such as who is paying for what, before your child picks a college.

—Emma Zurer, Marlboro College

Send more money.

—Greg Ponstingl, Pomona College

Force your kid to take business classes.

—Soren Packer, Indiana University

If you aren't going to give your kids money, give them food.

—Arinze Ukachukwu, SUNY—Albany

On Communications

If you are ever going to contact your child's professor, it should only be about a medical emergency.

—Elizabeth Daley, Bard College

I love getting letters in the mail that aren't junk mail, and I would love it if my parents would write to me every once in awhile about what's going on with life at home, how my siblings are doing, etc. That way I don't get the impersonal, "We're too busy to call" e-mail, and I don't have to deal with the sometimes inconvenience of a phone call. Instead, I can read the family news at my leisure and still feel as though my family hasn't forgotten about me.

—Alexander Lydon, Pomona College

Send your kid a gift basket every now and then.

—Soren Packer, Indiana University

If I do not call you, it is not because I don't love you. It is because nothing is going on. College is boring most of the time.

—Eva Chao, Scripps College

Don't expect me to be awake just because you are.

—Jessica Brand, SUNY—Buffalo

One voice mail message a day is sufficient.

—Elizabeth Daley, Bard College

Your initial contact with your college kid should be infrequent but available. They are undergoing a lot of changes and adjusting to a new life. Make sure to feel out the way they respond to your contact. If they are calling you a lot, then they are probably homesick or need a little reassurance and a few more phone calls. If not, then let them situate themselves and only check up on them once in a while. Don't feel as though you shouldn't be able to call them though, either. After all, you are a person, too!

—Amanda Lydon, Pomona College

Supply your kids with snacks, or send them home-cooked meals.

—Arinze Ukachukwu, SUNY—Albany

Don't tell me that I gained weight.

—Dieu Ha, Pomona College

On the Parent/Child Relationship

In my experience, many children that did not get along that well with their parents in their younger years begin to truly appreciate everything that their parents have done for them along the way once they reach college. My parents have become my support, my inspiration, and my best friends. All we needed was a little time apart to realize that we were the best things to ever happen to each other! Before college, I never called home or told my parents what I was up to; now I call them and write them e-mails constantly on my own incentive.

—Amanda Feinberger, Scripps College

Just let them live. At this point, they are old enough to make decisions. They may be right or they might be wrong, but you have to let them do it themselves and to just let them live.

—Danny Ingberg, Hofstra University

It'd be really helpful to know how you were just like me at one point in your life. Could you just please convince me that my inability to verbalize my interest in someone is like some past experience you had? That'd be great, thanks.

—Dieu Ha, Pomona College

The ideal parent should be "supportive but not clingy."

—Anonymous, UNC—Asheville

Stop nagging your kids about brushing their teeth. (My mom does that everyday still.)

—Van Vu, Claremont McKenna College

Let your kids arrive on campus before the first day of classes.

—Elizabeth Daley, Bard College

Parents, your job is done, whether you like it or not. Just send them gift certificates to delivery restaurants every once in a while.

—Daniel Ades, Amherst College

I know you mean well when you ask me if I'm going to church/temple/whatever, but sometimes, it's just as important to let me figure it out on my own as it is to have introduced me to said religion. So don't push me about it. Be happy that you raised me and be proud of the job you did.

—Dieu Ha, Pomona College

On the Future

You cannot plan my future, so let me make my own choices about my major and my career pland.

—Debby Brand, Pomona College

FROM ONE PARENT TO ANOTHER...

And now, some words from parents who have already sent a child off to college:

Before They Go...

Start to look at your relationship with your husband or wife before your children go to college. Sometimes if you have only one child and she leaves, you look up at your husband like, "Who are you?"

—Lonnie Cacchioni, parent of a Vassar Student

Photocopy all of their credit cards, their driver's license, and everything else in their wallet in case they lose it. We backed up their cell phone address book numbers on my computer before they left, too.

—Parry Aftab, an attorney and a single-parent mother of two recent college graduates

If you're divorced, be clear with the school and your ex-spouse about who gets what college-related mailings. If the children live with you, then you should be getting the mailings and the phone calls, regardless of who is paying the tuition.

—Pat Wilburn, a registered nurse and single mom of a college student

It's important to wean them of dependence on you for doing mundane but necessary things, (such as their own dirty laundry) way in advance of their departure. (I started first year in high school; they were glad to have responsibility over their own socks, but were dismayed to find the socks were subjected to the same black hole as when I had hold of the laundry.) And get them involved in cooking the family meal once every week months prior to their departure, so they will have some knowledge of how to navigate the culinary scene since by their third year they will want out of the dorms. Become their sous chef. If you are a good cook, or you're married to one, then your children might be miserable at first in college and miss home cooked meals. One way for them to return is through their stomachs.

—Lucille B. Pilling, a PhD in Public Health and mother of two college students

Even before the kids get into college, remember that it's difficult to pick a wrong college. So don't stress the admissions process too much.

—Alfred Poor, an industry analyst for technology
and parent of two from Bucks County, Pennsylvania

Make them coffee mugs with a silly picture from their childhood on it to take along with them. (You can do this at websites like www.Kodakphotogallery.com or www.snapfish.com.)

If they're driving to school, consider putting together a car safety kit, with jumper cables, a flashlight and extra batteries, flat tire inflator, snow removal brush, etc. and tuck it in the back of their car.

—Parry Aftab, an attorney and a single-parent mother of two
recent college graduates

Contact the college in the summer to find out what networking connections are available in the dorm room—wired or wireless—and what devices are approved and supported by the college IT staff. If the connection is wired, find out how many connections are available in the room. There was only one in our son's freshman double, but we were able to provide an Ethernet hub so that both he and his roommate could have their own connections. If you know how to configure network connections, plan to spend some time on move-in day taking care of this. If your child has to wait for the college to do the configuring, it can take weeks and your child may miss out on early advantages such as online registration for courses.

—Alfred Poor, an industry analyst for technology
and parent of two from Bucks County, Pennsylvania

On Academics

This advice is for your college student: Get to know one professor very well. They should invite him or her out to lunch or to your dormitory to have a meal with others in the group. Do some research for him or her. Find out what he or she thinks is interesting. Most faculty don't know students very well, and if you do this, you will stand out and be welcome.

—Herb Lin, a former professor, now at the National Academy of Sciences, and parent of a future a college student

If your child is interested in a particular college or major, suggest that they take courses at that college and/or in that major the summer of her or his junior year in high school. Once at school, encourage your child to take courses from the professors at their university who are known as great teachers—no matter what the subject is. Difficult core courses are often best taken in the summer semesters, if possible. (I discovered this myself in my recent graduate studies, and my sons agreed that "Mom was correct.") In other words, take statistics, biostatistics, organic chemistry, etc. over the summer. The reasons: concentrated shorter courses, facts are easier to recall as you take the subject daily, grading is on a more favorable curve, and it is over in six weeks!

—Lucille B. Pilling, a PhD in Public Health and mother of two college students

You'll want to tailor your support for the various class years. Freshmen have lots of separation anxiety issues and fitting in issues; seniors have pressure about employment and real-world issues looming. For freshmen: Don't have high expectations for grades—just adjusting to college life and getting average grades is a big accomplishment.

—Carolyn Walton, a journalist who lives on Cape Cod

Don't micro-manage course work. If your child asks you for advice on how to analyze German unification, DNA, or anything else, be flattered—but don't expect your words of wisdom to find their way into his or her paper. And don't call your child's professor, coach, or dorm assistant, either unless the problem is life-threatening. Problem-solving is a good skill to learn.

—Barbara Tischler, a parent of two college students and an Interim Head of the Upper School at Horace Mann School, a New York private school

On Finances

Do not give them a full allowance. It is perfectly possible for them to earn money while in college. I gave my sons a minimal amount and told them that I expected them to earn the rest of their pocket money. They did.

—Lucille B. Pilling, a PhD in Public Health and mother of two college students

On Dorm Life

Save all your quarters, and give them to your child whenever you see them. They will think of you fondly every time they do their laundry.

—Alfred Poor, an industry analyst for technology and parent of two from Bucks County, Pennsylvania

Dorm life is an experience of shock and awe for all involved. It's a subculture that few are prepared for. Fortunately, it is our children who have to live it, as they are better equipped than their parents to be flexible and open to the unfamiliar social mores. Don't ask too much about what goes on; trust your child to let you if they need help with problems.

—Alfred Poor, an industry analyst for technology and parent of two from Bucks County, Pennsylvania

On the College Experience

Warn your kids about drinking and drugs, don't assume they know.

—Lonnie Cacchioni, parent of a Vassar Student

Our children have many more choices than we had in college. The Chinese restaurant was the only one open past 9:00 P.M. and it closed at 11:00 P.M. These days, any college town will deliver anything from pizza to Mexican into the wee hours. It's a good thing.

—Alfred Poor, an industry analyst for technology and parent of two from Bucks County, Pennsylvania

We have a "college kid," but her course has been far from direct. Actually, if she had just stuck with a 4-year program, she'd be either done or going into her senior year; I can't quite work it out. But she's happy, so all is well.

—Neil Rubenking, parent of a college student from San Francisco

Watch out for the Freshman 15 (the infamous weight gain of 15 pounds that afflicts some students freshman year).

—Lonnie Cacchioni, parent of a Vassar Student

Instill in your child that they determine what they will get from their college experience. Through high school, their education was delivered to them, and all they had to do was respond. In college, the quality of education is largely determined by the effort that the student puts into the process. And it doesn't matter if they're in a class of 12 or 1,200. If they make the effort to meet the professor, and express interest in the subject beyond the minimum course requirements, you may find that all sorts of opportunities open up to you. If he or she gets into the best school in the country, they can still coast through and do the minimum and learn little more than they would at any other school in the country. The choice is available to any student at any school—even freshmen at enormous state schools—and if you can empower your child to think in those terms, they will benefit from it.

—Alfred Poor, an industry analyst for technology and parent of two from Bucks County, Pennsylvania

On Communication

It's okay if you child doesn't call for a few days. That usually means he or she is busy/engaged/happy. Don't worry.

—Barbara Tischler, a parent of two college students and an Interim Head of the Upper School at Horace Mann School, a New York private school

Some parents will have learned this when their children are in high school, but if you haven't yet, don't express too much praise or disapproval of your child's college associates, especially if they are roommates or boyfriends/girlfriends. When your child vents about conflicts and frictions in the relationships, be supportive but don't agree too much or condemn the other party. When your child and the other person reconcile, your harsh judgments won't be forgotten. On the other hand, too much praise can make it more difficult for your child to come to you for help with relationship problems, because you apparently will take the other person's side.

—Alfred Poor, an industry analyst for technology and parent of two from Bucks County, Pennsylvania

When it comes to the roommate, be cordial but not too curious. You will be provided the relevant information on a strictly need to know basis. When it comes to the boyfriend or girlfriend, follow the roommate instructions.

—Barbara Tischler, a parent of two college students and an Interim Head of the Upper School at Horace Mann School, a New York private school

When they call home hysterical about something, let them vent, let them cry, and listen, listen, listen. And hope that after venting they can start to figure out how they can handle the situation. Your child might vent negative feelings about a roommate or a friend that lead the parent to believe that this other person is evil and hated. What we don't realize is that after venting, and getting us all worried, your child is probably off partying with that person and having a great time

If you do get the hysterical phone call, do all of the listening and end with suggesting that they call you back the next day to tell you how things are working out. When they vent about their problems, they sometimes forget to tell us when things are better. And if things are not better, it helps them to know they can talk again the next day. Tell them you are glad they called, that it is okay to worry you, and that you know they will figure it out.

—Bebe Poor, a musician and artisan and parent of two from Bucks County, Pennsylvania

If you have the choice between getting phone service in the dorm room or providing a cell phone, go with the cell phone. Your child will be anywhere but the room most of the time.

—Alfred Poor, an industry analyst for technology and parent of two from Bucks County, Pennsylvania

On College Supplies and Care Packages

My advice is to send the kids lots of junk-food, often. The goal is not to bulk them up—it's to enhance their social life and make friends with neighbors in the dorms. If you worry about weight, send crates of apples, oranges, etc. Make sure that the food is perishable and comes in such volume and frequency that they will be forced to share it with many people.

—Steve Edelson, a Boston area engineer and
parent of a college student

I sent my kids to school with huge baskets of Tootsie Roll Pops and with large buckets of Twizzlers, thanks to Costco/Price club. I found that it helped them get situated faster the first year when their dorm mates stopped in for their stash.

—Parry Aftab, an attorney and a single-parent mother
of two recent college graduates

Don't buy the campus-delivered "care packages"—they tend to be lame, over-priced, and they don't have your personal touch.

—Alfred Poor, an industry analyst for technology
and parent of two from Bucks County, Pennsylvania

I sent flowers to both my daughter and my daughter's roommate a few days after they moved in. It was appreciated by her roommate and made them feel more like friends, rather than just strangers sharing a room.

—Parry Aftab, an attorney and a single-parent mother
of two recent college graduates

Equip your college student with a laptop instead of a desktop computer. It may never leave the room—as there are probably computers available all around the campus—but the space-saving aspect of the design is essential for cramped dorm rooms. The computer can also serve as an MP3/CD player if equipped with good speakers and/or headphones, so spend money on more storage and these accessories rather than buy a separate sound system. Get your child a USB "thumb" drive and make sure they know how to use it. This is the new floppy disk, and makes it easy to take your term paper over to the computer center to print it out. Oh, and a game console is an essential part of any dorm room, especially if the occupants have Y chromosomes.

—Alfred Poor, an industry analyst for technology
and parent of two from Bucks County, Pennsylvania

Buy all sheets and linens in the same color. This avoids their losing one and not having the set. Use duvet covers, instead of comforters. They are cheaper and easier to wash and dry. And don't leave home without a first aid kit, a sewing kit, and stain spot remover wipes.

—Parry Aftab, an attorney and a single-parent mother
of two recent college graduates

Pack in furniture. Milk crates, book shelves, and laundry baskets are useful in any room, and will be on hand when it's time to move again at the end of the summer. Under-bed storage boxes are also very handy in cramped rooms. Have you ever tried to find an empty cardboard box during spring moving week in a college town? Also use fabric storage items—duffles, soft luggage—that can be stored in minimal space when empty.

—Alfred Poor, an industry analyst for technology
and parent of two from Bucks County, Pennsylvania

When my kids left for school, I set up a watch for books and CDs I knew they liked on www.Amazon.com and would have their address already embedded in the address book there. That way, I could easily send them something quick and cheap but that meant something to them—and I could even do it from the road when I was traveling for work. I also sent them with disposable cameras and prepaid developing envelopes. When I wanted to treat them, I would give them a gift card for Banana Republic or the Gap that they could use online. Gift certificates for McDonald's are also good so they can still eat when their cash runs out. Movie ticket gift certificates are better than cash since you know how they'll use it. And remember to send batteries along with the other things in their care packages.

—Parry Aftab, an attorney and a single-parent mother
of two recent college graduates

When you're picking up your child at the end of the year, don't take their word for it when they say, "Oh yes, it'll all fit in the car—easily." Either get a qualified second opinion or bring a U-Haul truck!

—Linda Hodge, mom of a college student
and a former national PTA President

On the Parent-Child Relationship and Letting Go

Be prepared to do a lot of letting go and looking the other way.

—Lonnie Cacchioni, parent of a Vassar Student

It's okay to have rules when they come home that are different than what they have in college. You need your sleep, and you don't need to worry needlessly—there's enough of that already. Let go in areas you have no control over now—boyfriends, study habits, clothing, friends, hours they keep, and just keep open to talking about their emotional state—they'll need that.

—Carolyn Walton, a journalist who lives on Cape Cod

Your kid will do at least one stupid thing in the first year of college. As long as it's not (too) illegal, try to be supportive and, most important, try to remember what it was like to be 18 (translated: young and foolish).

—Barbara Tischler, a parent of two college students and an Interim Head of the Upper School at Horace Mann School, a New York private school

Sending them off to college is a grueling process of balancing closeness while trying to respect their need to spread their wings.

—Camilla Calhoun, an art gallery owner and novelist in upstate New York, mother of two boys who graduated from college

When they're coming home, take orders in advance for special meals they would like to have.

—Parry Aftab, an attorney and a single-parent mother of two recent college graduates

After knowing that you have to let them go, remember that you can visit them a lot. We had one child at William and Mary and one at Washington and Lee—two schools on opposite sides of Virginia. When I got to missing them, I would take a road trip and go see them. They would be busy but we would have nice meals or take walks between their classes and all of the other things they had to do. While they were busy, I would entertain myself in those great college towns or nap to recover from the hours and hours of driving. (Don't expect kids to drop everything or not have homework or other commitments just because you're visiting.) I tended to enjoy visits more that were not on Parents' Weekend. When we went for Parents' Weekends we would usually skip all of the official activities.

—Bebe Poor, a musician and artisan and parent of two from Bucks County, Pennsylvania

Be prepared for lots of ups and downs and just be supportive when the downs occur—they pass!

>—Carolyn Walton, a journalist who lives on Cape Cod
and parent of a college student

If you set limits at age 2, stuck to your guns at age 12, you (and your kid) will have the ethical and psychological strength to get through the choices and challenges that college represents.

>—Barbara Tischler, a parent of two college students and an
Interim Head of the Upper School at Horace Mann School,
a New York private school

Remember that, in many cases these days, leaving may not be forever anymore. I just wept, once again, at one of those "last" times as my 27-year-old took off after a year living at home, saving money for a move to Colorado. Caution: Don't be too rash about downsizing! They may return to stay for a while and they might bring their girlfriend! Leaving is both sad and a relief for them to have their own lives and for you to get a life beyond your offspring. Get together with friends, take walks with them, watch Marx Brother movies. Tears will morph into laughter as with all inevitable change.

>—Camilla Calhoun, an art gallery owner and novelist
in upstate New York, mother of two boys who graduated from college

On the Future
Relax. After all, you turned out (mostly) okay.

>—Barbara Tischler, a parent of two college students and an
Interim Head of the Upper School at Horace Mann School,
a New York private school

Encourage them to speak with counselors on campus about their emotional or employment and future issues. This gives them control of working things out for themselves with the help of a professional other than their parent.

—Carolyn Walton, a journalist who lives on Cape Cod

Not that they ever listen, he says, but New Jersey dad Bill Machrone has given his kids the following Dad's Rules for Success in College:

1. Be the first one done with the reading assignment. The questions from all the brickheads who didn't read it will help you clarify your thinking.

2. Sit up front in class.

3. Ask questions in class. Same effect as number 2; maybe worth half a grade point.

4. Start the paper a day sooner than you think you have to.

5. Keep your room clean. (Guys: Chicks will dig you. Girls: Your roommate won't be tempted to strangle you as you sleep.)

As for advice to his parents, Bill makes this list: Don't be Shocked When . . .

1. They come home after that first semester 10 lb. fatter or thinner

2. You don't recognize them because of their hair style, facial hair, hair color, body jewelry, etc.

3. You discover that they've discovered sex

4. All that neatly packed and organized stuff you sent is trashed or missing

5. You find an article of the opposite sex's clothing mingled with your offspring's dirty laundry

6. They've changed their major . . . again

7. And finally, if your kid is into music and doesn't yet have an iPod or other digital music player, get one. Leave the CDs home—a collection of 100 CDs (not uncommon) could cost $1500 to replace if it walks, and individual CDs will doubtless be lost, stolen, or ruined.

In closing, I'll leave you with my own wishful prayer for fellow parents of college students:

May your college kids never disappear long enough to cause you alarm.

May your insurance rates be kept to a minimum and your accidents, losses, and breakages be material, not physical.

May your children balance the arts and sciences and leave college with some marketable skill and a heart full of passion.

May they understand that in the real world, people clean their own bathrooms and make their own beds.

May they make good friends for life.

May you enjoy at least one moment of great pride of their accomplishments during their four years.

May you have some money left for your retirement when their formal education is complete.

And . . . may your empty nest continue to stay empty, except when it's filled with sweet and memorable visits.

Appendices

APPENDIX A

Family Educational Rights and Privacy Act (FERPA)

FAMILY EDUCATIONAL RIGHTS AND PRIVACY ACT (FERPA)

General

The Family Educational Rights and Privacy Act (FERPA) (20 U.S.C. § 1232g; 34 CFR Part 99) is a federal law that protects the privacy of student education records. The law applies to all schools that receive funds under an applicable program of the U.S. Department of Education.

FERPA gives parents certain rights with respect to their children's education records. These rights transfer to the student when he or she reaches the age of 18 or attends a school beyond the high school level. Students to whom the rights have transferred are "eligible students."

- Parents or eligible students have the right to inspect and review the student's education records maintained by the school. Schools are not required to provide copies of records unless, for reasons such as great distance, it is impossible for parents or eligible students to review the records. Schools may charge a fee for copies.

- Parents or eligible students have the right to request that a school correct records which they believe to be inaccurate or misleading. If the school decides not to amend the record, the parent or eligible student then has the right to a formal hearing. After the hearing, if the school still decides not to amend the record, the parent or eligible student has the right to place a statement with the record setting forth his or her view about the contested information.

- Generally, schools must have written permission from the parent or eligible student in order to release any information from a student's education record. However, FERPA allows schools to disclose those records, without consent, to the following parties or under the following conditions (34 CFR § 99.31):
    - o School officials with legitimate educational interest;
    - o Other schools to which a student is transferring;
    - o Specified officials for audit or evaluation purposes;

- o   Appropriate parties in connection with financial aid to a student;
- o   Organizations conducting certain studies for or on behalf of the school;
- o   Accrediting organizations;
- o   To comply with a judicial order or lawfully issued subpoena;
- o   Appropriate officials in cases of health and safety emergencies; and
- o   State and local authorities, within a juvenile justice system, pursuant to specific State law.

Schools may disclose, without consent, "directory" information such as a student's name, address, telephone number, date and place of birth, honors and awards, and dates of attendance. However, schools must tell parents and eligible students about directory information and allow parents and eligible students a reasonable amount of time to request that the school not disclose directory information about them. Schools must notify parents and eligible students annually of their rights under FERPA. The actual means of notification (special letter, inclusion in a PTA bulletin, student handbook, or newspaper article) is left to the discretion of each school.

For additional information or technical assistance, you may call (202) 260-3887 (voice). Individuals who use TDD may call the Federal Information Relay Service at 1-800-877-8339.

Or you may contact us at the following address:
Family Policy Compliance Office
U.S. Department of Education
400 Maryland Avenue, SW
Washington, DC 20202-5920

SEC. 952. ALCOHOL OR DRUG POSSESSION DISCLOSURE

Section 444 of the General Education Provisions Act (20 U.S.C. 1232g) is amended by adding at the end the following:

(i) DRUG AND ALCOHOL VIOLATION DISCLOSURES

(1) IN GENERAL - Nothing in this Act or the Higher Education Act of 1965 shall be construed to prohibit an institution of higher education from disclosing, to a parent or legal guardian of a student, information regarding any violation of any Federal, State, or local law, or of any rule or policy of the institution, governing the use or possession of alcohol or a controlled substance, regardless of whether that information is contained in the student's education records, if--

   (A)   the student is under the age of 21; and

   (B)   the institution determines that the student has committed a disciplinary violation with respect to such use or possession.

(2) STATE LAW REGARDING DISCLOSURE - Nothing in paragraph (1) shall be construed to supersede any provision of State law that prohibits an institution of higher education from making the disclosure described in subsection (a).'

SUMMARY OF SECTION 952

Section 952, Alcohol or Drug Possession Disclosure, another section of the Higher Education Amendments relevant to IHE prevention, authorizes IHEs to disclose to parents and guardians violations of institutional policies or rules in addition to local, state, and federal laws governing the use or possession of alcohol or a controlled substance if the student is under 21 and if the IHE determines that the student has committed a violation with respect to such use or possession.

According to Nicholson and Grow, the old legislation, Section 444 of the General Education Provisions Act, only allowed disclosure of violations of local, state, or federal laws governing the use or possession of alcohol or a controlled substance.

Section 952, originally part of the Warner amendment, so named for its sponsor Senator John Warner (R-Virginia), clearly allows IHEs to disclose violations of not only local, state, and federal laws but also institutional policies and rules governing the use or possession of alcohol or controlled substances.

Source: http://www.edc.org/hec/pubs/prev-updates/higher-ed-amend.html

APPENDIX B

The Clery Act

CLERY ACT SUMMARY

The Cleary Act requires colleges and universities to file reports on campus crimes.

Schools must publish an annual report disclosing campus security policies and three years worth of selected crime statistics.

Schools must make timely warnings to the campus community about crimes that pose an ongoing threat to students and employees.

Each institution with a police or security department must have a public crime log.

The U.S. Department of Education centrally collects and disseminates the crime statistics.

Campus sexual assault victims are assured of certain basic rights.

Schools that fail to comply can be fined by the DOE.

Source: www.securityoncampus.org

APPENDIX C

Parents' Trivia Test

ARE YOU "OUT OF SIGHT, OUT OF MIND" OR ARE YOU TOTALLY IN THE LOOP?

Once your child goes off to college, see how many of these you can answer correctly:

1. What is your child's e-mail address?
2. What color(s) is your child's hair currently?
3. What is your child's roommate's name?
4. What is the name of this roommate's hometown?
5. What do the roommate's parents do for a living?
6. What is your child's college advisor's name?
7. What is your child's GPA (if they are just starting, then answer for last test score or grade on a paper)?
8. Does your child belong to any clubs at school? Which ones?
9. What color is your child's blanket?
10. Does your child have any piercing or tattoos?
11. How many courses is your child taking?
12. How many credits?
13. Can you name the classes?
14. What time does the earliest class begin?
15. What is the name of your child's dorm (if not in a dorm, then street address)?
16. What is the school's mascot?
17. What month does your child finish school for the summer?
18. How much money does your child spend, on average, each week?
19. What is your child's favorite place to eat off campus?
20. What did your child do last Saturday night?
21. What's their favorite dinner in the cafeteria (if not on meal, plan then at home)?

Points

If you score:

    1–5 points: Time to reacquaint yourselves

    6–18 points: Sharing nicely

    18 or more: Get a life

For additional play: Reverse the game and have your child see if she can answer 21 questions about your life and your friends. Whoever gets the most points wins.

APPENDIX D

Websites for Parents

WEBSITES FOR PARENTS

General Advice

College Parents of America—A resource for college parents and college parents to be, this site covers everything from finding a scholarship to life on campus. If you join as a paying member you get access to their experts and some discounts for college related gear and services. www.collegeparents.org/cpa/index.html

Health and Wellness

American College Health Association—A clearinghouse for a variety of student health issues. Includes referrals for various treatments and information about college health care. www.acha.org

Campusblues—Resources for students that concern physical and mental health, money management, learning problems, and more. Tools include a list of colleges and the services they provide. www.campusblues.com

Drinking Responsibly—A downloadable brochure from the national distillers. www.centurycouncil.org/lib/downloads/parents_brochure.html

Education Development Center—An international nonprofit site that, in addition to other things, lists the universities and colleges that are issuing anti-drug, alcohol and violent behavior initiatives. You'll be able to look up a specific school and see what the schools' policy is. www.edc.org/hec/parents/#1

The Higher Education Center—Created by the Department of Education to help college and community leaders develop, implement, and evaluate programs and policies to reduce student problems related to alcohol, drug use, and violence. The site has a robust parents' section that talks in depth about parental notification policies. www.edc.org/hec/parents

Security on Campus—Delivers information including school-specific crime statistics. www.securityoncampus.org/

Gear

College Gear—The place to go if you want to wear it proudly, this site features a large assortment of college apparel, sports gear, frat gear and more. www.collegegear.com

Ecampus—A good place to buy and sell college textbooks. www.ecampus.com

Hipkits—Send a birthday or holiday basket of fun. www.hipkits.com

Stuff 4 college—If you're looking for a care package that's more than just candy, this one offers links for fruit baskets and other healthier fare. www.stuff4college.com

Studentbistro—Directory of outlets and outfitters offering special deals for students. www.studentbistro.com

TBXN—One more site designed to let students buy and sell used textbooks. www.TBXN.com

Travel

Student Advantage—Discounts on everything from movies to textbooks to travel are available when you join as a member. www.studentadvantage.com/discountcard

Student Universe—Special student travel rates on air and hotels. www.studentuniverse.com

Statistics

National Association for Educational Statistics—A comprehensive listing of all data related to post secondary education from a number of sources. www.nces.ed.gov/edstats

Financial Aid

Federal Student Aid—Get your application for federal student aid started here. The U.S. Department of Education's Federal Student Aid (FSA) programs are the largest source of student aid in America, providing nearly 70 percent of all student financial aid. www.fafsa.ed.gov/

Eavesdropping

College Boredom—Insight into the world of how some students choose to pass the time. www.CollegeBoredom.com

Dorm Cooking—A list of cookbooks and recipes geared toward college kids. www.recipelink.com/dormcooking.html

Ebaumsworld—Bizarre videos, photos and other college timewasters. www.ebaumsworld.com

Facebook—The electronic equivalent of the college viewbook, this site is the largest social networking site for college students. Unfortunately, you must have a .edu (college-linked) email address to enter. www.Facebook.com

Realcollegelife – Information on everything from renting a house to throwing a party. www.realcollegelife.com

Two more . . . These sites will all make you embarrassed to even know a college kid, but they give you a good idea about how student's let off steam. www.CollegeNut.com and www.CollegeDrunkFest.com

ABOUT THE AUTHOR

Robin Raskin is the former editor of *PC Magazine* and former Editor in Chief of *FamilyPC*. She's been a columnist for *USA Today Online*, and has authored three books about raising kids in a digital world. Her free-lance articles appear in many women's magazines including *RedBook*, *Real Simple*, *Parents,* and others. A champion of a safe Internet, Raskin lectures, consults and serves as a media spokesperson on the subject. She's also the Director of Communications at The Princeton Review.

Do you have other questions about parenting college-age kids? E-mail to robinr@review.com and we'll do our best to get them answered.

Independent 529 Plan.

Offering prepaid tuition at over 250 private colleges and universities... and counting[†]

Your child's private college education doesn't have to be so expensive. Independent 529 Plan provides an opportunity for you to control the rising cost of tuition.

- Prepaid private college tuition at less than today's price*
- Over 250 participating private colleges and universities[†]
- Valuable estate and gift tax benefits**
- Freedom from market risk and federal income taxes**

Enroll today and get the most out of Independent 529 Plan.

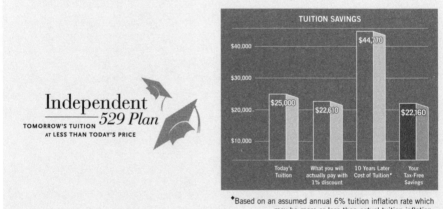

TUITION SAVINGS

$44,770

$40,000

$30,000

$25,000

$20,000 $22,610 $22,160

$10,000

Today's Tuition | What you will actually pay with 1% discount | 10 Years Later Cost of Tuition* | Your Tax-Free Savings

*Based on an assumed annual 6% tuition inflation rate which may be more or less than actual tuition inflation.

Take a look at the facing page for a complete list of member colleges!

For more information, or to request an enrollment package, visit **www.ind529parentsguide.org** or call us at **1-866-475-3204**.

TIAA CREF

FINANCIAL SERVICES FOR THE GREATER GOOD™

*Participation in Independent 529 Plan does not guarantee admission to any college or university, nor does it affect the admissions process. Owning a certificate may have an adverse impact on financial aid determinations.

**The law allowing for federal income tax-free qualified withdrawals is set to expire on December 31, 2010. Congress may or may not extend this law beyond this date. Future changes in the law may create adverse tax consequences, or lead to the termination of the Plan. TIAA-CREF and its affiliates do not provide tax advice. Please consult your tax advisor. Purchasers should read the Disclosure Booklet, including the Enrollment Agreement, carefully before making purchase decisions. Teachers Personal Investors Services, Inc. and TIAA-CREF Individual & Institutional Services, LLC Distributors. Tuition Plan Consortium, LLC is the program sponsor and TIAA-CREF Tuition Financing, Inc. is the program manager.

[†]As of September 2005

C34661

Alabama
Birmingham-Southern College
Faulkner University
Samford University
University of Mobile
Arkansas
Hendrix College
Lyon College
California
California Lutheran University
Chapman University
Claremont McKenna College
Harvey Mudd College
Mills College
Mount St. Mary's College
Occidental College
Pepperdine University
Pitzer College
Point Loma Nazarene University
Pomona College
Saint Mary's College of California
Stanford University
University of LaVerne
University of Redlands
University of San Diego
University of the Pacific
Westmont College
Whittier College
Colorado
Colorado College
Regis University
Connecticut
Fairfield University
Wesleyan University
District of Columbia
American University
Catholic University of America
George Washington University
Florida
Jacksonville University
Rollins College
Saint Leo University
University of Miami
Georgia
Agnes Scott College
Berry College
Clark Atlanta University
Emory University
LaGrange College
Mercer University
Oglethorpe University
Spelman College
Wesleyan College
Hawaii
Chaminade University of Honolulu
Idaho
Albertson College of Idaho
Northwest Nazarene University
Illinois
Augustana College
Bradley University
Elmhurst College
Illinois Institute of Technology

Knox College
Lake Forest College
Monmouth College
North Central College
Olivet Nazarene University
University of Chicago
Indiana
Butler University
DePauw University
Earlham College
Franklin College
Rose-Hulman Institute of Technology
Saint Mary's College
University of Evansville
University of Notre Dame
Valparaiso University
Wabash College
Iowa
Buena Vista University
Central College
Clarke College
Dordt College
Grinnell College
Graceland University
Loras College
Luther College
Northwestern College
Simpson College
Waldorf College
Wartburg College
Kentucky
Centre College
Transylvania University
Louisiana
Centenary College of Louisiana
Dillard University
Tulane University
Maryland
College of Notre Dame of Maryland
Goucher College
Loyola College in Maryland
McDaniel College
Mount Saint Mary's College
Massachusetts
Amherst College
Berklee College of Music
Boston University
Clark University
Gordon College
Hampshire College
MIT
Mount Holyoke College
Smith College
Springfield College
Wellesley College
Wheaton College
Michigan
Albion College
Hope College
Kalamazoo College
Minnesota
Carleton College
Gustavus Adolphus College

Hamline University
Macalester College
St. Olaf College
Missouri
Culver-Stockton College
Drury University
Hannibal-LaGrange College
Maryville University of Saint Louis
Rockhurst University
Saint Louis University
Stephens College
Washington Univ. in St. Louis
Webster University
Westminster College
Nebraska
Creighton University
Doane College
New Hampshire
Franklin Pierce College
New Jersey
Centenary College
Drew University
Princeton University
Rider University
Stevens Institute of Technology
New Mexico
College of Santa Fe
New York
Bard College
Canisius College
Daemen College
Elmira College
Hartwick College
Hobart & William Smith Colleges
Ithaca College
Marist College
Medaille College
Nazareth College
Niagara University
Pace University
Rensselaer Polytechnic Institute
Roberts Wesleyan College
Rochester Institute of Technology
Skidmore College
Syracuse University
University of Rochester
Vassar College
Wells College
North Carolina
Catawba College
Greensboro College
Guilford College
Lenoir Rhyne College
Methodist College
Salem College
Wake Forest University
Ohio
Ashland University
Capital University
Case Western Reserve University
College of Wooster
Denison University
Hiram College

John Carroll University
Kenyon College
Mount Vernon Nazarene University
Muskingum College
Oberlin College
Ohio Wesleyan University
Tiffin University
University of Dayton
Wittenberg University

Oklahoma
Oklahoma Christian University
Southern Nazarene University
University of Tulsa

Oregon
George Fox University
Lewis & Clark College
Linfield College
Pacific University
Reed College
Willamette University

Pennsylvania
Allegheny College
Alvernia College
Arcadia University
Carnegie Mellon University
Chatham College
Dickinson College
Drexel University
Franklin & Marshall College
Gettysburg College
Grove City College
Keystone College
Immaculata University
Juniata College
Keystone College
La Salle University
Marywood University
Moravian College
Muhlenberg College
Saint Francis University
Susquehanna University
Thiel College
Ursinus College
Washington and Jefferson College
Waynesburg College
Westminster College
York College of Pennsylvania

South Carolina
Charleston Southern Univ.
Claflin University
Columbia College
Converse College
Furman University
Presbyterian College
Wofford College

South Dakota
Augustana College

Tennessee
Belmont University
Carson-Newman College
Lambuth University
Rhodes College
Trevecca Nazarene University
University of the South
Vanderbilt University

Texas
Abilene Christian University
Austin College
Baylor University
Dallas Baptist University
Hardin-Simmons University
Lubbock Christian University
Rice University
St. Edward's University
St. Mary's University
Southern Methodist University
Southwestern University
Texas Christian University
Trinity University
University of Dallas
University of Mary Hardin-Baylor

Vermont
Middlebury College
Saint Michael's College

Virginia
Bridgewater College
Eastern Mennonite University
Hampden-Sydney College
Hollins University
Mary Baldwin College
Randolph-Macon Woman's Col.
Shenandoah University
Sweet Briar College
University of Richmond
Virginia Wesleyan College

Washington
Pacific Lutheran University
Seattle Pacific University
Whitworth College

West Virginia
West Virginia Wesleyan College
Wheeling Jesuit University

Wisconsin
Lakeland College
Lawrence University
Ripon College